By the Same Author

THE MYTH OF

The Golden Age

IN THE

Renaissance

L'aage d'Or.

L'aage premier d'une innocente sainte
A ces viuans aporta ce bon heur,
Que franchement sans loy, force, ou contreinte
On meintenoit la foy, le droit, l'honneur.
L'amour n'estoit suget au blasonneur,
Ains pouuoit on de s'amie estre aymé,
Hanté, baisé, sans creindre deshonneur:
Dont à bon droit l'aage d'Or fut nommé.

a 4

Harry Levin

THE MYTH OF
The Golden Age
IN THE
Renaissance

Oxford University Press

NEW YORK

#2969657

FOR HENRY HATFIELD

THE PATTEN FOUNDATION

MR. WILL PATTEN of Indianapolis (A.B., Indiana University, 1893) made, in 1931, a gift for the establishment of the Patten Foundation at his Alma Mater. Under the terms of this gift, which became available upon the death of Mr. Patten (May 3, 1936), there is to be chosen each year a Visiting Professor who is to be in residence several weeks during the year. The purpose of this prescription is to provide an opportunity for members and friends of the University to enjoy the privilege and advantage of personal acquaintance with the Visiting Professor. The Visiting Professor for the Patten Foundation in 1967 was

HARRY LEVIN

[✿]

Contents

[✿]

Preface

A LONGISH TITLE ought to indicate the contents of a book. Each of the concepts triangulated here—myth, golden age, Renaissance —has an aura of ambiguity, which should be dispelled before we proceed. We shall be proceeding on the assumption that there really was a Renaissance, that it did not occur in the Middle Ages or in America, but that it marked the cultural progression of Western Europe during the two hundred years between the mid-fifteenth and the mid-seventeenth centuries. As a movement it had antecedents reaching beyond Dante to the ancients and consequences reaching through the post-Baconian epoch into modernity. For many living since, the Renaissance itself has been the golden age, especially in literature. Yet we ought not to beg a question which has set historians at odds; rather we ought to distinguish, as clearly as we can, between historical and mythical ages. Books have been written on the golden age of philosophy, of drama, of music, of law, even of crime. To apply such a label means neither more nor less than to pass a value judgment on history and, incidentally, upon ourselves. Our first concept, myth, is the most elusive of all. But if use and abuse have lately blurred it, they have likewise brought out its positive meaning. We think of it, not as downright falsehood, but as collective fantasy embodying ideals and memories.

Every myth, and not least the one that invites our attention, is fictitious in the double sense of the term: it is a fabrication, a made-up tale. Hence, if we do not dismiss it for its demonstrable untruth, we must examine its make-up for intimations of symbolic truth. Where and when was it made, by whom and how, with what intent and effect, and—since nothing can come of nothing within men's minds—from what store of inherited materials? Though the answers to such questions may be conjectural, they may be substantiated by comparative studies. If we conceive of human expression as a spectrum of possibilities, then mythology stands with religion at an imaginative extreme. Civilization has been broadly pushing toward the opposite end, the scientific approach, the realistic transcription of direct experience. Yet these are differences of degree, which need not be mutually exclusive. Plato, pointing the way toward the rational, often fell back on myths to clinch his point. James Joyce, starting from an accumulation of data, set it in order by a sequence of appeals to the mythical. Criticism, in its perennial search for originality, too long overlooked or underrated those continuities which have made all literature one organic enterprise. Folklore, anthropology, and psychology have been bringing new insights to Aristotle's principle that the *mythos* is the soul of the literary work.

Some critics have been moving so far and so fast in this recent direction that, abandoning their task of discrimination, they would turn everything into a pallid reduction of what they presume to have been its archetype. Analogues from unrelated cultures, insofar as these are based on true analogy, may well be adduced to demonstrate the universality of a given myth. But there we must distinguish between the myth itself, which belongs to a particular culture, and the motif, the generic feature that various myths have in common. Even if we limit our perspective to that body of mythological lore which originated in Greece, was syncretized by Rome, and passed on to us through the Latin tradition, the territory before us is still so dense and expansive that we could quite easily lose our way. However, we have the reassurance of knowing that it has been charted and can be retraced. Relationships are conscious and explicit; testimony, for the most part, is documented and signed.

Though we could do little more than sample it here and there, we may hope to discern a representative pattern. In this instance, there can be no temptation to assume that our witnesses literally believed in the myths they evoked with such varied eloquence. Their religious beliefs came from other sources, leaving them to cultivate the classics for intellectual and esthetic purposes, and with increasingly secularistic results.

This process of acculturation is perhaps more remarkable than, in our habituation to it, we always remember. The Occident has lived with two mythologies side by side, one supporting its theological and ethical commitments, the other providing models and conventions for the arts. Traditionally a sharp line has been drawn between the one and the other, between Christian verity and pagan fiction. But the parallels are strong and the contacts are numerous. "All peoples that have a history have a paradise, a state of innocence, a golden age," as Schiller remarked. "Moreover, every single man has his paradise, his golden age, which he recollects with more or less rapture according to his more or less poetic nature." Schiller's remark stresses both the universal responsiveness to the theme and the individual variation among the responses. It takes us back to Genesis, the beginning of all things in whatever version; and when the outlook is reversed under modern conditions, it looks forward to a millennial ending. The expected rule of heaven on earth, the spiritual faith in a Millennium, is secularized into the temporal notion of a Utopia, which in turn affects political thought and programs of revolutionary action. Similarly, on a spatial plane, the backward glance at Eden has its classical counterpart in Arcadia and its exotic counterparts elsewhere, the farther the happier.

The myth of the golden age is a nostalgic statement of man's orientation in time, an attempt at transcending the limits of history. Since it concentrates mainly upon a prehistoric epoch, a foreworld once perfected and now lost, its usual corollary is a recoil from the belated decadence of the present epoch, whenever that may be. When the focus is shifted from the past to the future, the standpoint shifts to the idea of progress. In both cases—especially the latter, where specific plans can be envisaged—it posits an ideal relation between man and man. It holds up an anarchic vision of justice among men, peace among peoples, and love between the sexes. Love, its most affirmative value, is largely defined by the accumulating hatreds of the other ages. It is not to be equated with marriage; indeed there were no women in the original myth. The constant yearning for peace is the echo of a revulsion from war, which has determined the state of affairs more often than not. In much the same way, justice is negatively set forth as the absence of prior or subsequent injustice. All the evils of society are blamed upon the aggressions of property. Our ultimate forefathers were able to do without it, and of course without labor or trade, because of the garden-like fruitfulness of their natural environment. The shibboleth describing their way of life, "in common," is continuously balanced against the acquisitive catchwords, "mine" and "thine."

Christianity rationalized Adam's eviction from the earthly paradise with the doctrine of *felix culpa*; it was a blessing in disguise, since man was given an occupation; he could work out, in the literal sense, his salvation thereafter. For the loss of the golden age no compensations were seen. The utopian dream of prospective leisure, made possible by the development of technology, seems to have found its fulfilment in the nightmares of science fiction. At all events, the *ur*-myth led straight back from an urban locale to a state of nature, pastoral if not utterly primitivistic, trammeled with few institutions and no inventions. What then, freed from all cares and responsibilities, did men live for? For happiness, to be sure, but where did they seek it? Not in any religious sublimation—More draws the contrast strikingly in his *Utopia*—but in the sensory values of this world. If there is a single unifying concept which runs through the corpus of texts about the golden age, it is pleasure —pleasure unabashed, as Tasso is at pains to specify. Each of the many different versions, with some regional variance, seems to take place against the same setting: a pleasance or pleasant landscape, the *locus amoenus*. Such images were projections of ideas, skeptical and naturalistic in purport, fostering an emphasis on free will, an ethic of hedonism, a cult of beauty. This is why the golden age was so pertinent a myth for the Renaissance, as Américo Castro has pointed out.

"The lament for a golden age is only a lament for golden men," wrote Thoreau in his journal. In either case, it remains a lament, and its mode has been prevailingly elegiac. However, there have been occasions when elegy was transformed into carnival, most spectacularly at the courts and in the cities of the Renaissance. The humanistic revival of learning conjoined with the unprecedented efflorescence of the arts to act out the fancy that the golden age had returned. Though artists duly tried to paint the myth, they did not make as much of it as could have been expected. For reasons we shall be noting, it is essentially a literary subject, and there were few men of letters in whose works we could not find some sort of allusion to it. But, though it flourished on patronage and on the rhetoric of dedications and thanks, there were doubts at a more serious level; there were those who, adopting a more traditional stance, lamented the fate of living in the iron age. After all, the mythical golden age would have been the absolute antithesis of the Renaissance in several important respects. The former distrusted elaboration and favored simplicity. It looked upon art, with considerable suspicion, as an upstart antagonistic to nature. Most ironically, it had little use for knowledge. Other myths, and notably that of Prometheus, gave more adequate reflection to those intellectual curiosities which ushered in modern science.

In their monumental edition of Ben Jonson, C. H. Herford and Percy Simpson declare that "the most palpable flaw in the traditional conception of the Golden Age" was "its blank incapacity of growth." This is a surprisingly myopic pronouncement, in view of the capacity that conception has shown for adaptation to changes and innovations. No discovery can have made more impact on the European consciousness than the exploration of the Americas. At this crucial point, as we shall see, the old myth was transposed from a chronological to a geographical sphere. The voyagers reported on the natives of the western hemisphere in language which created a new myth, that of the noble savage, launched by Montaigne and assigned to so strategic a role in the ideology of Rousseau. The elements of our story tend to diffuse and to merge with other tendencies in the post-Renaissance period. Yet it is not without continuing relevance for the age of uranium, into which we have thus far managed to survive. Something like it seems to be motivating those pathetic youngsters who describe themselves as "flower people" today. Theirs is a vagrant quest for the good life. They revert to a pseudo-primitive idleness in order to repudiate a social involvement which they have found oppressive in its conformities. Their escape is only another pipe dream, yet it is also a meaningful protest. And they reassert a long tradition of disregarded wisdom in their slogan: "Make love, not war."

Something should here be said about the scope and method of the chapters that follow. Unlike most other myths, that of the golden age does not really narrate much of a story. Its cast of characters is supernumerary and anonymous, except for two unrelated figureheads who have little to do. Its actual function is to project an attitude. Consequently, it lends itself best to a sequence of generalizations, usually spoken as asides, ranging from casual allusions to speculative excursions, in works whose main concern is otherwise. Thus it blends in with Montaigne's reflections on the natives of the New World, and that essay in its turn becomes a kind of moral backdrop for a Shakespearean comedy. An underlying wishfulness brings the myth close to the very basis for all fiction, the poetic process itself; yet, even in this impetus toward escape, it has a way of turning back to the world and engaging in satire. A protean aptitude for adjustment, along with a generality inviting the widest application, helps to explain why it figures in so many contexts. If all of these were collected together, there would be an overwhelming amount of repetition; hence a student of the subject must approach it selectively; and, beyond the area of his selection, there is bound to be a large area containing instances he has missed. He can only hope that those he has touched upon are central or typical.

An exhaustive study of the topic announced by my title would be a life-work, preferably to be pursued at the Warburg Institute. Iconology, by tracing its images back to their generative ideas, with a special devotion to the cultural linkages between classical antiquity and the Renaissance, has set a stimulating example for students of literature. There is further incentive in the fact that we stand closer to our material, since all of it is verbal. But if we are centering upon thematic analysis, on pursuing a protracted and continuous pattern of thought through the divers meanings it has held for different writers, we cannot pretend to deal adequately with any single writer or with the full esthetic depth of his writings. The breadth of the panorama, the interplay of relationship, will have to compensate; and if some names are merely cited in passing, it will not be for the gratification of dropping them, but in the hope that some other curious reader will pick them up and carry on from there. Our terrain is a middle ground between literary criticism and the history of ideas—not too much of a limbo today, I trust, when the humanistic disciplines are finding new stimulus through convergence. Since the subject matter is so rich, and so much of it ought to be considered at first hand, I have tried to quote as often or paraphrase as closely as possible. Apparent repetitions will be seen, in context, to present significant variations.

My regard for the interwoven texts far exceeds my confidence in the interweaving commentary. Together they are intended to serve as an illustrated outline; but most of the quoted passages could probably speak for themselves as a chrestomathy or a *florilège*. The scheme of organization, operating within a framework determined by historical lines of development and subdivided by national and linguistic continuities, also pays as much attention as has seemed feasible to conceptual or topical relations. The persistent vehicle that bears the burden of changing significance is the *topos*, the rhetorical set-piece. The exemplary treatment of its permutations was given by Ernst Robert Curtius in his *Europäische Literatur und Lateinisches Mittelalter* (Bern, 1948). It is to be noted that this compendious work does not include the golden age among the *topoi* it retraces. For the seeming omission there are good reasons, which will be discussed in their place. The myth had no great currency in the Middle Ages; it had evolved in Greece and crystallized in Rome. Most of its Greco-Roman manifestations are reprinted, translated, and summarized in the standard compilation of A. O. Lovejoy and George Boas, *A Documentary History of Primitivism and Related Ideas in Antiquity* (Baltimore, 1935). This subsumes and augments the earlier undertaking of Ernst Graf, "Ad aureae aetatis fabulam symbola," *Leipziger Studien zur Classischen Philologie*, VIII (1885).

The volume of Lovejoy and Boas was to have been the first in a projected series conveying the history of primitivism into modern times. Later volumes have not appeared, although Professor Boas has made some additional contributions, notably his *Essays on Primitivism and Related Ideas in the Middle Ages* (Baltimore, 1948). In retrospect, it seems doubtful whether the post-classical developments could have been treated on the same scale or in the same way. I have attempted to summarize the myth as it was known to the ancients, while formulating some of the problems it raises, in my introductory chapter. My concluding chapter is a sketchy endeavor to look ahead from the seventeenth century to the Enlightenment and toward our own day. Latter-day interest, as expressed by Novalis or Dostoevsky, has been sporadic but striking. The body of this book has to do with the Renaissance, mainly as it proceeded through the Romance cultures to England. If the English documentation has outweighed the rest, that is primarily because of its accessibility to me. The diffusion of the myth has spread it wider than my competence to track it down. I am fascinated to learn about *Erophíle*, the Romaic tragedy by George Hortátzis, strongly influenced by Tasso, through the translations of F. H. Marshall in *Three Cretan Plays* (Oxford, 1929). Certain Slavic versions are attested by František Graus in "Social Utopias in the Middle Ages,"

Past and Present, 38 (December, 1967), and Ante Kadić, "Marin Oržić, Croatian Renaissance Playwright," *Comparative Literature*, XI, 4 (Fall, 1949).

It was a sign that the golden age had been relatively neglected, when it was barely mentioned in so authoritative a survey as Douglas Bush's *Mythology and the Renaissance Tradition in English Poetry* (Minneapolis, 1932). This particular lacuna was conscientiously filled in by the doctoral dissertation of F. Y. St. Clair, "The Myth of the Golden Age from Spenser to Milton" (Harvard, 1931), which unfortunately was never published. The article of Paul Meissner, "Das goldene Zeitalter in der Englischen Renaissance," *Anglia*, LIX, 3/4 (July, 1935), offers a brief account of relevant aspects, and the published thesis of Erika Lipsker-Zarden, *Der Mythos vom goldenen Zeitalter in der Schäferdichtung Italiens, Spaniens und Frankreichs zur Zeit der Renaissance* (Berlin, 1933), is usefully descriptive if not analytic. The inaugural lecture of Mia I. Gerhardt, *Het Droombeeld van de Gouden Eeow* (Utrecht, 1956), is, within its compass, suggestive. The study of Paulus Svendsen, *Gullalderdrøm og Utviklingstro* (Oslo, 1940), is comprehensive, though oriented toward Scandinavian culture. Walter Veit emphasizes Germany and confuses the *topos* with Judeo-Christian conceptions in *Studien zur Geschichte des Topos der Goldenen Zeit von dem Antike bis zum 18 Jahrhundert* (Cologne, 1961). The theme has been treated from a social vantage point by H. J. Massingham in *The Golden Age: The Story of Human Nature* (London, 1927), as an undercurrent of intellectual history by Hiram Haydn in *The Counter-Renaissance* (New York, 1950), and as a reaction to sexual taboos by Wayland Young in *Eros Denied* (London, 1965). The recent book of A. Bartlett Giammati, *The Earthly Paradise and the Renaissance Epic* (Princeton, 1966), makes an illuminating approach to a neighboring theme.

Each of these studies has, in its own field, suggested examples which have extended my reading, and I am grateful to them for spurring me on to attempt a more general interpretation. I am glad that the monograph of Elizabeth Armstrong, *Ronsard and the Age of Gold* (Cambridge, 1968), came out just in time for me to mention it here, though sorry I could not digest it more fully and reconsider my page or two on Ronsard in its intensive light. Many of the authors whom I have merely saluted deserve the thorough reconsideration that Mrs. Armstrong has accorded her poet. She has compared his view of the golden age with that of his French contemporaries, and has enriched her study with pictorial as well as literary illustrations. But, though she shows an interesting disparity between Ronsard's use of the myth for courtly flattery and his private transplantation of it to the countryside, a more extensive range of comparison would show that he had been anticipated by convention in almost every instance. Seeking to strengthen her claims for Ronsard's originality, Mrs. Armstrong discusses the association between Don Quixote's discourse on the golden age and the handful of acorns that sets it off. "Would even he have been able to produce this particular association of ideas," she asks, "had Ronsard not pioneered it a generation before?" It would be my answer that Cervantes had many nearer sources, and that Ronsard was by no means a pioneer in this respect.

My own venture was animated by the experience of giving a Harvard seminar in the comparative literature of the Renaissance, and finding through the course of several years that the golden age had become its leitmotif. When Indiana University honored me with an invitation to deliver the Patten Lectures (February 15–March 22, 1967), it presented not only an occasion for trying my notions out on a distinguished and hospitable audience but also an arrangement for bringing them out in a book. My customary researches in the Widener and Houghton libraries had been supplemented, during the fall of 1966, by a most pleasant and profitable sojourn as visiting scholar at the Henry E. Huntington Library in San Marino, California. Harvard University facilitated my sabbatical plans with a grant from the Joseph H. Clark Fund. My preliminary sketch, "The Golden Age and the Renaissance," appears in a collection edited by Carroll Camden on the centennial of Rice University, *Literary Views: Critical and Historical Essays*

(Chicago, 1964). Two articles on related concepts are reprinted here as appendices. The first, "Paradises, Heavenly and Earthly," originally the Founder's Day address at the Huntington Library on February 28, 1966, was first printed in the *Huntington Library Quarterly*, XXIX, 4 (August, 1966); slightly revised and somewhat amplified, it has been republished in *Encounter* XXXII, 6 (June, 1969). The second appendix, "Some Paradoxes of Utopia," was contributed to a symposium at Union College, and has appeared in a pamphlet on Edward Bellamy among the College's series of *Union Worthies* (23).

To all of these sponsors, whose encouragement was manifested in so many ways, I would express my deep gratitude. I wish there were some way of recording my incidental debts: to students whose questions taught me to take a fresh look at familiar subjects, to scholars in other fields who welcomed my intrusions and generously shared their expert knowledge. For valuable suggestions and criticisms I feel particularly indebted to four colleagues: Morton Bloomfield, Stephen Gilman, Walter Kaiser, and Agnes Mongan. Elizabeth Ann Farmer, with her usual competence, has typed the manuscript. Elena Zarudnaya Levin, with more than her usual patience, has checked the references. Unhappily I cannot thank the colleague to whom I feel the greatest obligation, the late Renato Poggioli. Our long academic collaboration and personal dialogue were enlivened during his last years by the circumstance of working on parallel projects. His was so much larger, and he had it so well in hand, that near the outset I offered to set mine aside. His characteristic response was to view the two undertakings as complementary, and to encourage me with helpful advice. The major contribution that was promised by his masterly essay, "The Oaten Flute," in the *Harvard Library Bulletin*, XI, 2 (Spring, 1957), a reinterpretation of the pastoral through perceptive revaluations of individual works, had not quite been completed when he died in 1963. However, a substantial manuscript exists in good condition, and soon we may look forward to its publication by the Harvard University Press.

The reader should be alerted to one or two mechanical details. He will observe no footnotes on these pages. The decision to avoid them was reluctantly and regretfully taken; but, given the nature of the disquisition, it was feared that they would pose an endless temptation to digress. Accordingly, the notes in the rear are the simplest bibliographical references, linked with the text by page numbers and key phrases. They keep a record of specific acknowledgments to critical and scholarly discussions which have relevance for, or had influence on, this one. Yet most of the quotations are from primary documents, and in many cases from early editions. A special effort has been made to use contemporaneous English translations of continental authors, where they exist. Frequently, when exact phrasing is important, the quotation is in the original language; and where no translator is acknowledged, I am responsible for the translation. No attempt has been made to regularize the sometimes exasperating inconsistency of older English spelling and punctuation, except for modernizing the long *s*, following our useage with *i* and *j* and with *u* and *v*, and expanding such typographical abbreviations as the ampersand. The frontispiece, reproduced through the permission of the Harvard College Library, is from the fine collection of French illustrated books of the sixteenth century gathered by Philip Hofer for the Department of Printing and Graphic Arts. It belongs to a series of woodcuts illustrating an epitome of Ovid's *Metamorphoses*, and is briefly described in Appendix C.

H. L.

Wellfleet, Massachusetts
July 18, 1968

THE MYTH OF

The Golden Age

IN THE

Renaissance

[I]

PREHISTORY

Our story begins, somewhat prior to the beginnings of history, with the primordial formula of the storyteller: *once upon a time*. We are invited to stretch our minds backward as far as we can conceive of human existence, beyond its historical records to its mythic traditions, insofar as these have been preserved or revived through poetry, the arts, and the other organs of culture. The invitation should not be less attractive because it offers some degree of respite from the pressing responsibilities of our times. Temporarily casting aside the burden of time itself, it beckons us toward that timeless sphere where experience is regulated by ritual and individuals merge into archetypes—and where, as Homer tells it, "all existence is a dream of ease." The Nietzschean myth of the eternal return, as it has been traced across an extensive terrain of anthropology by Mircea Eliade, attests the depth and breadth of this appeal to the collective unconscious. History may or may not repeat itself; mythology could scarcely exist without repetition; and the imagination has rounded its cycle, again and again, by returning to its storied point of departure: *in illo tempore*. Those were the days . . . The reader who turns away from his morning newspaper to literature may well feel more comfortable with the past than with the present. But if he reads very widely or deeply, he knows that any given period of the past, so long as it was the present, had its own discomforts, and also that it probably had its own yearnings for still more distant periods.

3

We cannot look back to an age which did not look back toward *illud tempus*, time immemorial, half-forgotten days of yore, melted snows of yesteryear, *antan*. That ultimate recollection has always been sealed and separated from its commemorators by a cataclysm of some kind. Such was the giant race before the flood; such was life in the garden before the fall; such was the *douceur de vivre* before the revolution. After so many aeons of more or less painful vicissitude, man instinctively longs to reestablish contact with what he has never ceased to regard as his aboriginal situation. The elder statesman, Nestor, may shake his head, recalling his grandsires and reminding his juniors that they are lesser men than their fabulous forebears. But the old Yankee farmer is more realistic when he remarks, "Things ain't so good as they used to be, and they never were." Their memory keeps receding like a mirage; yet it remains, as Sir Kenneth Clark has stated, "the most enchanting dream which has ever consoled mankind, the myth of a golden age in which man lived on the fruits of the earth, peacefully, piously, and with primitive simplicity." Consoled—the formulation is apt in suggesting the wastelands of actuality that loom behind this vision of well-being. The dream might be described by folklorists as an etiological fable, explaining how men came to be alienated from nature and why they have lived too seldom in peace and plenty, justice and freedom, leisure and love.

The consequence is their desire to recapture that primal freshness, to restore that innocence which later ages have blemished. The earliest age of mankind is associated with the verdure of springtime, with the spontaneity of childhood, and often with the awakening of love. Long before and long after Petrarch, poets have been chanting variations on the theme: "*Nel dolce tempo della prima etade . . .*" Novelists, discovering for themselves the principle that ontogeny recapitulates phylogeny, have concentrated more and more intensively on the joys and pangs of adolescence. In his book of reminiscent sketches, *The Golden Age*, Kenneth Grahame refers to his adults as the Olympians, with the implication that children are the true Saturnians, reliving the infantile fantasies of the race.

4

"*Wo Kinder sind*," said Novalis, "*da ist ein Goldnes Zeitalter*." Nostalgia for a happier day would be a sterile emotion, if it merely sighed for what was not; encouraged by the rotation of the seasons, it is transfigured into a hope for recurrence. The Judeo-Christian tradition moves from paradise lost to paradise regained, from Eden through the wilderness to Canaan, the land flowing with milk and honey, and hence from retrospection to prophecy. It looks forward from the peaceable kingdom of Isaiah, where swords are beaten into plowshares while the wolf dwells with the lamb, toward the Apocalypse, with its city of resplendent gold, the New Jerusalem. And when these visions shift from the past to the future, they harbor terrors as well as hopes; Antichrist must battle with the Messiah, and Doomsday precede the kingdom of God on earth.

Our primary concern, however, is not millennial but primitivistic. Not only must we begin at the very beginning, but we shall be repeatedly coming back to it. Now cultural primitivism—which we need not distinguish here from chronological primitivism, since we shall be involved with chronology soon enough—has been paradoxically defined by its most authoritative students, Arthur Lovejoy and George Boas, as "the discontent of the civilized with civilization." Its exemplar is the queen who plays milkmaid or the artist who goes native on a South Sea isle. As the definition should imply, the positive thrust of this attitude has been provoked by a negativistic recoil: that is to say, the praise of times past, its *laus temporis acti*, is an implicit critique of nowadays. Moreover, the predilection for what it fancies to be primitive is essentially a sophisticated, not to say a sentimental, state of mind. That man is happy, it asserts, who lives far from affairs, like the pristine race of mortals.

> *Beatus ille qui procul negotiis,*
> *ut prisca gens mortalium . . .*

And, having distinguished sharply between the alternatives of business and leisure, *negotium* and *otium*, Horace continues with a townsman's nostalgic description of the countryside and concludes by revealing that his spokesman is a moneylender, who will be back at his counter after a short vacation. Those sentiments have been emulated by weekenders and exurbanites ever since. The way of rural life especially envied by the city-dwelling poet is the leisure he imagines the shepherd to enjoy, fondly imagining—if we may judge from the immense accumulation of poems devoted to this notion—that shepherds spend more of their efforts in chasing shepherdesses than sheep. It is not for nothing that the homely word for herdsman, *swain*, has become synonymous with lover. Other humble outdoor occupations, such as fishing, have occasionally vied with the tending of sheep or of goats as subjects for poetic idealization; the Renaissance produced a few piscatories along with its innumerable pastorals. But the classic ideal of pastoralism, refining upon the folkways of a sheep-grazing culture, would be hallowed by its coalescence with the Christian symbolism of the pastor and his flock. The emblem of Jesus, the lamb, tinges Chaucer's picture of "The Former Age," when he commemorates "The lambish peple, voyd of alle vyce." The pasture is the playground of Spenser's spokesman, Colin Clout, in *The Shepheardes Calender*:

> *O happy* Hobbinoll, *I blesse thy state,*
> *That Paradise hast found, which* Adam *lost.*

The pastoral, as a literary form, was primitivistic rather than primitive: sentimental rather than naive, in Schiller's terms, since the poet employed such conscious artifice to signalize his relationship with nature. The bucolic—to give the genre its Hellenistic title—was an Alexandrian invention, practised with particular elegance and elaboration by the cosmopolitan Theocritus, who set his rustic scenes on his native island of Sicily. In Latinizing such idylls, it was Vergil who transplanted their setting to an isolated locality which, from a Roman vantage-point, would seem more remote and rugged. Arcadia, the mountainous hinterland of the Peloponnesian Peninsula, is celebrated in the Homeric hymn to Pan, the tutelary god of its singing herdsmen, as a land of many springs and the mother of flocks. Yet the shadow of Rome falls directly on Vergil's first eclogue, when his spokesman Tityrus voices his thanks to Octavius for having intervened to save his farm from confiscation. And with the poet's farewell, in the tenth and last eclogue, he detaches himself from his Arcadian companions and wistfully identifies himself with the departing onlooker: *"utinam ex vobis unus . . . fuissem."* There, as at other moments, the Vergilian heartcry seems to sound like the voice of the modern artist, with his elegiac tone, his backward glance, and his innate self-consciousness. "Would that I were truly one of you!" he exclaims in effect. Would that we might somehow close that rift between the isolated self and its natural environment!

The pastoral mode has been discussed by criticism and scholarship on a scale commensurate with the role it has played in the history of western literature. For so limited and so limiting a medium, its fortunes have been spectacular, and indeed could not be comprehended except through the emotional charge that it has single-mindedly and repetitively conveyed. "Pastoral is an image of what they call the Golden Age," wrote Alexander Pope at the age of sixteen. Following a neo-classical precept, he was starting his own poetic career by composing a series of pastorals. The eighteenth century had its urbanized critics who would disagree with his dictum, and who would uncritically believe in the genuine rusticity of a Theocritus. Doubtless there have been exceptions to Pope's rule; more logically he might have turned it around, and noted that the idea of the golden age was a pastoral image. But he made an important point by formulating a connection between the spatial and the temporal concepts, between the great good place and the good old days, between the ideal landscape—Arcady, Sicily, or wherever else—and the ideal epoch, whenever that may have been or might be. *Utopia*, our name for the best-known model of all model commonwealths, means nowhere. Its namer, Sir Thomas More, intended a pun in Greek on *Eutopia*, the good place, that happy realm which never existed on land or sea or in the air. In much the same fashion, taking up a hint from Charles Renouvier, we might speak of *Uchronia* or *Euchronia* to signify either never or the good time.

The Ciceronian lament over modern manners, "*O tempora! O mores!*," has its sequel in the wish of Boethius that modernity might go back to the ways of antiquity:

> *Utinam modo nostra redirent*
> *In mores tempora priscos!*

Undetachably our lives stand rooted in the firm realities of here and now. Restlessness may project our thoughts in unspecified directions: "Anywhere out of the world," to echo the phrase that Baudelaire echoed from Thomas Hood. But if our longing to escape—or, more positively, to better our condition—has any goal, however dimly envisioned, it must be located elsewhere or otherwhile. Standing here and wishing to be there, we are given a choice, at least by imagination; we may opt for some distant part of the world, a terrestrial paradise, or for an otherworld, a celestial paradise. Living now and preferring to live then, we are not likely to get beyond an imaginative exercise; but again we are faced with a double option. If we reject the present, we must choose between the past and the future, between an Arcadian retrospect and a Utopian prospect. The spatial and the temporal distances may prolong one another, as they do in exotic imaginings that took place far away and long ago. Both of them fall within the orbit of primitivism. On the other hand, both the expectation of an afterlife and, on a more worldly plane, the resolve to build a heaven on earth through social planning share a common expectancy, which might be viewed as chiliasm or millennialism. (See figure.) These are the possibilities that lay open to the visionary, whose area of speculation is bounded only by what a German scholar calls wish-space (*Wunschraum*) and wish-time (*Wunschzeit*).

Any willed alternative to things as they are is likely to present itself as an amelioration of them. Landscapes of other worlds tend to vary according to the various cultures that have imagined them. Conceptions of the best of times, of Uchronia, tend to shade off almost imperceptibly into heavens and hereafters. Yet, on the whole, there has been a striking consistency in the ideals of the good life

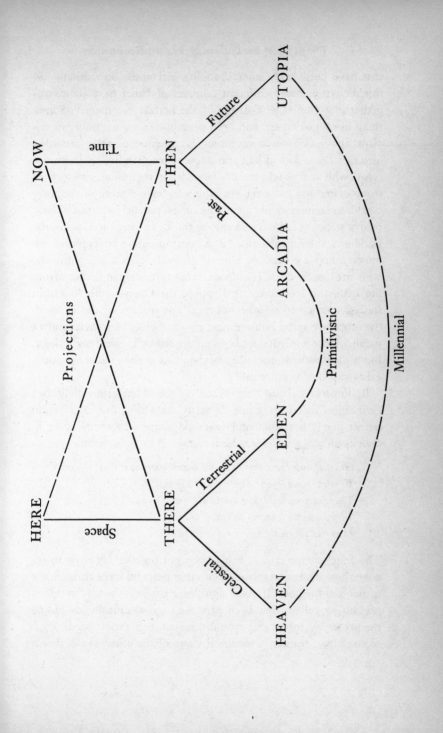

that have been held under changing circumstances; writers and thinkers from many different climates of belief have joined together in a mutual wish-dream of the perfect community. Something like a golden age had been presupposed by a number of ancient civilizations as a mythological prelude to their recorded histories. Some sort of halcyon stage, when men lived on intimate terms with their gods, usually heralded a regression into a more troublesome and more recognizable era. Such a myth of the foreworld, sometimes involving a more or less parallel sequence of four or five stages, is to be found among the Egyptians, the Hindus, the Buddhists, the Zoroastrians, the Aztecs, and other adherents of the most venerable creeds. As a motif of folklore, to be caught in the wide net cast by Stith Thompson, it has turned up in versions from the Irish, the Icelandic, the Lappish, the Chinese, the American Indian, and numerous other sources. The analogy of the *Völuspá*, the prophecy in the Norse Eddas, may not quite be an independent parallel, since it might have been influenced by classical mythology. But a plentitude of examples, as abundant as the golden age itself, exists to prove its universality.

Its impact is already registered on the oldest relics of literate civilization that have come down to us. On a clay tablet from Sumer nearly four thousand years old, there is an adumbration in cuneiform script which has been translated by S. N. Kramer:

> *Once upon a time, there was no snake, there was no scorpion,*
> *There was no hyena, there was no lion,*
> *There was no wild dog, no wolf,*
> *There was no fear, no terror,*
> *Man had no rival.*

The fragmentary tale, as it has been put together, goes on to recount how dissension intruded into that peaceful scene through the quarrels of the gods. Its most significant aspect is the way in which preexisting felicity has been expressed by specifically excluding the predatory forces that would threaten it. A similar tendency is so constant a feature in medieval views of the other world, that it

has been designated by Howard Patch as "the negative formula."
Thus the Anglo-Saxon poem about the phoenix, which has precedents going much farther back, dwells upon those characteristics
of the Old English climate which might be more happily avoided
in a more tropical land:

> *No rain or snow,*
> *or breath of frost or blast of fire,*
> *or freezing hail or fall of rime,*
> *or blaze of sun or bitter long cold,*
> *or scorching summer or winter storm*
> *work harm a whit.*

Such denials open the way for oblique satire or protest. Any enumeration of those ills whose absence was the precondition of bliss,
obviously, reflects back again from the illusory past to the less than
satisfactory present and, more immediately, to the beholder who is
less than satisfied with what he beholds. Roughly speaking, the
golden age is all that the contemporary age is not. Consequently,
any specification of the factors making for its initial beatitude comprises a revealing index of subsequent values and of the changing
interests of other ages. One is reminded of those Victorian albums
wherein young people's characters could be read through their
responses to such challenges as "your idea of happiness."

We need hardly ask ourselves why man, in exalting his racial
memories, transferred the gold standard from economics to ethics
by way of esthetics. Karl Marx has some mordant pages on this
transvaluation in his *Critique of Political Economy*. The paradox
is that the simple life should be denoted by such a sumptuous term
and, more profoundly, that the same precious and ambiguous substance should be regarded as both a touchstone for goodness and
the root of all evil. Literally, the poetry of the ancients is aglitter
with golden objects; the language of the Greeks is rich in compounds and epithets which spread that aureate glow. Pervading
their myths, it gilds the apples of Atalanta, the shower of Danaë,
the fleece of Jason, the bough of Aeneas. Taken metaphorically, it

affords an evaluation of the highest excellence; the beauty of Aphrodite is characterized as golden by Homer; and Lucian reduces the characterization to absurdity by describing people made of real gold. Socrates patiently explains, in the *Cratylus* of Plato, that the adjective χρύσεος means good or noble. Similarly, the Latin *aureus* comes to be the equivalent of *optimus*. Whenever we allude to the golden mean, the golden rule, or the golden legend, we accept the value judgment that singles each of them out as the best of its species. The garden of Eden seems to have been adjacent to the land of Havilah, "where there is gold," as we are told in the book of Genesis. "And the gold of that land is good."

Speculations dazzle and disconcert us by ranging from early religions, which—like Pindar—associate gold with the sun, to Freudian psychoanalysis, which associates it with faeces. Because it stood at the head of the hierarchy of metals, it played a dominant part in the tangled network of quasi-religious and prescientific assumptions that prompted the hypotheses and experiments of the alchemists. The position to which they assigned it was comparable to the one that the physicists assigned to the atom, before it was disintegrated by nuclear physics. As the only pure mineral, gold was the fundamental basis of matter itself, the *prima materia*. When it liquified into potable gold, it became an elixir of life, a sovereign remedy for all bodily complaints. Its final and unattainable transfiguration was nothing less than the philosophers' stone, the talisman of absolute mastery over the physical world. Gold is more familiar to us—though still rare enough to exert an ambivalent force—as the measure of material wealth, whether reckoned by ingots or by coins. "No loadstone so attractive as that of profit," observed Robert Burton, "none so fair an object as this of gold." As our basic symbol for the profit motive, its luster gets morally tarnished. "Gold is not merely powerful, it is almost all-powerful," complained Petrarch in a letter, "and everything under the heavens above is subject to its domination." Aeneas blamed the fall of Troy on the cursed thirst for it (*"auri sacra fames"*). The twilight of the Nordic gods was the outcome of the struggle for the Rhinegold.

Whether or not such metal was the earliest to be mined or minted, as Marx argued, its essential purity was unalloyed by considerations of practical usefulness. Silver has usually been coupled with it, sharing its moral ambivalence to a lesser extent and suffering slightly from the esthetic comparison. Brass (the alloy known to archaeologists, in its Italianized variant, as bronze), carried the imputation of hardened nerve that is adjectivally connoted by *brazen*. Iron has connotations which are harder and harsher; yet, since it indicates a crucial step on the way to civilization as we know it, with all its potentialities for construction and for destruction, it should connote the plow as well as the sword. The bronze age and the iron age, of course, are recognized by archaeological science; the golden age and the silver age, alas, have a purely mythical significance; and the metals themselves have no place in those myths, except as chronological metaphors. "Mythology's golden age was humanity's stone age," remarked the Swedish poet, Viktor Rydberg. Some of the characteristics attributed to the denizens of the golden age, according to the conjectures of Lewis Mumford, may have really been present in the culture of neolithic man. The distinctive trait of any endeavor to reconstruct the first epoch of humanity, whether by poets or by anthropologists, is the fact that it necessarily must have antedated the developments and the encroachments of technology.

The sequence of four metals has the ethical sanction of the Old Testament, as well as of the Classics. In Plato's *Republic*, Socrates categorizes his ruling class as golden, and contrasts it with the silver, the brass, and the iron qualities of inferior temperaments. "For brass I will bring gold," Isaiah promises, "and for iron I will bring silver." The monstrous statue in Nebuchadnezzar's dream, with its head of gold, its breast of silver, belly of brass, legs of iron, and feet of clay, has portended a declining succession of kingdoms for a long line of prophets extending from Daniel. Classical literature, from the outset, abounds in allusions to prehistoric ages, and to a euphoric *modus vivendi* which could favorably be compared with that of the Elysian Fields or of the Fortunate Isles. It seems to have been Hesiod who first linked the age itself with the golden metaphor, and plotted the progression of succeeding ages. His canonical version of our theme—we may well call it the *locus classicus*—occurs in his *Works and Days*, that farmer's almanac of early Hellas, alongside of other cosmogonic fables: notably those of Prometheus and Pandora, with their respective implications regarding the consequences of intellectual curiosity. Since it was Pandora who brought trouble into the world, and since like Eve she was the first of her sex, it follows that there were no women in Hesiod's golden age. As a matter of fact, he does not term it an age (αἰών), nor does he use the magic number four.

He sings of five generations, the first of them a golden race (χρύσεον γένος), mortal men living like gods and loved by the gods while Kronos was reigning in heaven. Free from care, they dwelt in ease and peace among their flocks and on land which yielded its fruits without being forced. After long lives and painless deaths, they became benevolent spirits, and were replaced by a silver race which was weaker, inconsiderate toward fellow men and neglectful of the immortals. Meanwhile the reign of the Titans had been overthrown by the Olympians; it was Zeus who put an end to the silver generation, creating a brazen race which was stronger and more warlike, and which ended by destroying itself. Lacking mates, these generations could not have propagated, but were separately recreated after each dissolution. At this point, the deteriorating trend is interrupted by a nobler interlude. Zeus creates the famous race of heroes who become demigods, performing the great exploits of Thebes and Troy, and surviving to abide forever in the far-flung islands of the blest, where Kronos is reestablished as their ruler. That reversion seems to be somewhat out of keeping with the larger pattern of degeneration, and the note of military glory is at odds with the pacifistic sympathies that are voiced before and afterward. George Grote has interpreted the disparity as an unsuccessful attempt to reconcile the myths of a heroic age with the poet's didactic parable. Significantly, his fourth race has no metallic ascription, and it is omitted by most of those who retell the tale.

The fifth generation, which would normally be considered the fourth, is the worst of all, the iron race. It is still going strong, and this is where we came in. While lamenting its travail and sorrow, while denouncing the violence and dishonor of its social relationships, Hesiod takes occasion to underline the moral lesson that he has been preaching. Would that it had been otherwise, would that he himself had died earlier or had been born later! He terminates his pessimistic narration by prophesying that evil will prevail; Aidos and Nemesis, the personifications of shame and indignation, will forsake the earth. Their defection heavenwards may have prepared the way for the stellar heroine introduced into the *mythos* several centuries afterward by one of Hesiod's imitators, the Stoic poet Aratus. The latter, in his astronomical poem, *Phaenomena*, assumes the continuous descent of the four races, as well as their successive deterioration. His principal contribution is to narrate how the maiden goddess of justice, Dike, who dwelt among men during the first and even the second generations, was so appalled by the bloodshed of the third that she fled to heaven (in the wake of Hesiod's abstract deities). There she found a sanctuary in the zodiac, where she now appears as the constellation Virgo, thus combining the attribute of chastity with that of equity. All the more conspicuous in the sky because those virtues are lacking here below, she will shine down continually upon poets, who will invoke her under the starry appellation of the virgin Astraea—a sign that the gods have withdrawn from participation in men's affairs.

Such, in bald abridgment, was the myth that Greece bequeathed to Rome, where it underwent two strategic modifications at the controlling hands of Vergil. The first belongs to that process of conflation whereby the Romans adapted the religion of the Greeks to their own. In this case, the archetypal figure was Kronos (Κρόνος), the Titanic son of Heaven and Earth, whose cannibalistic treatment of his own children came to be construed as an allegory of time (Χρόνος). One of them, Zeus, escaped to take command of Olympus and to banish his father in turn to Crete. Hesiod's glimpse of the exiled Kronos presiding over the haven of the demigods, far across the sea, is the link that connects him with Saturnus, the Roman god of planting (*satus*), who was welcomed to joint rule by two-faced Janus, the indigenous god of portals and beginnings. Saturn's festival, the Saturnalia, happened to be the most popular manifestation of holiday cheer and the carnival spirit, at once a relaxation of rules and an eternal return. J. G. Frazer has suggested that it might have embodied some happy-go-lucky legend of carefree days under a merry monarch; hence it could be viewed as a temporary revival of the golden ages men talk about. One of these was evoked by the *Aeneid*, in a scenic description which is contrasted with a view of the rising city.

Aurea quae perhibent illo sub rege fuere saecula.

King Evander, himself a refugee from Arcadia, has been welcoming Aeneas to Rome, pointing out that his citadel now stands where the oak-trees anciently engendered a race of savages. Saturn, fleeing from the wrath of Jove (or Zeus) to the Hesperian shores of Italy, had settled in that region and called it Latium because it offered him a hiding place (with a pun on *latuisset*). The hidden god became a culture-hero, to be happily and nostalgically recollected during less peaceful reigns, who had civilized the natives by giving them laws and teaching them the arts of agriculture.

The second twist that Vergil gave to the myth is even more farreaching in its purport. This is the mysterious *Fourth Eclogue*, whose many reverberations have been perplexing its commentators for two millennia. By expressly turning for inspiration from the Sicilian muses of Theocritus to the prophetic books of the Cumaean Sibyl, Vergil deliberately courted that mystery. Technically, this is a genethliacon or natal ode. Addressing his friend, the consul Pollio, the poet hails the birth of a son for whom a glorious lifetime is foreseen—so glorious that interpretation has not rested content with the identification of the child as Pollio's. Some of the interpreters would attach the poem to the fortunes of Mark Antony and his son by Cleopatra, Alexander Helios; some, proceeding farther in that direction, would descry an Egyptian cult of the sun itself. Others would discern a motive for the congratulations in a recent marriage within the family of Octavius Caesar, whose own career would do more than any other to fulfill the lofty expectations that Vergil expresses here. That line of explication is borne out by the passage in the *Aeneid* where the shade of Anchises predicts that Augustus Caesar will restore the golden age to the Latian fields once ruled by Saturn. The arresting novelty of these predictions is that they transport the *aurea saecula* from the past to the immediate future. They reverse the downward movement of the four ages and look upward, look onward to a time of cyclic regeneration.

The eclogue, inspired by the sibylline oracles to sing in loftier strains, gazes into the latest (*"ultima aetas"*), not the first age, whose best remembered figures, the Virgin and Saturn, are now seen to be coming back. The great line of the centuries is born anew (*"magnus ab integro saeclorum nascitur ordo"*). With the anticipated descent of this new generation from heaven, the iron race will drop off and a golden race will spring up again throughout the world. Nature will experience a general rebirth, an unforced flowering, and herds once more will graze unharmed by vicious beasts. Typically, the tough oaks will exude dewy honey; to be literal, they will sweat with it (*"et durae quercus sudebunt roscida mella"*). Apollo will be king, and presumable sponsor of an efflorescence in the arts. Yet the age perforce will likewise witness acts of heroism; it will have to launch a second Argo and to fight another Trojan War. Then, when all the wars are finally over, the ships of pine will quit the seas. The plowmen, having no more need to cultivate the soil, will unyoke their oxen. Nor will it be necessary any longer to dye wool for clothing, for the obliging sheep will produce their fleece in assorted colors. The inevitability of this rosy advent is decreed by the Fates themselves, who are crying out to hasten it: *"Talia saecla, . . . currite."* And, with his proud announcement of it, the poet challenges Pan himself to a singing contest in Arcady.

Vergil has thus transformed the pastoral into an official eulogy:

the simplistic conventions of primitivism are rallied to the support of the Augustan principate, the *Pax Romana*, and the march of empire. Historically, the era of Augustus would be labelled a golden age, not in the Hesiodic sense but for its civilized institutions and cultural achievements. These began to shine with peculiar brightness in the silver years of dynastic decline. Yet in the following century Calpurnius Siculus did not hesitate to borrow Vergil's phrasing for an auspicious eclogue hailing the accession of the Emperor Nero. During the fourteenth century Petrarch would hail the tribunate of Rienzi as a restoration of the golden age, and so would the self-appointed tribune. The Pollio eclogue had virtually created a minor genre, a means for the court poet to flatter his sovereign, as well as a device for balancing the moderns against the ancients; and we shall be catching obsequious echoes from it as we witness later periods praising themselves and striving to realize their ideas of greatness. However, its greatest impact was inadvertent. The salute to the babe whose birth would usher in a new order, coming in conjunction with the reappearance of Virgo, would lead pious Christians to identify the goddess Astraea with the Virgin Mary and to read the poem retrospectively as a prefiguration of the nativity of Christ forty years afterward.

> *Rapt into future times, the Bard begun:*
> *A Virgin shall conceive, a Virgin bear a son.*

Pope, in his sacred eclogue "Messiah," was conflating Vergilian reminiscence with the messianic prophecies of Isaiah. But the Roman approximation had been close enough to gain the unique prestige that haloed Vergil during the Middle Ages, as a pagan writer who had apprehended some glimmering of the Christian revelation, *anima naturaliter Christiana*. To this coincidence, in part, he owed his position as Dante's guide in the *Divine Comedy*. Therein it is even supposed that Statius was converted to Christianity by reading the *Fourth Eclogue*, which Dante reechoes:

> *Secol si rinnuova;*
> *torna giustizia e primo tempo umano. . . .*

And the pagan overtone lingers among the sacred harmonies of Milton's hymn "On the Morning of Christ's Nativity":

> *For if such holy song*
> *Enwrap our fancy long,*
> *Time will run back and fetch the age of gold.*

If Hesiod first enunciated our myth, if Aratus endowed it with a feminine protagonist, Vergil reoriented it, both geographically and chronologically, when he acclimatized it to Italy. But it was his younger contemporary, Ovid, who crystallized it into a *topos*, who realigned its traditional elements in the grandly rhetorical set-piece that would be imitated, plagiarized, paraphrased, parodied, reinterpreted, controverted, distorted, and metamorphosed into so many shapes by the writers we shall be considering. As a compendium of Greco-Roman mythology, Ovid's *Metamorphoses* has been among the most fruitful and stimulating of literary sourcebooks. More than that, it constitutes a vast paean to the vitalizing and transforming power of nature itself, whose unflagging energies unify the endless changes of the particular narratives. Ovid's depiction of the four ages, not unnaturally, comes just after he has recounted the creation of the cosmos.

> *The* Golden Age *was first, which uncompeld*
> *And without rule, in faith and Truth exceld.*

These are the opening lines in the early seventeenth-century translation of George Sandys. "Uncompelled" was more affirmatively put by Ovid in "*sua sponte* (of its own accord)," as opposed to "*sine lege* (without rule)" or "*nullo vindice* (with no magistrate)" —the last omitted by the English translator, perhaps because it will be paralleled by "*sine judice* (with no judge)." There are no fears of punishment, no threatening laws. So far the man of the golden age has been negatively presented; we have learned that he is not a prisoner in the dock; and we have been obliquely asked if we can say as much for ourselves.

> *To visit other worlds no wounded pine*
> *Did yet from hills to faithless seas decline.*

By synecdoche the pine will have become a mast and thence a Vergilian ship, and will seem to be the worse for that metamorphosis. Since there is as yet no navigation, there can be no trade. Better still, there are no fortifications, no weapons, no alarums of war. The age-old vision of security and tranquillity has been placed before us by a vigorous deployment of the negative formula. The key-word seems to be *nondum*: not yet were men coerced by those pressures with which we are all too well acquainted. This is the prelapsarian situation that James Joyce sets forth at the opening of *Finnegans Wake* when, among the other tragedies that have not yet had time to happen, Sir Tristram has not yet been a "passencore" (passenger/*pas encore*) on that fateful voyage with Yseult. Such litanies of future woe are so frequent that Ernst Bloch, in his vast and immensely suggestive anatomy of human wishes, *Das Prinzip Hoffnung*, classifies them as *Noch-Nicht-Bewussten*, things not yet known.

Ovid's negations turn into blithe affirmations as soon as he permits us to contemplate the bucolic scene. True, he reminds us that the earth is still unplowed, that it is unwounded by the rake, and that it yields its crop without constraint (*"nullo cogente"*). Nonetheless, we are overwhelmed by its spontaneous bounty; we recognize some of the most typical flora; and our euphoria is undisturbed by any mention whatsoever of fauna. Acorns, the staple of Arcadian diet, are much in evidence, enhanced by the poet's awareness that they have dropped from the outspread tree of Jove: *"Et quae deciderant patula Iovis arbore glandes."* We have not seen the last of these unpretentious nuts. Ovid himself will revert to them, and to the golden age, when he arrives at the vegetarian doctrine of Pythagoras in the last book of the *Metamorphoses*. Trees always seem to stand out in sharper relief against a Mediterranean landscape, partly because they are relatively sparse, and partly because they are beautifully symbolic: the olive, the cypress, the laurel, the palm. For Ovid it is the ilex, or holm-oak, which becomes the bearer of honey, and completes an idyllic presentation recalling to us the land of Canaan:

With Milke and nectar were the Rivers fill'd,
And Hony from greene holly-okes distill'd.

As for the weather, it was eternal spring: *"ver erat aeternum."* This marks an improvement over the Italian weather that Vergil has praised in his *Georgics*, where there was persistent spring and summer during unaccustomed months: *"Hic ver adsiduum atque alienis mensibus aestas."* The silver age would bring in the other seasons, just as in the biblical story, where they are the price paid for the expulsion from Eden after the fall. "The penalty of Adam," for Shakespeare, is "The seasons' difference." Whereas the continual growth of plants and flowers all the year round is, according to Bacon, "the privilege of the golden age." This privilege may be its greatest impossibility; it is also one of its most potent attractions; for to exist without seasons is to be suspended in a state of timelessness, which would be humanly inconceivable except in an earthly paradise. Actually, our notions of time and of weather are as intimately related as their cognate Latin expressions, *tempus* and *tempestas*; in the Romance languages both are signified by the same word (*tempo, tiempo, temps*). The texture of life is bound to differ under differing atmospheric conditions; but, whatever those may be, they determine its structure.

Ovid's version of the silver age is less than half the length of his exordium on the golden age. It deals summarily with the displacement of Saturn, thrown down into Tartarus by Jove, who thereupon curtails the everlasting spring and introduces the winter, the summer, and the irregular autumn. The consequent extremes of heat and ice compel men to shelter themselves by building houses. Since the soil is no longer spontaneously fertile, tillage is concurrently introduced and the ox is subjected to the yoke. The next, the brazen age, is covered by a single sentence marking the introduction of warfare, not yet as wicked as it will become. This makes a brusque transition to the peroration on the iron age, which is treated at the same length as the golden age. Hesiod's account of the golden age itself was considerably shorter than his accounts of the subsequent ages, which lengthened as he swung from rhapsody into diatribe. Ovid's adaptation of the fourfold scheme, by foreshortening the two intervening gradations, brings out the polar opposition between what is respectively symbolized by gold and by iron. References to the silver and brazen ages are few and far between in other writers. The golden age is often conjured up for what may seem to be its own sake; but there is always an implicit cross-reference, and frequently an explicit allusion, to the iron age. The historical paradigm fades into the background, while the moral antithesis comes to the fore.

The Ovidian iron age is the golden age in reverse, as adumbrated in the companion piece and harking back to the original premises. Now every crime breaks out; shame, truth, and faith take flight; into their places steal the vices, fraud, malice, treason, force, and "the wicked love of gain (*amor sceleratus habendi*)." There is more about the folly of chopping down pines in the mountains for the purpose of constructing sea-going vessels. In recounting how the land was subdivided and how it had originally been shared, the poet glances back to the primeval stage, using a rather more positive phrase which will have some notable repercussions: "*communemque prius.*" Previously the soil, like the light and the air, was common to all. To parcel it out or fence it off, so Vergil affirmed in the *Georgics*, would have been considered a sacrilege before the ascendancy of the Olympians. It was then that Ceres first taught men husbandry, since the acorns and wildings were growing scarce. It was then too that Jove took away the honey from the trees and imposed other deprivations on men in order to stimulate their own resources for industry and enterprise. Here Vergil, the gentleman farmer, seems to be confessing a certain nostalgia for a pre-agricultural mode of living, a preference for the Saturnian outlook as against the Olympian. Yet Saturn's part is a confusing one, since he is elsewhere represented as having imported the techniques of farming to Italy. In less poetic accounts, both Greek and Roman, primitives are civilized by labor and inventions.

Ovid goes on to demonstrate why the iron age is so appropriately titled. Not content with the fruits of the soil, men have plunged into the bowels of the earth in a search for treasures which can only become incentives for further evils. The precondition of the golden age—Ovid has declared, when attacking the power of gold in his *Amores*—was that riches were allowed to remain concealed in the earth. Why should men be digging for them, or sailing the seas, or erecting fortified towns? he inquires of a personified Human Nature (*"hominum natura"*). Boethius was to ask an analogous question, and Chaucer was to twist it into a curse in his own Boethian poem, "The Former Age":

> But cursed was the tyme, I dar wel saye,
> That men first dide hir swety bysinesse
> To grobbe up metal, lurking in derknesse,
> And in the riveres first gemmes soghte.

The ambiguity of that accursed and coveted ore, the very paradox of gold itself, was memorably epitomized by Boethius in the epithet *"pretiosa pericula"*—which Chaucer translates and glosses as "precious perils" and Milton rephrases as "precious bane." Suspicion was so widespread among the poets that the pioneering minerologist of the Renaissance, Georgius Agricola, would feel it incumbent upon him to answer their objections, citing Ovid in his metallurgical treatise, *De re metallica*. Mining had seemed an act of desecration, as flying would seem for so long, and as even navigation did to an anterior day, because it pried too audaciously into nature's secrets. Civilization advances by violating such taboos against forbidden knowledge. But the reproach of Ovid was not mere obscurantism; it transmitted a pastoral curse against an industrial society. His iron age was no metaphor, and its gold was more baneful than its iron (*"ferroque nocentius aurum"*).

> Curst Steele, more cursed Gold she now forth brought
> And bloody-handed Warre, who with both fought.

The internecine conflict spreads, turning friends into enemies and destroying the family from within. Piety lies prostrate, and Astraea

—the last of the immortals to do so—abandons the earth. And the poem moves on to its next metamorphoses, the battles of the giants and the deluge.

Since Ovid's poems are so pervasively amorous, it may seem ironic that he has nothing to say about love in the golden age; but it is not surprising, since he was held back by the Hesiodic tradition that had excluded females. In the *Ars amatoria*, making one of his bitter taunts against the venality of his contemporaries, he does compress the paradoxical implications of gold into a play upon words: "*Aurea sunt vere nunc saecula . . .*" Truly this is the golden age, since the highest honor—love itself—is procurable by means of gold. Comparable sentiments are voiced by his fellow elegists. Horace reacted against the civil wars by counselling escape from Rome, modulating the usual recollection of the golden age into plans for a voyage to the blessed islands. Vergil's *Fourth Eclogue* may have been a patriotic answer to Horace's *Sixteenth Epode*. Tibullus, recoiling from the city's commercialism, which turns men into iron, pursues his love to the country, which he apostrophizes in terms of the golden age; but he goes out of his way to avoid the phrase itself, albeit he adds the interesting detail that the houses then (houses then?) had no doors. Empedocles had oracularly hinted that the age had been ruled by Venus, and Theocritus had rhapsodized the loves of golden men, but it is not until a late and anonymous elegy that we find eroticism held up as an attraction: "*Liber amor . . .*" Whilom love was free; no woman was suspected by her mate; she was chaste enough if she knew what to deny in public. Masculine broadmindedness, in this unclear case, seems to connive in feminine hypocrisy. In general, the assumption that our sires indulged in promiscuity—or what John Donne would call "plurality of loves" —was left for the Renaissance to develop.

Juvenal, in his satire against womankind, does assume that she existed in the days of Saturn. He paints an unlovely portrait of her —"often more uncouth than her acorn-belching spouse (*et saepe horridior glandem ructante marito*)"—but he credits her with the lost virtue of fidelity. The external aspects of this portrait fall into the category that Professors Lovejoy and Boas describe as hard primitivism. That was well exemplified by Lucretius, whose cave-dwelling aborigenes seduced their women with bribes of fruit and what else but acorns? Juvenal is as harsh as possible toward his own age; elsewhere he declares that it is worse than iron, that nature has no name for it, no metal to designate it. Yet, as a satirist, his harshness is softened by his commitment to a code of ethics which seems all the more virtuous because it has been flouted so flagrantly. Pudicitia, the personification of shame or modesty, lingered on earth in the days of his cave-women because—however repellent they might have been—they were chaste. Now, since the silver age has witnessed the emergence of adultery, she has flown to the heavens with Astraea. As an object-lesson in Stoic morality, the golden age formed a backdrop for the philosophy of Seneca, who reminisces about it in his tragedy *Hippolytus* and is presented reminiscing about it in the apocryphal tragedy of *Octavia*. In his most influential essay, the *Ninetieth Epistle*, he appeals to the norms of frugal nature as his authority against the corruptions of hypercivilized luxury, and to the humanistic wisdom (*sapientia*) of Diogenes against the scientific ingenuity (*sagacitas*) of Daedalus.

Citation and illustration could be multiplied further; but perhaps we have reviewed enough examples to understand how the *topos* of the four ages—and, more specially, the golden age versus the iron age—became a commonplace of classical discourse. Its provisions, as they had been codified by Ovid, were to be reiterated by others to the point of monotony. Yet, during the long-drawn-out course of reiteration, the topic was to display a fascinating capacity for adapting itself to changed viewpoints and new situations. The sketchiness of the outline facilitated its adaptation and hence its perpetuation. It had been defined by repudiating warfare and injustice, trade and travel, labor and property. As man's experience ripened, there were bound to be adjustments, revaluations of some things he had rejected, modifications in his conception of a better world, and even the possibility of attaining some of its components.

The myth had a broad application because it was so abstract; the story it tells is highly generalized; it is less of an adventure than a state of mind. Its few concrete details became its most recurrent motifs. Consider its vegetarian fare: man's earliest food, the nutriment of Arcadia, the humble fruit of Jupiter's strong tree, the inevitable acorn. It was so habitually instanced that the ancients had already grown tired of it, and Cicero cites a Greek proverb: "Enough of the oak-tree (ἅλις δρυός)!"

Recalling that the Latin *glans* is not only the etymon of our word *gland* but also the anatomical term for the forepart of the masculine genitalia, we are tempted to posit some glandular reason for the acorn's extraordinary persistence, a modest innuendo of generative powers. By the Renaissance it had become such a poetic cliché that Petrarch could write about those acorns which everybody praises while shunning them (*"quelle ghiande / le qua' fuggendo tutto 'l mondo onora"*). Góngora could exercise his gifts for elegant variation, and for transforming nature into art, by describing the evergreen oak as the canopy of the golden age (*"pabellón al siglo . . . dorado"*) and the coarse nourishment it produced as the offering of the best world, the primal brightness:

> el tributo, alimento, aunque grosero,
> de el mejor mundo, de el candor primero.

Even the Anglo-American poet of the twentieth century, if he adopts the stance of Ezra Pound, is still "bent resolutely on wringing lilies from the acorn." Thus the fundamentals of life are modified in the elaborations of literature. A useful handbook for painters and stage-designers, showing them how to personify the abstracttions, the *Iconologia* of Cesare Ripa, describes the four ages as they appeared in a comedy performed before the King of France, Henri II. The Golden Age was "a very beautiful damsel attired in gold, with boots of the same material, bearing in one hand a honeycomb and in the other an oaken bough with acorns." The allegorical *dramatis personae* that follow her were older women, less and less attractive, and clad in increasingly martial panoply. The attributes of the Età dell' Oro juxtapose the opposites of soft and hard primitivism, the sweetness of the honeycomb and the hardness of the oak. Need it be remarked that her cloth of gold is a prerequisite of royal opulence, rather than a token of rigorous simplicity?

The myth itself has no real protagonist, conceivably because those who dream of it are its truest participants. Astraea plays a distant and passive role, disappearing to reappear in the sky as the sixth sign of the zodiac, having acquired wings and bearing a sheaf of corn. Saturn, the eponymous hero with the scythe, does little more than preside; he remains an elusive and self-contradictory figure, probably because of his syncretic origin and his checkered past, his dethronement in Greece and apotheosis in Rome. As Kronos, he has been heavily involved in conflicts with parents and with children. With a slight alteration of his name, he becomes Chronos, the god of time, which is of the essence in our myth. When he crosses over from Crete to Italy and is fused with Saturnus, he is forced into several contradictions. As a founding figure and a civilizer, he instructs the Latians not only in farming but also in voyaging and trading; he sets up institutions and even mints gold —a far cry from the primitivistic anarchy for which he will be more celebrated. The fact that his temple became the public treasury is one of the *Roman Questions* that puzzled Plutarch, who suggests that the custom may have derived from the legendary prosperity of the Saturnian reign. "Now the abundance of fruits which the earth yeeldeth, and the vent or disposition of them, is the very mother that bringeth foorth plentie of money," Plutarch speculates, in the Elizabethan translation of Philemon Holland.

The influence of Saturn is sublimated to the intellectual plane through his association with the planet, and through the neo-Platonic rationalization of the golden age, as expounded by the sixteenth-century mythographer, Vincenzo Cartari:

> For say the Naturalists, the soule of man when she entreth into the humane bodie, bringeth with her from the spheare of Saturne the force of knowledge and discourse, so that the Platonickes understand by Saturne, the mind, and the inward contemplation of things celestiall, and therefore called the time wherein he lived the golden age, as a time, entertaining quiet, concord, and true content.

The ancient astrologers had consigned the artists and men of letters to the planetary sphere of Mercury; but the Renaissance transferred them to the sphere of Saturn; and Marsilio Ficino identified the congenital melancholia of the saturnine temperament with the madness of genius, Plato's *manía*. Despite these exaltations of astrology, mythography continued to regard Saturn as a mundane deity, whose preoccupations were less astral than economic. The Romans wanted to store their public funds in the Temple of Saturn because everything had been common to everybody during his rule ("*cunctis universa communia*"), Boccaccio tells us in his *Genealogiae deorum*. In the standard manual of Natalis Comes, *Mythologiae*, we read again that all things had been common to all because of the rich fruitfulness of the soil. Although Comes mentions Tibullus, he could not have derived his statement ("*Omnia . . . omnibus . . . communia*") from the Roman elegist. Ovid had used the adjective *communis* and Vergil had stressed the absence of boundaries, while Seneca spoke of men enjoying nature "*in commune.*" But the key-phrase seems to have originated in the *De officiis* of Cicero, which recognizes no sanction for private ownership in nature, states that all belongings are shared within the family ("*una domus, communia omnia*"), and Latinizes a proverb cited by Plato and Aristotle: "All things in common among friends (*amicorum . . . communia omnia*)."

This comity had been extended to all believers in Christ, when Saint Peter made his conversions in the Acts of the Apostles: "And all that believed were together, and had all things common." A sense of Christian brotherhood reinforced the pagan impulse to abolish property. Conversely, it is amid the foliage of the golden age that we discover the roots of Christian socialism and—as the very term implies—communism. A closely related dictum is added to the *topos* in its post-classical manifestations; this is the refusal to differentiate between mine and thine, *meum* and *tuum*. The interchange of possessive pronouns has its counterpart in the gospel of Saint John, when Jesus prays to God for his followers: "And all mine are thine, and thine are mine; and I am glorified in them." But a secular context, somewhat mockingly, comes closer to the prior notion of sharing worldly goods. In the *Trinummus* of Plautus, when a prodigal son seeks financial relief from his father, he argues that "what's thine is mine, and of course all of mine is thine (*nam quod tuomst meumst, omne meumst autem tuom*)." The belief of the early Christians in the dignity of the poor would bring further reinforcement to the Ovidian denunciation of wealth and suspicion of ownership. The watchword, "*Amicorum communia omnia*," was so well established by the Renaissance that Erasmus chose it to open his collection of adages. His commentary linked it with the *meum/tuum* antithesis by recalling that Socrates, in *The Republic*, found the chief cause of civil strife in the citizens' disagreement over such expressions as *mine* and *not mine* ("τὸ ἐμὸν καὶ τὸ οὐη ἐμὸν").

The satirist of the German Pre-Reformation, Sebastian Brant, included the contempt for poverty among the cargo of follies in his ship of fools. In the *gulden welt* men did not scramble for money (*gelt*); they did not despise those who lacked it; nor, since their neighbors had nothing to covet, did they say: "Would thine were mine (*wer myn das din*)!" All men were equal, since their equality was grounded upon their indigence. The vista of plain living and high thinking that opens up in Brant's *Narrenschiff* is amplified by the English metaphrase of the Scottish priest, Alexander Barclay:

> *Than was theyr fode scas, theyr lyvinge lyberall*
> *Theyr labour comon, they knew no covetyse*
> *All thynge was comon than amonge them all*
> *The law of nature from them expellyd vyce*
> *Without violence or rigour of justyce*
> *But none of all these our firste progenytours*
> *Theyr myndes blyndyd with gatherynge great tresours.*

Here a new note is sounded; the golden age is ascetic and industrious; labor, albeit common, is habitual from the outset; it is not a penance for a later falling-off; once deprecated by the classical hedonists, it is now extolled by Christian moralists. Brant's contemporary, Antonio de Guevara, went a step farther in his *Dial of*

Princes, updating our first progenitors by picturing them hard at work on their farms, which are privately owned.

> In the first age and golden world, al lived in peace, eche man toke care for his owne landes, everie one planted and sowed their trees and corne, every one gathered his fruites and cut his vines, kned their bread and brought by their children, and finally all lived by their owne proper swet and travaile, so that they al lived without the prejudice or hurt of any other.

Whereupon the Spanish moralist, as Englished by Sir Thomas North, deplores the wickedness that has brought about the present misery, precipitating a series of reversals, turning plows into weapons, and corrupting men. What Guevara smells is human perspiration, not honey from the oak. "And finally that sweat they had to profit in their own goods, they turned to bloud sheading to the domage of the common wealth." There is a hint of capitalistic development in this rechannelizing of energies, or at least a foreshadowing of John Locke's apologia for property, which is based on the postulate that "God gave the world to men in common," and which demonstrated how they managed to fence themselves in by industry and rationality.

Erasmus, in his elaborate treatise on simplicity, *The Praise of Folly*, asserted that the simple lives of the golden age had been guided by instinct and nature (*"naturae ductu instinctuque"*). Locke, the expositor of enlightenment, substitutes reason for instinct in his *Treatises of Government*, defining the state of nature as "men living together according to reason, without a common superior on earth with authority to judge between them." But this is mere hypothesis for Locke, and it is all too quickly relinquished before the threat of force, the state of war, which persuades them to ratify a social contract. The anarchic state of nature at the beginning was roundly summed up in the corrosive sentence of Thomas Hobbes:

> In such condition, there is no place for industry, because the fruit thereof is uncertain, and consequently no culture of the earth, no

navigation, nor use of the commodities that may be imported by sea; no commodious building, no instruments of moving, and removing, such things as require much force; no knowledge of the face of the earth; no account of time; no arts, no letters, no society; and, which is worst of all, continual fear and danger of violent death, and the life of man solitary, poor, nasty, brutish, and short.

We have travelled a considerable distance to watch Hobbes invert the negative formula and answer the primitivists by enumerating the benefits of civilization that were unavailable to primitive man. His realism has prevailed, on the whole, and most of us would be reluctant to exchange our lot for the kind of society that comes under the investigations of anthropology. Yet we carry a heavy burden of misgivings. When we look backward to the Renaissance, which marks for us an apogee of culture, we find it looking back to Greece and Rome more often than it looks ahead to us. And when we too look back at Greece and Rome, we find that the view is still retrospective. The dimness of the ultimate horizon favors the irenic presupposition that once upon a time the life of man was sociable, abundant, pleasant, gentle, and long.

[I I]

ETHICS

Since we never see as far as we look, our attempts at retrospection are filled in with moments of anticipation, just as our retrospect of the golden age *in illo tempore* presupposes the prospect of an iron age, this iron age of ours. We could hardly have touched on the classical view of times past without presupposing our own views, to some extent; and since our present center of attention is the Renaissance, we must be continually looking backwards and forwards. Already, while indicating how certain watchwords of early Christendom would find their way into the later versions of the classical *topos*, we have been anticipating the medieval view. We could have been looking farther back toward Eden, the garden of gardens, whose very name in Hebrew signified pleasure. Something like a synthesis was broached by the more classical-minded of the Church Fathers, notably Lactantius. Not that his *Divine Institutes* were half-hearted in their patristic zeal against the false worship of pagan gods. It was the one and only God, they affirmed, who "gave the common earth to all men, so that they might lead a common life." The poetic tradition of a reign of justice under the good old Saturn should therefore be accepted as truth. Evil came into the world when Jupiter and the false gods dispelled the golden age. "When justice was rejected," Lactantius maintained, "then cupidity, unfair laws, defiance, avarice, ambition, pride, impiety, and other vices held sway."

But it is overhasty to assume, by way of rapid historical summary, that the Catholic Church assimilated the belief in a golden age. The

Middle Ages were far from ecumenical in the modern sense of the term. One of their universal doctors, Alanus de Insulis, was evidently attracted to the idea; but he seems to have been unorthodox, almost to the point of heresy, in his willingness to give nature her due. Another, Saint Thomas Aquinas, epitomized the Ovidian convention in a commentary upon Boethius. Bernard of Cluny was willing to invoke the *aurea tempora* in his poem, *De contemptu mundi*, but merely as a premise for satire on women. Monkish writers versed in the Latin poets used the theme occasionally for secular ornamentation. Modoin, the Bishop of Autun, dedicated an eclogue to the Emperor Charlemagne which reechoes the Vergilian predictions for a glorious reign. The wandering scholar Hilarius took the liberal mores of the golden age as a precedent for addressing a homosexual lyric to an English boy; would-be paganism was harmonized with an ecclesiastical strain by echoing the notorious pun of Pope Gregory the Great on *Anglicus* and *angelicus*. The transition from classical to medieval culture, as it has been magisterially retraced by Ernst Robert Curtius in *European Literature and the Latin Middle Ages*, characteristically tended to fall back upon the *topoi*, those great commonplaces of thought and expression which became fixed and have recurred in literary contexts from Homer through Dante. It is significant that the golden age is not among the recurrent topics that Curtius has gathered together and studied in rich detail.

Among those themes, the one that comes closest to ours is the *locus amoenus*, the pleasant place or pleasance. This description of an ideal landscape, which goes back to Vergil's Elysian Fields and was standardized by manuals of rhetoric, offered a standing invitation to the fancies and talents of later authors. Its endemic pleasantness was enhanced by a confused etymology which derived *amoenus* from *amor*, so that the *locus* could be regarded as a perfect background for dalliance. Such places, summoned up in the mind's eye again and again, have a tendency to look pretty much the same. As Alfred Jeanroy remarked of the settings for Troubadour love-poems: "*Toujours le même paysage.*" Yet closer scrutiny will always reveal nuances of topographical variation which, however slight, can be meaningfully illuminated by thematic analysis. As a spatial concept, the *locus amoenus* could be handed on in more or less static form. The golden age, as its temporal counterpart, was charged with the sort of kinetic energies that would burst forth in the Renaissance. Boethius, that belated Roman, imprisoned and condemned to death by the Goths in 522 A. D., had sought appropriate consolation by recalling the *prior aetas*. Jean de Meun reanimated the topos in the late thirteenth century, with his revival, completion, and transformation of the conventional allegory by Guillaume de Lorris, *The Romance of the Rose*. During the seven hundred and fifty years between the memory-haunted Boethius and the forward-looking Jean de Meun, the golden age might be said to have gone underground.

The exception that proves the rule is a Latin eclogue of the ninth or tenth century by a poet otherwise unknown, Theodulus. Though it has been virtually forgotten, it was long and widely utilized as a text in the schools. It consists largely of a pastoral dialogue between the respective personifications of falsehood, Pseustis, and truth, Alithia. Falsehood propounds a series of classical myths, which Truth confutes in each case by presenting a Christian analogue and being sustained at the end by Phronesis or Judgment. In an exchange of two quatrains, the pleasing fiction of Saturn's age is discredited by the tragic facts about our first parents in the garden of Eden. As a staple of the curriculum, this debate or *conflictus* was both influential and typical in the sharp distinction it drew between mythical falsehood and religious truth. Dante would still be strict in maintaining that line, and setting the myth within the perspective of doctrine. Guiding him through the Inferno, Vergil cannot mention the island of Crete without being reminded of Saturn, who was King there when the world was chaste. But Vergil's recollection is incidental to his description of a portentous statue, which is composed of the four metals eked out with clay. Here the reminiscence is from the book of Daniel, and the implication is prophetic for the history of mankind. Tears drip from all the statue's parts except its golden head. The limbs of iron and clay are supposed to stand for the spiritual and the temporal authorities.

Statius, encountered in the *Purgatorio*, also has his classical recollections, but he is careful to apply them figuratively. The earliest time was as beautiful as gold ("*Lo secol primo quant' oro fu bello*"). He rationalizes the charm of its modest regimen by saying that hunger made its acorns savory, while thirst made the water of its streams taste like nectar. When the three pilgrims finally reach the summit of the Mount of Purgatory, they are admitted to the Terrestrial Paradise, where they are welcomed by its presiding spirit, Matelda. This, she explains, is the site where the roots of humanity blossomed in innocence, where the spring blooms eternally with fruit, where the celebrated nectar flows. When the ancient poets sang about the golden age and its blissful condition, she suggests, perhaps they were dreaming about this place. And the poignance of the suggestion is underlined by the unspoken comparison between their Parnassus and this purgatorial mountain.

> *Quelli che anticamente poetaro*
> *L'età dell' oro e suo stato felice,*
> *forse in Parnaso esto loco sognaro.*

After Matelda has spoken, Dante turns to his companions, the two Roman poets. He notices that they are smiling, for they have accepted the final construction that she has put upon their earlier beliefs. Christianity, superseding paganism, could feel no need for the golden age, since it had its own equivalent. Nevertheless the two scriptures, the Greco-Roman and the Judeo-Christian, went on coexisting and interpenetrating. By the fourteenth century, moralists were reinterpreting Ovid's *Metamorphoses* in parallelism with the biblical tales. The golden age prefigures the earthly paradise, where men lived at their own behest, without feeling hunger, thirst, heat, cold, evil, pain, or distraction:

> *En ce deliteuz paradis*
> *Vivoit lors homs a son devis,*
> *Sans faim, sans soif, sans chaut, sans froit,*
> *Sans mal, sans paine et sans destroit.*

"*Sans labourer*" is added to this negative litany in another version of the *Ovide moralisé*; plainly the moralist seems to have known and felt the burdens of labor; and we feel we are not very far from the Middle Ages when we are told that castles and towers were lacking, along with warfare and weaponry. But though we are used to seeing the golden age built up by knocking down the self-image of the iron age, we can hardly be certain whether it is Saturn or Adam who is being banished here from his primal retreat. There is no problem, obviously, in making Deucalion's flood coincide with Noah's; further efforts to make Ovid's heathens behave like Christians seem more far-fetched. Yet the moralistic impetus was so strong that, even after the Classics had regained their esthetic pre-eminence, they were treated hermeneutically by the mythographers of the Renaissance. When Arthur Golding translated the *Metamorphoses* into Elizabethan fourteeners, he moralized the fables with marginal glosses:

> *Moreover by the golden* [*age*] *what other thing is ment,*
> *Than Adams tyme in Paradyse, who beeing innocent*
> *Did lead a blist and happy lyfe untill that thurrough sin*
> *He fell from God? From which tyme foorth all sorrow did begin.*

The medieval poets used the allegorical mode as a means of returning to the garden state. Guillaume de Lorris surrounded it with all the aura of courtly idealism in the original *Roman de la rose*. It is more naturalistic—and therefore, under the circumstances, less innocent—in the continuation of Jean de Meun, condemned in its day for heretical tendencies. As a hardened satirist Jean has his soft spot for the paradisiacal age, which his personified Genius depicts in full cognizance of all its Vergilian and Ovidian features, along with some interesting afterthoughts. Not only did men live "*comunaument*," doing whatever they pleased; not only was the spring everlasting ("*printems pardurable*"); but there was no night, no measure of time, neither future nor preterite ("*tuit li trei tems i sont present*"). When Saturn was supplanted by Jupiter, who laid down rules, things went from good to ill and bad to worse; now, in the

iron age, the sheep are drably black and white, instead of being
gaily colored like Vergil's. The crucial innovation comes at a point
when the hero, the generic Lover, is being advised by his Friend,
who invokes the golden past in order to criticize the amatory
usages of the present. In the old days, love was free and unembar-
rassed. Just as there were no kings nor princes, so there was equality
among lovers, for love—as Ovid had argued—is incompatible with
mastery:

> Qu'onques amour e seignourie
> Ne s'entrefirent compaignie.

Free love, *liber amor*, had figured in one exceptional Latin poem;
but the possibilities for sex in the golden age had not heretofore
been fully exploited. The responsibility for bringing them out rests
squarely with Jean de Meun, and his radical program has been described by Curtius as "erotic communism." This, at any rate, is the
attitude of Jean's procuress, whose uninhibiting motto is "All
women for all men and all men for all women (*Toutes pour touz
e touz pour toutes*." Consequently, in spite of the uncharacteristic
avoidance of women in Ovid's presentation of the theme, they appear in sixteenth-century illustrations to the *Metamorphoses*, where
affectionate couples sport in the shade of the oak-trees. Once the
cult of Aphrodite was admitted, a reference to the golden age
could be confounded with a voyage to Cythera. John Cleland's
woman of pleasure, Fanny Hill, could describe a house of pleasure
with this eighteenth-century circumlocution:

> The authors and supporters of this secret institution would, in the
> height of their humours style themselves the restorers of the golden
> age and its simplicity of pleasures, before their innocence became so
> injustly branded with the names of guilt and shame.

Since pastoralism is an urban phenomenon, the rise of cities was
destined to revive it, particularly among the city-states of Italy.
Two poetic narratives of Boccaccio, the *Ninfale fiesolano* and the
Ameto, are—strictly speaking—nymphals rather than pastorals; they

people the primeval groves of Tuscany with tutelary nymphs pursued by lovelorn huntsmen; in looking back to improvise a regional mythology, they look forward to hail the founding of a metropolis, Florence. Now, insofar as Florence became the cynosure of the Italian Renaissance, allusion to the golden age became its particular trademark. E. H. Gombrich has shown how its ruling family, the house of Medici, cultivated this legendary association, how their circle of poets and humanists thanked them for their patronage in munificent Latin rhetoric, which was self-consciously borrowed from the *Fourth Eclogue*. "The manner and way to rule and to raigne in the right kinde" was the chiefest of the courtly virtues that Baldassare Castiglione would soon be expounding at Urbino, "Whiche alone were sufficient to make men happie, and to bring once againe into the worlde the golden age, which is written to have bin when *Saturnus* raigned in the olde time." Since the Medici were burghers and bankers rather than feudal aristocrats, they could more appropriately be praised for the arts of peace than for military triumphs. With the consolidation of their regime, they adopted the habits and gestures of a traditional aristocracy. Their triumphal processions subserved their civic interests, and fitted in with the rollicking street scenes of the carnival—that Florentine resurgence of the Saturnalian impulse. But they liked to assume the panoply, and to go through the motions, of war in their jousts and tournaments.

The magnificence of Lorenzo de' Medici was officially made visible in the year of his accession to leadership, 1468, when he appeared as the central figure in a diplomatic tournament held at the Piazza Santa Croce. The motto in chivalric French on his pennant, *le tems revient*, was a proclamation of municipal and cultural renascence. The fulfilment of that promise is attested, on a more humanistic plane, in a letter written during the very year of Lorenzo's death, 1492, by one of the leading beneficiaries of his patronage, Marsilio Ficino, to the mathematician Paul of Middelburg. Ficino, ardent Platonist that he was, associated Hesiod's four ages with Plato's four talents, and had no hesitation in evaluating the talent of his own age: "For this golden century, as it were, has brought back to light the liberal arts, which were all but extinguished: grammar, poetry, oratory, painting, sculpture, architecture, music, the ancient chanting of songs to the Orphic lyre, and all this in Florence." In the next century Giorgio Vasari, who himself painted frescoes of the golden age on the walls of the Palazzo Vecchio, would begin his life of Botticelli with the declaration that the time of Lorenzo the Magnificent had been "truly a golden age for men of genius." That *Zeitgeist* is reflected in Botticelli's painting, most expressly in the Primavera, through a complex and delicate symbolism which has been analyzed and documented by Aby Warburg. The cult of spring was linked with the flowering of youth in the city of flowers whose patron goddess was Flora, and whose most popular carnival song was Lorenzo's own *Giovinezza*.

When his second son was elected to the papacy, through which —as Leo X—he would extend the bounties of the renewed golden age to Rome, the new pope's native town outdid itself in spectacular celebration. The climax of the carnival was a procession designed by a local humanist, Jacopo Nardi, and executed by the artist Pontormo. Its triumph was conveyed by no less than seven chariots. The first carried figures personifying Saturn and Janus with their condign attributes, attended by elaborately undressed shepherds on horseback; the next five cars gave majestic representation to other episodes from ancient legend. The seventh and climactic episode is thus depicted by Vasari in his life of Pontormo:

> After these six came the car, or rather, the triumphal chariot, of the age or epoch of gold, wrought with the richest and most beautiful artistry, with many figures in relief executed by Baccio Bandinelli, and with very beautiful paintings by the hand of Pontormo among which those of the four cardinal virtues were highly praised. From the center of the car rose a great globe in the form of the world, upon which a man lay prostrate on his face as if dead, his armor all rusted, and from the open fissure of whose sundered back emerged a small boy all naked and gilded, representing the revival of the golden age and the end of the iron age, which expired and was reborn

through the election of the pope . . . I should not omit the fact that the gilded infant, who was the child of a baker, died shortly afterward through the suffering that he endured in order to gain ten crowns.

Whether the gold paint poisoned the poor child or caused his body to suffocate, it must have taken a certain amount of incidental sacrifice to make a Florentine holiday. But Vasari does not pause to moralize the spectacle of that abortive birth. He concludes by quoting briefly from Nardi's verses for the occasion, which have elsewhere been printed in full. Their main conceit is a simile of the phoenix, reborn from the emblematic stump of a green bay tree, just as the golden age is born again out of the iron age. Such allusions set the tone of the Medicean iconology, as it was embodied in masques and festivals of ever-mounting elaboration. A canzonet about the golden age was sung at the nuptials of Cosimo I, Duke of Tuscany. A personification of Flora represented eternal spring at the opening of the Uffizzi Theater. When a Medici scion married a Farnese daughter, their wedding at Parma featured the Golden Age on a *carro trionfale* with two white doves, and a young man singing a lengthy aria—one could almost reconstruct the lyric. Saturn and Astraea returned again and again to grace these occasions of state.

The most poignant of these stately celebrations was one which never actually took place. Its celebrant, the scholar-poet Angelo Poliziano, also paid his compliments to the reigning house of Gonzaga when he dramatized the myth of Orpheus for presentation at the court of Mantua. The *Favola di Orfeo* is a milestone, both as an experiment leading toward opera and as the secularization of a religious mystery celebrating a culture-hero of the Renaissance. Inevitably gravitating to Florence, where he had undergone his humanistic formation, Politian spent most of his relatively short career as one of the brightest lights in the constellation of Lorenzo the Magnificent. His poetic show-piece is the long sequence of *Stanze per la Giostra*, stanzas written in *ottava rima* for a joust in which the leading champion was to be Lorenzo's younger brother,

Giuliano de' Medici. The poem is dedicated to Lorenzo, whose well-known—if somewhat paradoxical—fondness for country life seems to have inspired its appealing laudation of rustic ways. Inevitably, this leads back to the golden age and its ancestral breed, who were sheltered by large and leafy oaks, dispensing honey from their trunks and acorns from their boughs. Politian neatly condenses the versatile role of the oak-tree into a graceful couplet:

> Lor casa eran fronzute querce e grande,
> Ch' avran nel tronco mèl, ne' rami ghiande.

Not yet did mothers weep over sons killed in wars; not yet had the wicked thirst for cruel gold come into the fair world. Though men and women lived affectionately together, it was not until afterward that lust entered their breasts, and the fury that wretched people call love:

> Lussuriosa entró n'e petti e quel furore
> Che la meschina gente chiama amore.

This passing evocation, which occupies two of Politian's 125 *stanze*, is a succinct and polished restatement of the relevant conventions. The narrative presents Giuliano as Iulio, the youthful huntsman, whose scorn for love incurs the revenge of Cupid; whereupon Iulio becomes enamored of a heroine reminiscent of Simonetta Cattaneo, Giuliano's mistress, who had lately died. Before the story could be completed or the tournament staged, Giuliano himself had been murdered in the nefarious Pazzi conspiracy of 1478. Lorenzo survived to put it down, and Politian set his poem aside to write a Latin history of the plot. *La Giostra* survives as a lyrical—if not a heroic—fragment, a kind of *cuirasse esthétique* or ornamental breastplate, where the artifice of the metal-worker has simulated and magnified the natural contours of the masculine torso.

Politian was his master's master in poetry. Yet Lorenzo's verses, though they do not have such an exquisite finish, have a sturdy fluency of their own. His expressed desire to touch the soil or to avoid the seductions of gold was not less genuine than the irony of his role as a merchant prince retreating from mercantile Florence to his hillside villa at Fiesole. Accordingly his longest sequence, mainly in *ottava rima*, is entitled *Selve d'amore*: literally woods of love, but a sylva is more technically a short poem with some pretensions to rusticity. Slightly more than a fourth of these stanzas are taken up with a revery on the golden age, which is rather more than a digression, since it plays a strategic part in the psychological continuity. After the enamorment of the poet, his madonna disappears; his intervening revery helps to prepare him for her final reappearance and Platonic transfiguration. Given her presence, he muses, his dear fatherland need not envy the *età dell' oro*, the *isole fortunate*, or the *paradiso terrestre*; and his musing reaches the conclusion that the perfected golden age subsists in the lover's feelings; its gold has been refined in the warmth of his lady's response.

> *L'oro di quella età quasi divina*
> *Nel dolce foco di mia donna affina.*

Lorenzo takes the other aspects of the golden age in his stride. He makes a detailed and picturesque survey of the animal kingdom at its best; there is no hunting here, for man is not yet carnivorous. This arch-capitalist can extoll a world which lived *communamente* and recognized no difference between *tuo* and *mio*. Even Hamlet would have been happy in those days, since being and seeming were then at one. Since nobody cared about time, since nothing was old or new, it was a principle of nature that what pleases today should always please ("*Quel ch'oggi piace, piacer sempre suole*"). That was indeed *la dolce vita* until it was spoiled by Prometheus, who learned too much, not to mention Epimetheus, who learned too little. Reliance on a mean between extremes is characteristic of Lorenzo's moderating outlook, especially in his subjective refinement of love, which he differentiates—like Politian—from the pangs of desire or the torments of passion.

The convergence of the golden-age myth and the pastoral genre, which Pope would take so readily for granted, had not really come about until the Renaissance. Its only classical precursor was Vergil's

Fourth Eclogue, which—although it would be endlessly imitated —had itself been an admitted departure from the bucolic strain. More decisively than any other writer, it was Jacopo Sannazaro who conflated the myth with the genre, while at the same time he linked his eclogues together by prose passages in the tradition of the late Greek romances. *Arcadia*, his title and his setting, largely through the popularity and influence of his work, has become synonymous with the world of escape, the *locus amoenus* of fiction. Sannazaro found a refuge from busy Naples in that idyllic terrain; his spokesman, the townsman Sincero, is escaping 'rom unrequited love; but he finds no enduring solace among the shepherds, and he ends by returning to the city. The prose links form a confession, as it were, of the poet vacillating between two worlds. The poems are thickly interspersed with motifs from the golden age, and there are moments when it looks as if the hoped-for renovation were at hand, with Astraea ready to redescend. More often we hear the shepherds express their yearning for that faraway time, and even their current discontent over the penury that has reduced their rations to acorns. A plaintive epilogue—accompanied by the *zampogna* or oaten flute—laments the death of the muses, the withering of the laurels, the silence of the woods, the disappearance of nymphs and satyrs.

The assumption that the golden age may still flourish, albeit in some region far remote from us, is so persistent and so enticing because that is the only route by which we can ever hope to attain it at first hand. The hope, of course, must turn out to be an illusion; for the very premise of the myth is its sense of belatedness, the romantic sentiment—which even Hesiod professed—of having been born too late into a world too old. The city-dweller, if he escapes to the countryside, must overhear the countryman bemoaning his lot, and thence conclude that there can be no escape from the liabilities that flesh is heir to. The shepherd who talks about the golden age throws doubts upon his own felicity. The world-weary intellectual, after spending a season in Arcadia, feels the pinch of reality all the more keenly. This consideration does not lessen the appeal of

Arcadianism, which is so intimately connected with the early development of the novel, and to which we shall be reverting in connection with Sidney. To glance beyond that toward later manifestations, curiously enough, is to see release harden into restraint. Near the end of the seventeenth century, an Arcadian Academy was established at Rome, in reaction to the excesses of baroque style. Like most academies, it became a stronghold for reaction on all fronts. At its meetings, the academicians masqueraded as shepherds. In the name of a return to pristine simplicity, they imposed a rococo taste for an overrefined neoclassicism.

Meanwhile, the artificial pose struck by the pastoral had been acted out. Its living paradox provided both a favorite theme and a novel mode for the pageantry of the ducal courts. The theatrical innovator was Tasso, and his innovation was the sylvan fable (*"favola boscareccia"*) of *Aminta*, performed with reverberating success at the court of Ferrara in 1573. The elements of the plot could not have been simpler: the lovesick shepherd, the reluctant maiden, the rebuffs and reversals of courtship. Since the hero and the heroine are never on stage together, the play would not strike a modern audience as highly dramatic. Each of them is drawn out by a confidant; the physical action, which takes place offstage, is relayed through narration by these lesser characters; while a chorus of shepherds interposes a commentary which, we should not be too surprised to learn, made a greater impression than anything else at the first performance. The sustained effect could hardly be other than lyrical, from the prologue by Cupid to the epilogue by Venus, though it is tempered with courtly compliments to the Duke of Ferrara, Alfonso d'Este, and with topical opinions from the poet himself, who could be identified with the shepherd Tirsi. The moral is a testimonial to the powers of the god of love, who can lift his servants up from the depths of wretchedness to the joys of his amorous paradise (*"il suo amoroso paradiso"*).

Silvia, the heroine, is a votary of Diana, and prefers hunting to the advances of the hero, Aminta. She hates his love, as she tells her confidant, Dafne, because it hates her chastity. The key-word she employs, *onestate*, has the same meaning as the word *honesty* applied to a woman in Shakespearean English. The ensuing demonstration, like Falstaff's military catechism on honor, will argue that it is no more than a word: a shibboleth, a fetish, a mere breath. Having repulsed Aminta, the nymph is attacked by a satyr; and when Aminta saves her from ravishment, she repulses him. Outraged dignity makes amends for dishevelled nudity when she enjoins him: "Touch me not, shepherd, I am Diana's (*Pastor, non mi toccar, son di Diana*)." All this is necessarily related at second hand; the obstacles and misunderstandings that lead to the dénouement could be more plausibly narrated than enacted. The discovery of a blood-stained garment, supporting the announcement that Silvia has been killed by a wolf, drives the despairing Aminta to resolve upon suicide. But again she turns out to be safe; and when she hears the bad news about him, she relents; she realizes that what she has called *onestate* has been *crudeltate* (cruelty). Happily, it is not too late after all, since Aminta's desperate gesture is cushioned by the grassy pastures below the cliff from which he has chosen to leap. The lovers, having both undergone mock-deaths, are revived and united through Amore or Cupid, the providential god in the pastoral machine.

Clearly, the happy ending has not been reached without some degree of turmoil. Tasso's shepherds are at least as far removed from the golden age as Sannazaro's. At the outset, when the more sophisticated Dafne is rebuking Silvia for preferring sport to love, she compares this naive preference to the infantile tastes of *la gente prima*, who had nothing better to eat and drink than acorns and water. Nowadays, what with the blessings of grain and grape, such provender should be left to the animals. The introductory monologue of the cynical satyr, attributing his failure in love to his poverty, deplores the commercial encroachment of the towns on the woods and fields. He can but emulate the shrug and the pun of Ovid in the *Ars amatoria*: truly this is the golden age, since gold alone conquers and rules.

> *E veramente il secol d'oro è questo,*
> *Poi che sol vince l'oro e regna l'oro.*

The satyr may be suspect as a moralistic commentator, but soon thereafter Tirsi reaffirms the basic antagonism of town and country, and Dafne sets the nostalgic mood of the drama by sighing: "The world grows old and, growing old, grows sad."

> *Il mondo invecchia,*
> *E invecchiando intristisce.*

Dramatically, *Aminta* could be played on a very shallow stage. Poetically it opens up, with a sudden burst of verbal music, to disclose a vista of ever-retreating depth. After the first act, the chorus gives voice to Aminta's impatience, and their song is probably the most purple of the many similar passages before us. "*O bella età de l'oro,*" it apostrophizes, or in Samuel Daniel's translation:

> *O happy golden Age,*
> *Not for that Rivers ranne*
> *With streames of milke, and hunny dropt from trees . . .*

And the apostrophe runs through the special traits, both affirmative and negative, that have traditionally given the age its reputation. But, the choric ode surprises us by maintaining, it was not golden because of its voluntary fruits, its eternally flowering spring, or its lack of ships and wars,

> *But onely for that name,*
> *That Idle name of wind:*
> *That Idoll of deceit, that empty sound*
> *Call'd* HONOR, *which became*
> *The tyran of the minde,*
> *And so torments our Nature without ground,*
> *Was not yet vainly found.*

There, for Tasso, was the crucial *nondum*; not yet had an erotic taboo been imposed by the code of honor; and Silvia would not then have been able to resist Aminta by appealing to it under its feminine aspect of *onestate*. Where the precondition of Juvenal's golden age was the presence of Pudicitia, the precondition of Tasso's is her absence. His second stanza moves from his protestation against shame to his affirmation of a permissive attitude, contrasting the hard laws of honor with

> golden lawes like these
> Which nature wrote. That's lawfull which doth please.

Having joined his predecessors in stating what the golden age was not, Tasso now has the courage to introduce legislation. The succeeding stanzas contrast the pursuit of pleasure through the practice of free love with the repressive morality that would cast a veil of shame over the source of sensual delights. The argument culminates with the request that Honor limit his surveillance to the spheres of the mighty, allowing ordinary people to live and love like the joyful race of old. By way of coda, Tasso adds a paraphrase of Catullus, the perennial invitation to love (*"Vivamus, mea Lesbia, atque amemus"*), with the lover's reminder to his coy mistress that time is running out:

> *Soles occidere et redire possunt:*
> *nobis cum semel occidit brevis lux,*
> *nox est perpetua una dormienda.*

Tasso intensifies the carnal shudder by conceiving the sunset as a death and a rebirth (*"il Sol si muore e poi rinasce"*). Daniel's English approximates the original Latin more closely:

> *Let's love: the sun doth set, and rise againe,*
> *But whenas our short light*
> *Comes once to set, it makes eternall night.*

The reign of free love, like that of communism, is not without its problems; the principal one is whether love can ever be wholly free, whether certain bonds are not implied by its very definition. The conception of the golden age as an amorous paradise had been chiefly the contribution of Jean de Meun. It had been embroidered with speculations by other writers during the three centuries between *Le Roman de la rose* and *Aminta*. One of Tasso's literary rivals whom he was accused of imitating, Sperone Speroni, had cited the marriage of Saturn and Ops "*nella età dell' oro*" among a series of precedents for the incest in his tragedy of *Canace*. But it was Tasso who codified the example of hedonistic behavior presumably set by the first generation of men into a single precept, a golden law ("*aurea legge*"). "If it is pleasing, it is permitted (*S'ei piace, ei lice*)."

This is a far cry from the golden rule of Christianity, and even farther from the moral orthodoxy of the Middle Ages, which condemned Semiramis to hell because—as Dante phrased it—she had made lust permissible in her law ("*libito fe' licito in sua legge*"). On the other hand, to do whatever one pleases ("*agere quicum licitumst*") was the pagan counsel of Plautus in the *Menaechmi*; but that has been the habitual license of comedy, where misrule is temporarily allowed to prevail. When Ben Jonson declares, "Naught that delights is sin," he is conscious of the guilt he is disclaiming. John Marston, who deliberately assumed an Italianate tone, comes closer to Tasso: "For we hold firm, that's lawful which doth please." Such formulations are not put forward without an air of bravado, since they fall among the lapsed prerogatives of the golden age, and to revive them is to challenge the *status quo*. Rosemond Tuve has pointed out a similar conflict of principles in the writing of Jean de Meun: "As in Tasso, prelapsarian 'freedoms' are selected, admired and praised for the most grossly wrong and postlapsarian reasons." Whether a judgment of this order can be viewed as right or wrong depends upon an acceptance of the fall. Once that dogma is called into question, it follows that an ethic can be deduced from the state of nature. Then the sole criterion for distinguishing good from evil is personal liberty, as John Donne insisted with his usual interplay of paradoxes:

> *The golden laws of nature are repeal'd*
> *Which our first fathers in such reverence held;*
> *Our liberty's revers'd, our Charter's gone,*
> *And we're made servants to opinion.*

Donne's raillery at the tyranny of opinion is more bitter than Tasso's expostulation against honor. But Donne himself was to shy away from the consequences of ethical relativism and turn back to the absolutes of religious faith. And when the mystagogic Henry Reynolds translated Tasso's ode, he was so nonplussed by the golden law that he simply left it out of his English translation. At the Cavalier extreme, Richard Lovelace could deftly twist it into a libertine plea for total permissiveness:

> Thrice happy was that golden Age,
> When compliment was constru'd Rage,
>   And fine words in the Center hid;
> When cursed No stain'd no Maids Blisse,
> And all discourse was summ'd in Yes,
>   And Noght forbad, but to forbid.

It would seem difficult to carry the process of emancipation much farther. Yet it seems appropriate that a woman should have the last word in this debate, and that the eternal feminine should be conjoined to the everlasting yea. Mrs. Aphra Behn spoke for herself and her sex, and for the Restoration, when she made her metaphrase:

> O cursed Honor, Thou who first did damn
>   A woman to the sin of shame!
>   The base debaucher of a generous heart . . .

Whether Tasso was more than half-serious, when he launched his winged words, seems fairly doubtful. *Il disonore dell' onore* seems to have been a topic for the clever young poets of his manneristic generation, who were working at some distance from the courtliness of Castiglione or the moderation of Lorenzo de' Medici. Tasso's *magnum opus*, the heroic romance of *Jerusalem Delivered*, throws a brief and sinister light upon his wavering conception of the golden age. This becomes a snare and a delusion for his Christian heroes, who are lured beyond the Fortunate Isles to an Isola di Piacere, a pleasance indeed, where sirens try to divert them from their crusade with familiar blandishments:

> *This is the place wherein you may assuage*
> *Your sorrows past, here is that joy and bliss*
> *That flourish'd in the antique golden age;*
> *Here needs no law, here none doth aught amiss.*

But the knights are steeled in resisting such temptations to gather the rosebuds of transitory love (*"cogliam d'amor la rosa"*). Though their great Rinaldo has succumbed, though he dallies with the enchantress Armida, the Crusaders shame him into rejoining them, and in her grief she destroys her palace of pleasure. It was not on the basis of what pleased him that Rinaldo made his moral choice; or rather, it was on the basis of higher pleasure; for Tasso went on to write a philosophical dialogue, *Del piacere onesto*, the title itself a contradiction of the terms he had used in *Aminta*, demonstrating that the desire for honor and glory was the highest pleasure. Even if the moralist be a naturalist—and the dialogue was suspected by the Inquisition—he must calculate degrees or distinguish kinds of pleasure. A masque for the Medici, produced by Vasari a few years before Aminta, presented both Onesto Piacere and Inonesto Piacere among its *dramatis personae*. The freest spirit in sixteenth-century Italy, Giordano Bruno, took Tasso's chorus as a text for one of the subversive dialogues in his *Expulsion of the Triumphant Beast*, a manifesto of naturalism in ethics. Ocio or Leisure defends the golden age by attacking Fatica or Hard Work, who has extinguished it by introducing property, mine and thine, and other cares. But Sofia, goddess of wisdom, points out that the first men were as stupid as beasts; Momo, the god of censure, reasons that their comparative freedom from present-day wickedness was not the same as positive virtue; and it is Leisure who gets expelled from the council of the gods.

Wide as was the fame of Tasso's *Aminta*, it was soon surpassed by the studied rivalry of the Ferrarese professor of rhetoric, Giovanni Battista Guarini, with his much reprinted pastoral drama,

The Faithful Shepherd. Tasso had dashed off his play within a few months; Guarini labored over his for nearly a decade; it came out thrice the length of its model and vastly more complex. Dryden noted how much less natural and more affected the *Pastor fido* seemed than the *Aminta*. But Jonson testified, through Lady Wouldbe in *Volpone*, that English authors plagiarized from Guarini almost as much as from Montaigne.

> He has so moderne, and facile a veine,
> Fitting the time, and catching the court eare.

The setting for *Aminta* was an idealized north Italian landscape, with some reference to the river Po. The setting for *Il Pastor fido* is Arcadia itself, to which we are introduced by the guardian deity of its sacred river, Alfeo. Guarini, though his shepherds are more capable of malice than Tasso's, harbors fewer doubts about the accessibility of the golden age. The Arcadian prologue announces (in the English translation of Sir John Fanshawe, which is seldom as literal as it is here):

> unto this onely nook
> O' th' iron world, when she her flight had took
> From sinfull men, the golden age retir'd.

But even in Arcadia there can be trouble. Silvio, the male counterpart of Tasso's Silvia, is a coy huntsman who resists the love of Amarilli. It is not until he accidentally shoots Dorinda that he feels a tender pang for the other sex. The plight of a male defending his virginity, while it may not be absurd in itself, was easily reducible to absurdity because of the double standard in sexual relations, as Fielding was to prove in *Joseph Andrews*. But Silvio is merely the hero of the underplot; the faithful shepherd is ultimately Mirtillo, whose fidelity to Amarilli is unimpaired by her inclination for Silvio—or by the attempt of the wanton nymph Corisca, who loves Mirtillo herself, to compromise Amarilli. It will be seen that the doubling of the plot greatly multiplied the numerical possibilities for coupling off; likewise it increased the opportunities for machination, as opposed to chance or coincidence, in determining the fortunes of the characters. The troubles of Arcadia exist as threats to be melodramatically warded off by *peripezie*, reversals, plotted surprises. The sacrifices so grimly exacted by Diana will be averted because her standards of chastity and fidelity will be upheld, despite appearances to the contrary. The oracles will be fulfilled, though by unforeseeable turns. The ending will be, could not be other than, happy.

It is obvious that this dramatic pattern, while it may continue to function at the level of popular entertainment today, would invite the polemics of the meticulous pseudo-Aristotelians who guarded the canons of literary criticism in Guarini's day. Perhaps his real importance lay in his ability to meet their arguments cogently, through his preface and a pair of critical treatises. Freely admitting that the new genre was neither tragedy nor comedy, he argued that the one was outmoded and the other debased, and sought in their place to set forth a rationale for tragicomedy. His confidence has been more or less borne out, not least by the reception of the *Pastor fido*, which was read and imitated across Europe, and constituted more of a threat to morals—said Cardinal Bellarmino—than all the heresies of Luther and Calvin. The same admixture of sensuality and sententiousness is observable in John Fletcher's pastoral tragicomedy, *The Faithful Shepherdess*. Fletcher seeks to outdo Guarini by redoubling his double plot; he borrows and overuses such devices as the symbolic wounding. Through various disguises and enchantments, he makes it even harder to keep in mind the several identities of his shepherdesses. Basically this makes little difference, for the Sullen Shepherd in any case: "Now lust is up, alike all women be." And the faithless shepherdess, Chloe, lives up to his appraisal:

> *It is impossible to ravish me,*
> *I am so willing.*

A spectrum of relative faith and honesty extends across the play from the nymphomania of Chloe to the frigid celibacy of Chlorin, the faithful shepherdess. Even she, while playing the vestal priestess with the others, seems to flaunt her own pudicity, to be somewhat morbidly concerned with the technicalities of virtue, to practise coyness as a penance for shamelessness.

Despite Bellarmino's well-founded disapproval of such potential prurience, it may not be irrelevant that the *Pastor fido* dates from the Counter-Reformation; for, in a sense, it applies the flourishing art of casuistry to the field of sexual morality; in striving to reconcile the increasing demands of impulse and appetite with the institutionalized dictates of conscience, it places too much stress upon the external conformities. When Amarilli is accused of a transgression which, significantly enough, she has not committed, she is told that she has transgressed

> *Not Natures law perchance*, Love where thou wilt.
> *But that of Men and Heav'n*, Love without guilt.

(Not "*Ama se piace*," but "*Ama se lice*.") The moral antithesis between nature and custom, φύσις and νόμος, which was already time-honored among the Greeks, is neutralized by Guarini's conformable dictum that, during the golden age, "Husband and lover signifi'd one thing (*marito e vago*)." It was precisely the purport of Tasso's chorus to lay bare that gap between custom and nature. Guarini's golden-age chorus, which precedes his last act, is as bland as its opening diminutive, extolling milk as the food of the little-baby world ("*pargoletto mondo*"). From a technical standpoint, it is so parrot-like an imitation that it copies Tasso's rhyme-scheme word for word. Yet, when it arrives at the pith of the matter, it plays safe. For Tasso, if anything pleased, it was permitted: "*S'ei piace, ei lice*." For Guarini, it is pleasing if it is permitted: "*Piaccia se lice*." This is a much more cautious, more conventional—if not sycophantic—position, as contrasted with the bold individualism of Tasso's line. But Torquato Tasso, uneasy at court and long incarcerated for madness, had a signally unhappy career, which would be dramatized by Goethe as a parable of misunderstood genius. Goethe's Tasso hears from the princess he so admires, Leonora d'Este, that his cherished speculation is no more than a poetical fantasy. The golden age has long gone by; indeed it never existed. When he asserts, "What's pleasing is permitted (*Erlaubt ist, was gefällt*)," he is corrected with "What's proper is permitted (*Erlaubt ist, was sich ziemt*)." Futile to ask how men decide what is fitting and proper. We are back once more in the domain of orthodoxy.

A thoroughgoing traditionalist like Edmund Spenser could believe that a sense of propriety was inherent in human nature, though latterly there might have been a falling-off in temperance and the other virtues he celebrates. Hence an endangered heroine fears that a lustful brigand may "make his will his law." And when two ladies spend the night in a cottage with their gentle squire, Spenser feels it incumbent upon himself to reassure the reader:

> But antique age yet in the infancie
>> Of time, did live then like an innocent,
>> In simple truth and blamelesse chastitie,
>> Ne then of guile had made experiment;
>> But, voide of vile and treacherous intent,
>> Held vertue for it selfe in sovereine awe:
>> Then loyall love had royall regiment,
>> And each unto his lust did make a lawe,
> From all forbidden things his liking to withdraw.

There is a certain degree of tension here between liking and being forbidden, which is resolved by the exercise of self-control. The more adventurous minds of the Renaissance were more interested in what might happen when instincts were pursued and taboos were questioned. The ethos of More's Utopians, as we shall be seeing, is premised upon what Freud would call the pleasure principle. But it remained for a monk—to be sure, a quondam monk, who entered the world and turned doctor of medicine—to reject the sanctions of asceticism and make the strongest assertion on behalf of the senses. The surrogate of François Rabelais, in the *First Book* of his gigantic anti-romance, is another monk, Frère Jean des Entommeurs. This Friar John of the Funnels (as he will be denominated

in the exuberant translation of Sir Thomas Urquhart) can be num-
bered among the religious only by courtesy. He is not much given
to studies, unlike his creator; yet, like Rabelais, he expounds a
heterodox theology, if it be theology at all. Genial and voluble,
hard-drinking and hard-fighting, Frère Jean is a man of action
rather than contemplation. As the doughty right arm of the giant
Gargantua, in the victorious battles against the forces of King
Picrochole, he emerges the true hero of the *First Book*, whose concluding chapters deal with his reward.

When Gargantua distributes the spoils, Frère Jean refuses to
serve as governor of a province, declaring with candid insight that
he does not really know how to govern himself. Instead, he will
take advantage of the opportunity to realize a lifelong dream, if
not an ambition, and to found an abbey after his own heart. The
medieval fantasy of a land of Cockaigne, pressing its material comforts upon the wallowing pilgrim, was a gesture of recoil from
monkish restrictions, a poor man's golden age. The great good
place of Rabelais, the Abbaye de Thélème, is similarly grounded
in anti-monastic satire; more constructively, it ends by embodying
the cultural ideals of the French Renaissance. Thus it is located in
the valley of the river Loire, a *locus amoenus* not far from Rabelais'
birthplace, and it is conceived as a magnificent chateau—a hundred
times more sumptuous, if this be conceivable, than Bonnivet or
Chambord or Chantilly. Its appointments, which are specified *con
amore*, frame the accomplishments of its inmates: the libraries for
books in six languages, the picture galleries, the perfumed tapestries,
the gardens with their fountains, the pools and lists and courts for
tennis and handball, the stables for hunting and falconry. To gain a
glimpse of the Thelemites themselves, we have only to recall those
handsome portraits of courtiers by the Clouets. The bejewelled
ladies, wearing scarlet stockings and gold-embroidered gowns, set
a new style for nuns. Though the sexes are separately housed,
couples may show their mutual sympathies by dressing alike.

They are free to marry and to depart. There are no walls and no
clocks, no constraints of place or time; the negative formula helps

us to appreciate what it might feel like to live in a cell and observe monastic hours. Frère Jean's monastery is a *manoir*, where the vows of poverty, chastity, and obedience are released by affluence, marriage, and liberty. Eating, working, and sleeping are regulated not by statutes but by one's wish and free will (*"leur vouloir et franc arbitre"*). Gargantua has laid down but a single rule, "Do what thou wilt (*Fay ce que vouldras*)." Nothing more is necessary because "people who are free, well bred, well informed, and used to good company, have a natural instinct and incentive which always prompts them to virtuous acts and keeps them from vice, and it is called honor." Manifestly, this is not the kind of honor that Tasso would be protesting against; it is the code of the ideal gentleman, the *honnête homme*. The privileges of this establishment are designed for a select society, like a club. Indeed there is an inscription at the portal to warn off bigots and hypocrites, lawyers and usurers, scribes and pharisees, and other suspicious types. The name of the abbey reinforces the impact of its single golden law, since θέλημα means will in New Testament Greek. The handmaid Thelemia, personifying free will in the fifteenth-century allegory of Francesco Colonna, *Hypnerotomachia*, had helped to guide the hero Polifilo through the mazes of his erotic pilgrimage. It is human desire that is served by the Abbaye de Thélème—not the will that is venerated in the Lord's Prayer, the divine will in which Dante found man's peace.

The naturalistic outlook, while emancipating the individual, confronted him with ethical complications. There has been no lack of latterday moralists who, with Matthew Arnold, blame the difficulties of modern living on the hard-won habit of "Doing As One Likes." Whether Frère Jean's experiment was successful we shall never know, since the tale of *Gargantua* was written after the first tale of the giant's son, *Pantagruel*, so that the friar plays no part in the immediate chronological sequel. Possibly we catch a hint as to how a human being might qualify for membership in the exclusive Abbey of Free Will when the aging Gargantua, now King of Utopia, sends a letter to young Pantagruel, who is a student at Paris.

This is the famous salute of Rabelais to the revival of classical learning, the exfoliation of new science, the discovery of continents overseas, the invention of printing if not of gunpowder; and it is alerted to the contemporary excitement of humanism superseding scholasticism. In the next book, the *Tiers Livre*, Pantagruel will set forth on his quest for the Holy Bottle, rejoined by Frére Jean and joined by the shrewd and sophisticated Panurge. The latter, most resourceful of rhetoricians, knows how to wield the appropriate *topoi*. In his encomium on borrowing and lending, he harks back to the golden age, which he praises for its unlimited credit. In his harangue on codpieces he is led, via associations with armor and warfare, to a denunciation of this iron age. But, for Rabelais himself, there is no need either to exalt the past or to denigrate the present. He is replete with the fullness of here and now.

GEOGRAPHY

THE PEOPLE OF THE GOLDEN AGE have left us no monuments of genius, no splendid columns, no paintings, no poetry; they possessed nothing which evil passions might not obliterate, and when the heavens were rolled together as a scroll the curtain dropped between the world and their existence.

So EMERSON NOTED, from a commencement speech. And if the golden age left no monuments, its only documents are such fabrications as we have been reading. Given its release from labor, and from the other human anxieties that have left their mark upon history, we could hardly have expected it to have expressed itself in the form of concrete memorials or to have concerned itself much about our curiosity. Consequently, we are not in touch with it, as we are with what the past has erected and inscribed for the archaeologists and the historians to interpret. Its inaccessibility is the guarantee of its perfection. Horace had suggested an escape from history to geography, when he proposed that the faithful should leave strife-torn Rome and seek the Islands of the Blest. There, according to Hesiodic tradition, the golden age continued to exist. For argonauts who would risk the forbidden audacity of taking to sea, Seneca had counselled in a chorus of his *Medea*, there were better worlds to be found beyond Ultima Thule. If the Canaries were to be identified with the Fortunate Isles of classical myth, then the abode of the blessed would have to be sought further westward. Transatlantic navigation was originally concerned with finding the way to an older world; in fact Columbus was convinced that, on his third expedition, he had discovered man's oldest habitat, the Terrestrial Paradise. That another set of Indies lay between Europe and the Orient, that indeed two continents intervened, was a very gradual realization.

"Tomorrow to fresh Woods and Pastures new." The Middle Ages had buried the golden age under the conception of Eden; the Renaissance not only revived the original conception, but ventured forth on a quest to objectify it. When its locus shifted from the temporal to the spatial, it became an attainable goal and a challenge to the explorers. Heretofore the cult of the simple life, having nowhere else to look except toward the inscrutable past, had been an expression of chronological primitivism. Now it could be a manifestation of cultural primitivism, for better or for worse, insofar as it was brought face to face with genuine primitives. Nothing like them had thus far been imprinted upon the European consciousness, which was therefore bound to eke out its first impressions by drawing upon its imagination—and, even more, upon the precarious analogy of a well remembered myth. The privilege of undergoing a fresh experience is one thing, and the problem of writing about it is another. The discoverer who has looked upon *terra incognita* must explain it in terms which those who have never been there can readily comprehend. Furthermore, human awareness is conditioned to single out familiar sights and sounds, and often to confuse the unfamiliar with what may fit more easily into our preexisting scheme of things. Even if our eyes and ears have seen and heard correctly, the results of our observation must be reported in language, and language is the creature of convention. No wonder that a gap exists between the traveler's tale and the credence of its listeners.

Columbus and his crew reported that, while sailing offshore in the West Indies, they could hear the singing of nightingales. Some of them even reported encountering mermaids. Unfortunately, neither mermaids nor nightingales are indigenous in our western hemisphere, nor were they in the fifteenth century. The nightingale of Columbus was a kind of auditory mirage, as Leonardo Olschki has pointed out in his literary history of geographical discovery. Ornithologists have made suggestions as to the actual species of the bird whose call bemused the Spanish mariners. What would be more interesting to know is the psychological process whereby, on that occasion, wanderlust was overtaken by nostalgia. This is a small yet striking example of the way in which presupposition colored the first encounters of the Europeans with the New World. Nothing they had previously experienced could have prepared them for their initial view of the Amerindïans. However, they could draw upon a rich backlog of fabulous lore about aborigenes, namely the myth of the golden age. Hence it is not surprising that, whenever the voyagers undertook to describe the inhabitants of the new lands they had been exploring, the Ovidian *topos* was likely to come into play, almost as if it had been touched off by a reflex action. Life at its barest and least sophisticated was somehow decked out with a set of trappings inherited from the learned conventions of literature. These, at best, provided a metaphor, which dignified the simplicities of the tribe. At worst, they gave rise to a series of sentimental misconceptions, by some of which we are still haunted. "Again and again," as H. N. Fairchild has shown, "we shall find Noble Savages likened to men of the Golden Age."

The Italian chronicler of the Columbian expeditions and the earliest decade of discovery, who is known in English as Peter Martyr, wrote about the natives of Hispaniola: "They lyve without any certayne dwelling places, and without tyllage or culturying of the grounde, as wee reade of them whiche in olde tyme lyved in the golden age." Since there were no signs of property-holding in Cuba, he noted: "These natives enjoy a golden age, for they know neither *meum* nor *tuum*." What struck the European eye most perceptibly, of course, was the absence of European paraphernalia. Since the negation of existing customs and institutions had been the principal method for describing the golden age, a large amount of coincidence was inevitable. The most observable trait of the islanders was their comparative lack of clothing and artifacts. Lacking iron, they could not belong to the iron age. Their propitious climate, stimulating the natural bounty of the soil and ripening their corn two or three times a year, obviated much of the need for labor and lent substance to the legend of an eternal spring, along with kindred legends about the proximity of the earthly paradise or the fountain of youth. When Peter Martyr pauses to reflect, he makes it clear that his comparison is based upon a sense of freedom from the trammels of the Old World:

> The inhabitantes of these Ilandes have beene ever so used to live at libertie, in play and pastime, that they canne hardly away with the yoke of servitude, which they attempted to shake of by all meanes they may. And surely if they had received our religion I woulde thinke their life most happie of all menne, if they might therewith enjoy their auncient libertie. A few things content them, having no delight in such superfluities for the which in other places menne take infinite paynes, and commit manie unlawfull actes, and yet are never satisfied, whereas manie have too much, and none enough. But among these simple soules, a fewe clothes serve the naked: weightes and measures are not needful to such as cannot skill of craft and deceite, and have not the use of pestiferous money, the seed of innumerable mischeives: so that if we shall not bee ashamed to confesse the trueth, they seeme to live in that golden worlde of the whiche olde writers speake so much, wherein menne lived simply and innocently without enforcement of lawes, without quarrelling, judges, and libelles, content onely to satisfie nature, without further vexation for knowledge of things to come.

Notwithstanding, these simple souls are troubled with the ambition to enlarge their *locus amoenus*. Like most other Caribbean tribes, they prove to be unworthy of their classical prototypes by engaging in war. The Elizabethan translator, Richard Eden, offers a running commentary on Peter Martyr's *De novo orbe* by subjoining a pithy sequence of marginalia. He may be underlining the obvious when he notes at one point, "Fables muche lyke ovide his transformations," and at another, "Mine and thine the seedes of al myscheefe." But what impresses him most, becoming his major theme as he turns to the later explorations, is the universal presence of gold and the amiable nonchalance with which it is disregarded by the Indians: "Golde every where," "Gold no more esteemed then stones." As a patriotic Englishman, writing from a perspective of Anglo-Spanish rivalry, Eden is particularly critical of the "thirste of golde," which motivated the Spaniards—his glosses insist—more than their zeal for spreading the faith. "Desire of gold founde that which religion could not finde."

The onus of such criticism falls upon the Conquistadors and their notoriously cruel exploitation of the Mexicans and the Peruvians. It is well attested by the defender and historian of the Indians, Fray Bartolomé de Las Casas, whose missionary career was to put into practice the impulse that Peter Martyr had recorded in passing: "Undoubtedly, these folkes should be the happiest in the World, if onely they knew God." Yet Columbus himself, in one of his letters to his royal patrons, shrewdly promises them the best of both worlds, intermingling the prospect of untold riches with the propagation of Christianity: "Gold is the most precious of all commodities, gold constitutes treasure, and he who possesses it has all he needs in this world, as also the means of rescuing souls from purgatory and returning them to the enjoyment of paradise." The moral ambivalence of the golden lure was appreciated by the English, if not by the Spanish; and Eden could expatiate upon it, and upon the commercialization of justice, in his preface to Biringuccio's *Book of Metals*: "nowe that lady that reigned in Saturns dayes, is becomme the slave to hym that was then her bondeman in that golden worlde, so named, not for the desyre that man had to golde, but for the innocencie of lyvyinge in those dayes." Michael Lok, who completed Eden's translation of Peter Martyr's decades, draws a somewhat pharisaical contrast between the colonial policy of New Spain and that of the Virginia Company. In the later sections that he rendered, the carefree way of life before the conquest has become a remembrance in the past tense:

They had the golden age, mine and thine, the seedes of discord, were farre removed from them: the rest of the yeere from seede time, and harvest, they gave themselves to tennis, dancing, hunting, and fishing: concerning judiciall courts of Justice, suits of law, and wrangling, and brawling among neighbours, there is no mention at all.

The historic tragedy would be reduced to operatic burlesque by Sir William Davenant with *The Cruelty of the Spaniards in Peru*. Therein the exploited Incas are introduced singing and dancing, and endeavoring vainly to recapture the happiness of their native condition:

> *Whilst yet our world was new,*
> *When not discover'd by the old;*
> *Ere beggar'd slaves we grew,*
> *For having silver hills, and strands of gold . . .*
> *We danc'd and we sung*
> *And lookt ever young,*
> *And from restraints were free,*
> *As waves and winds at sea.*

The succeeding reign of terror is exemplified by the following stage direction:

Two Spaniards are likewise discover'd, sitting in their cloaks, and appearing more solemn in ruffs, with rapiers and daggers by their sides; the one turning a spit, whilst the other is basting an Indian Prince, which is roasted at an artificial fire.

Happily, the Prince's compatriots are rescued and the Spaniards are put to flight by the unexpected arrival of the English, with a cavalier twist of historical fact which the playwright justifies by claiming poetic license, and the opera concludes with the edifying spectacle of the English and the Indians shaking hands. In sober actuality, Drake and Ralegh had not been less eager for gold than Cortez or Pizarro. It was one of the issues over which England fought the Spanish Armada and sent its freebooters into the Spanish Main. Sir Walter Ralegh's *Discovery of Guiana* was a prospectus for a gold rush which failed to materialize. Vastly as Spain had profited from the wealth of the Indian mines, its adventurers were lured on farther and farther by the illusive tales of El Dorado, which their tortures may have wrung from their victims. That epithet ("the gilded one") had originally designated a man, a *cacique* or kingly priest whose tribal followers were said to cover him with gold dust in an annual ceremony. Then the name was transposed to his legendary capital, Manoa, which floated somewhere on a hidden lagoon—but where? Conflicting reports kept it moving, from the Amazon to the Orinoco River and farther west, and many treasure-seekers were lost in the attempted pursuit. Ralegh, to be followed by Milton, located it in Guiana: "I have been assured by such of the *Spanyardes* as haue seene *Manoa* the emperiall Citie of *Guiana*, which the *Spanyardes* cal *el Dorado*, that for the greatnes, for the riches, and for the excellent seate, it farre exceedeth any of the world."

Ralegh's adventurous spirit was to be confined and condemned, and apparently no European ever laid eyes on that floating city. Its opulence remained as mythical as the Hesiodic simile with which the travelers gilded their accounts. Amerigo Vespucci was an unreliable witness, whose veracity has been impugned by Las Casas and others since. He seems to have been more of a publicist than a navigator, and we must admit that he performed a remarkable feat of publicity when he succeeded in attaching his name to two continents. In discussing the mores of the mainland, he offers —perhaps at second hand—the usual observations: no commerce, no private property, everything in common, *et cetera*. On his own he puts forth the interesting comment that the South Americans "live according to nature, and are more inclined to be Epicurean than Stoic." We are accustomed to looking through the soft focus of primitivism rather than the hard one, to viewing the indigenes as children of pleasure rather than duty; but Vespucci amplifies this distinction with the suggestion that they are putting classical ethics in practice. The extent to which the Indians were classicized, in the European mind, is indicated by some of the illustrations to the voyage literature. In the widely circulated compendium on South America by André Thevet, *Les Singularitez de la France Antarctique*, the Brazilians are shown in delightful woodcuts, sitting under the pineapple-trees and looking like sculptured Greek demigods.

The late Geoffroy Atkinson made an examination of more than five hundred travel books and geographical surveys which had been published in France before 1610. His study, *Les Nouveaux Horizons de la Renaissance Française*, quotes and summarizes extensively; and his explorers and geographers fall repeatedly into the vocabulary of the golden age. The phrase itself, along with the remark that "*tout y est commun à chacun,*" is especially ubiquitous. The cartographer Jodocus Hondius made use of the concept as a political category, distinguishing between peoples ruled by chieftains and others still enjoying full liberty, "maintaining all things in common among them, in the manner of those who lived at the time of the golden age, which the poets mention." Marc Lescarbot, in his *Histoire de la Nouvelle France*, praises a community of savages for having perfected a way of life which is worthiest of man as a sociable animal, "life of the antique golden age, which the holy Apostles wanted to restore." But though they spiritualized life with their gospels, they did not carry through their social program, Lescarbot goes on. When these savages have any food, they share it with one another; they possess that mutual charity of which Europe has been deprived since the pronouns *mien* and *tien* came into existence; their hospitality is a reminder, to this observer, of the ancient Gauls. Attention focuses on the Americas with a particular interest for us. Yet French voyagers found similar characteristics among the Tartars and Brahmins and in the autochthonous races of China and Africa.

Whether this is a testimonial to the uniformity of mankind or to the universality of our daydream, it does not show a highly developed perception of ethnic diversity. It comprehends all breeds within a classic pattern of human nature, differentiated by their respective degrees of closeness to or distance from nature itself. The Portuguese told the same stories of Brazil. The English explorers and settlers of North America had comparable reports to make of the local Indians, as related in the maritime chronicles of Richard Hakluyt and Samuel Purchas. On a voyage of reconnaissance sponsored by Ralegh, Philip Amadas and Arthur Barlow stepped ashore at what is now North Carolina, where they were graciously received by the denizens:

> We were entertained with all love and kindness and with as much bounty after their manner as they could possibly devise. We found the people most gentle, loving, and faithful, void of all guile and treason and such as lived after the manner of the Golden Age. The earth bringeth forth all things in abundance as in the first creation, without toil or labor.

That expedition was the first harbinger of the Virginia colony, so named in courtly allusion to Queen Elizabeth, whose stellar role in the English revival of our myth we shall have further occasion to marvel at. Not the least of her royal attributes was to be patroness of the navigators and colonizers. A poem about Guiana, reprinted by Hakluyt, entreats her:

> *let your breath*
> *Go forth upon the waters and create*
> *A golden World in this our yron age.*

Michael Drayton paid his compliments in *The Muses' Elizium*, wherein Eliza's England has all the standard features of the Elysian Fields—except that, with due allowance for its northerly climate, the weather is not an eternal spring but an eternal summer. (Mythology adjusts to the English winter, as Byron timed it, "Ending in July / To recommence in August.") Elsewhere, at the very beginning of his *Polyolbion*, Drayton rediscovered the golden mean in Britain's atmospheric conditions: "The Summer not too hot, the Winter not too long." And William Camden, in the introductory survey of his *Britannia*, cites Byzantine authority for comparing the rich fertility and blessed pleasantness, ("*beata amoenitas*") of the British Isles to the amenities of the Fortunate Isles or Islands of the Blest, "where poets write that all things smile in a perpetual spring." To trace the ecology of the golden age is to shed some light on the varying atmospheric conditions under which it is called upon to flourish. Thus an account of Bermuda ascribed to Captain John Smith speaks of continual spring, but one of Hakluyt's relations about Guiana hedges by speaking of both spring and summer, as did Peter Martyr in referring to the seasonal atmosphere of Hispaniola. Drayton's ode "To the Virginian Voyage," which is addressed to Hakluyt, extenuates matters by reminding him that the winters are short in "Earth's onely paradise." There "the golden age / Still natures lawes doth give."

With the settling of the new continent, the slogan was taken over by the colonists as an image of themselves. Just as the Puritans sought for their paradise in the wilderness, so Cotton Mather regarded the degeneration of the times as the prelude to another golden age, somewhat less uninhibited than Tasso's. "In short, the first *Age* was the golden *Age*: to return unto *that*, will make a man a Protestant, and, I may add, a Puritan." It has its honored place in eighteenth-century rhetoric, in the ideology of the constitutional founders, on the great seal of the United States, and consequently on the dollar bill, which bears an inscription adapted from Vergil's *Fourth Eclogue*: "*Novus ordo saeclorum.*" It fitted in with the prospects and the bonanzas of nineteenth-century expansion, moving westward toward California—that state which derives its name so appropriately from an enchanted island, inhabited by tall, bronze-colored Amazons, in a sequel to the popular romance of *Amadís of Gaul*. The regional historian H. H. Bancroft, in a volume entitled *California Pastoral*, rhapsodized about the Mexican period:

> Never before or since was there a spot in America where life was a long happy holiday, where there was less labor, less care of trouble, such as the old-time golden age under Cronus or Saturn, the gathering of nature's fruits being the chief burden of life, and death coming without decay, like a gentle sleep.

European witnesses could transfer their sympathies from the Indians to the citizens of the blooming republic. In the words of one French pamphleteer, François Barbé-Marbois: "The golden age, a fiction of the Old World, is realized in the New." The interplay of innocence and corruption, which is so persistent a theme for American novelists, has been geographically correlated with the relationship of the two hemispheres. Chronologically it has its coordinates in the two ages, gold and iron. The imagery of Arcadia and the golden age is interwoven with the motif of Eden and the fall throughout Nathaniel Hawthorne's old-world novel, *The Marble Faun*. Henry James's expatriates in *The Europeans*, returning to suburban America, have a properly supercilious cliché for it: "It's primitive; it's patriarchal; it's the *ton* of the golden age."

Thoreau had incarnated the primitive strain, when he sought his private golden age and worked out the frugal simplifications of *Walden, or Life in the Woods*. There, in the house constructed by his own hands, he dreamed of "a larger and more populous house, standing in the golden age," with "the prostrate Saturn of an older day" greeting his guests at the doorstep. Emerson set the patriarchal tone as lecturer, preacher, rhapsode, with his oracles of public amelioration: "Resources of America! why, one thinks of Saint-Simon's saying, 'The Golden Age is not behind, but before you.' Here is man in the Garden of Eden . . ." Such optimism was negated by Herman Melville; his vision of his country is iron in its grimness; but his ideals of felicity are voiced in his reminiscences of the South Seas. The happy valley of Typee in the Marquesas, as he evokes it through negative enumeration, represents the antipodes of the pressure and the constraint—above all, the financial obligations—that he felt in bourgeois society:

> There were none of those thousand sources of irritation that the ingenuity of civilized man has created to mar his own felicity. There were no foreclosures of mortgages, no protested notes, no bills payable, no debts of honour in Typee; no unreasonable tailors and shoemakers, perversely bent on being paid; no duns of any description; no assault and battery attorneys, to foment discord, backing their

clients up to a quarrel, and then knocking their heads together; no poor relations, everlastingly occupying the spare bed-chamber, and diminishing the elbow-room at the family table; no destitute widows with their children starving on the cold charities of the world; no beggars; no debtors' prisons; no proud and hard-hearted nabobs in Typee; or to sum up all in one word—no Money! "That root of all evil" was not to be found in the valley.

The American vista that emerges from between these lines may be somewhat distorted, but it helps to explain why the hopes of the Golden Day turned too quickly into disillusionments. The era of big business and industrial inflation that opened up after the Civil War, if it was not the iron age, was Mark Twain's *Gilded Age*. The evanescence of the American Indian had spurred the search for noble savages onward across the Pacific to Polynesia. Diderot had anticipated Melville, in his trenchant *Supplément au voyage de Bougainville*, by sharpening the dialectic between the self-sufficient natives of Tahiti and their would-be civilizers, the missionaries. The irony comes full circle when we stop to consider that the West Indians were not such innocents as they had been taken for by the crew of Columbus. Were they not responsible for infecting Europe with a new venereal disease? Thence, among the blessings of civilization, syphilis was conveyed overseas by European sailors and passed on to the hitherto untainted South Sea islanders.

But we must not allow the shadow of coming events to deflect our gaze too far from the point where the voyage literature converges with *belles lettres*. This convergence seems to have had its immediate impact in France, whose culture was equally rich in colonial interests and classical traditions. The seminal restatement of our myth, which had been preserved in the later Middle Ages through the *Ovide moralisé*, had been made in French by the *Roman de la rose*. One of the many adaptations of the *Metamorphoses*, in the late fifteenth century, was aptly titled *La Bible des poètes*. The golden age is among the tropes that were brandished by the *rhétoriqueurs*; their chief, Lemaire de Belges, traced the genealogy of the French kings back to the reign of Saturn. Contrariwise, an anonymous poetic satire of somewhat earlier date, the *Contrefait de Renard*, blamed the dissolution of the golden age on the establishment of the French monarchy. Clément Marot, as a courtly practitioner of the pastoral, composed a Vergilian eclogue hailing the birth of a son—the future François II—to the Dauphin. In translating the first two books of the *Métamorphoses*, he set forth the four ages in rather labored couplets. He was more at ease when he treated the subject in a rondeau, which has lasted as his main contribution to the anthologies, *De l'amour du Siècle Antique*, with its refrain harking back to the good old days: "*Au bon vieulx temps.*" A moralistic poem by one of his followers, Béranger de La Tour, purports to be the monologue of the first man, looking back upon a long life which has been coextensive with the golden age.

We should not forget that the heroine of the best-known pastoral romance, *L'Astrée*, was a Gaulish namesake of the goddess of justice, whose ancient heyday is recalled by Honoré d'Urfé in his dedication to the "*pasteur souverain*," Henri IV. The convention of royalty posing as shepherds was a well established routine at the French court under the Valois, though it would not have reached its apogee until Marie Antoinette had set up her dairy at Versailles. Yet in a *bergerie* or pastoral masque by Pierre de Ronsard, a chorus of shepherdesses hails their presiding shepherdess, Catherine de' Medici, as the benefactor who has recreated the golden age:

> *Si nous voyons le siècle d'or refait,*
> *C'est du bienfait*
> *De la Bergere Catherine*

Then a chorus of nymphs salutes Prince Charles as the shepherd Carlin, who is destined to revive the best years of old Saturn. The shepherd Navarrin, as played by the ten-year-old Henry of Navarre, later to be crowned as Henri IV then declaims a set-piece on the golden age, when gold was powerless ("*Hà! bel âge doré, où l'or n'avoit puissance!*"), when the fields were unfenced, the lands common, the crops spontaneous, and grievances conspicuous by their absence. The pace of these court entertainments, as well as the frequent successions, compelled Ronsard to use the same phraseology over and over, while applying it to different kings. In *Les Sereines*, a masquerade at Fontainebleau, the siren song dates the golden age from the kingship of Henri II, the father of Prince Charles, who will soon be reviving it. A fifth eclogue comprises a dialogue between Carlin, who is now Charles IX, and Xarcin, the future Henri III. Carlin is sighing for that golden season of the earlier Charleses ("*les pasteurs Charlots*"). Xarcin endeavors to reassure him by prophesying that the good time—the springtime—will come back, with milk in its rivers and honey in its oaks. Such expressed misgivings were well founded, for the reign of *le grand pasteur Carlin* was to be marked by the culminating outrage of the religious wars, the Massacre of Saint Bartholomew's Day.

To Catherine de' Medici, who—as Queen Mother—was to be a strategic figure in the Catholic plot, the courtier-poet had previously dedicated a poem lamenting the demise of the golden age, *Des misères de ce temps*. Compliments to royal personages alternate with complaints on the poet's plight throughout Ronsard's voluminous *ouvrage*, and his evaluation of his contemporaries shifts accordingly. His *Hynne de l'or* is inscribed, with a play upon the surname, to Jean Dorat, fellow member and preceptor of the Pléiade. The mock-hymn to the power of gold turns into a lamentation on the high cost of living in this far-from-golden age, when hungry men of learning find that their Greek and Latin will not assuage an empty stomach:

> Car de bien peu nous sert le Grec et le Latin,
> Quand la faim nous assaut l'estomac au matin.

In the epistle to Jean de Brinon, *Les Armes*, the pun is on *fer* and *l'enfer*; this hellish iron age of cannon and gunpowder is contrasted with the age of acorn-eating commonage, when there were no such words as mine and thine—or, for that matter, kill (*Tue*) and strike (*Assomme*). And Ronsard, whose deafness kept him from serving in the bloody campaigns of his embattled time, resurrects the old curse against mining and invention. The polarity of gold and iron, as we have seen, can be a premise for both satire and flattery. Ronsard is extremely mercurial, sometimes oscillating from the one to the other within the compass of a single poem. His *Hynne de la justice* bitterly denounces the iron age's afflictions, and ends by appealing to the Cardinal-Prince of Lorraine as the potential restorer of the happier dispensation. Here the goddess of justice is the blindfolded Themis with her scales; no mention is made of Astraea, possibly because Astrée was a name for one of the mistresses to whom Ronsard devoted his sonnet sequences. To a former mistress who planned to marry another lover, he directed a bitter-sweet elegy, again recalling the days of Saturn, whom he invokes with a domestic epithet as the husband of the mother of the gods ("*le mari de Rhée*"). Pleasure was free in those days because love was; there were no marriage contracts nor dowries, no rings, priests, or laws; Hymen was not a god.

> *Lors Hymen n'estoit dieu, et encores le doy*
> *Ne cognoissoit l'anneau, le prestre, ny la loy.*
> *Le plaisir estoit libre . . .*

In an imaginary dialogue by Guy de Brués, Ronsard is represented as taking an orthodox position against his more skeptical colleague, Jean-Antoine de Baïf, who speaks for a naturalistic ethic grounded in Ovid's *topos*. The real Baïf avowed his hopes for a return of "*le bon siècle*," when poets were sages and musicians as well, and composed a charming if not profound sonnet associating "*le siècle . . . de celle gent dorée*" with the countryside and his love. Joachim Du Bellay made Mary Queen of Scots his Astraea, in a sonnet calling for peace between France and England, and—in a salutation to Henri II—employed the same personification for the revival of learning under his predecessor, François I:

> *Tu a defaict ce vil monstre Ignorance,*
> *Tu a refaict le bel age doré:*
> *Par toi premier au monde est revenue*
> *La belle Vierge aux vieux siecles songneue.*

Ronsard, steeped in classical mythology, lost none of the opportunities for conjuring with it that came to him through the vicissitudes of a picturesque career. He was committed, through his adherence to the Pléiade and the principles outlined in Du Bellay's *Défense et illustration de la langue française*, not to the imitation of the classics but to emulation and challenge. Myths were not decorations, to be superficially applied; they were correspondences for living experiences, which could be brought home to Christendom, to France, and to the poet's lifetime. Since the myth of the golden age is a way of viewing one's lifetime, however ambivalently, it could frame the other mythical references. But, by using it as an official greeting for one short-lived and ill-starred sovereign after another, he wore it fairly thin.

In such a mood of revulsion as had led Horace to consider flight from Rome, he wrote *Les Isles fortunées*, calling upon his friend, the humanist Muretus, and other disappointed men of letters to join him in setting sail for those fortunate islands which Jupiter had set aside for his favorites when the gold and silver ages had given way to the rusty stain of murderous iron:

> *Que Jupiter reserva pour les siens,*
> *Lors qu'il changea des siècles anciens*
> *L'or en argent, et l'argent en la rouille*
> *D'un fer meurtrier qui de son meurtre souille*
> *La pauvre Europe!*

Up to a point Ronsard seems to be going through a set of literary motions, gracefully repeating the Horatian gesture in a personal context. Beyond that point, when he glances back at poor Europe, we realize that his imagination has been travelling across the Atlantic. The crucial step, which he takes in his *Discours contre Fortune*, is to interlink the conventional myth with the reality of contemporary exploration. Here he is addressing Durand de Villegagnon, the soldier of fortune who attempted to found a Huguenot colony on an island in the bay of Rio de Janeiro. Ronsard, discouraged with his own fortunes in France, is seriously tempted to join the expedition. At all events, he has some advice to offer. It is a mistake, he tells Villegagnon, to civilize your innocent native, who is now just as devoid of clothing as he is of malice (*"D'habit tout aussi nu qu'il est nu de malice"*). Not recognizing the names of virtue and vice, nor any laws save those of nature, he lives at his own pleasure. These Americans share whatever they have as freely as water, with no lawsuits to create invidious distinctions.

> *Et comme l'eau d'un fleuve, est commun tout leur bien,*
> *Sans procez engendré de ce mot* Tien *et* Mien.

Leave them alone, Ronsard begs Villegagnon. Do not teach them to fence their fields, or to be ambitious and acquisitive. They are now living in their golden age. Do you want to turn it into iron? They will curse you for that.

The decisive confrontation between the thoughtful European and the uncivilized American happened in the *Essais* of Montaigne. With authoritative self-knowledge, he had chosen a pair of balances as his emblem; for the mode of discursive prose to which his reflections have given their tentative name is indeed a subtle equilibration of ideas. If tradition is questioned by their skepticism, then their experimental outlook is balanced by a respect for custom, so that the implications and repercussions of Montaigne's thought are always far in advance of his own position—insofar as it can be specified. The scale is nervously poised between Montaigne the observer, the *grand seigneur* and man of affairs on the one hand, and on the other the thinker who retired to his tower outside of Bordeaux, where the wisdom of the ancients was quoted on the very beams that held up the roof of his study. Among the multitudinous quotations that serve as guideposts through his rambling paragraphs, seventy-two are from Ovid, twenty-two of them from the *Metamorphoses*. In Montaigne's essay on the instruction of children, he attributes his earliest taste for books to the reading of those fables in Latin at the age of seven or eight. Yet, in his essay on physiognomy, he declares himself a naturalist, more interested in invention than allegation; and it is equally typical of him that, when he confronted the newly discovered *homo americanus*, he set aside the travel writers and sought out first-hand information. His principal informant was a member of his own household, who had spent ten or twelve years with Villegagnon in so-called Antarctic France; and this testimony was authenticated, briefly but empirically, by a direct interview with three Brazilian Indians.

The question that Montaigne puts to himself, in his momentous essay on the cannibals, concerns the nature of what we call barbarism. He is well aware, though he makes no issue of it, that the Greeks invented the notion to stigmatize the non-Greeks. The stigma is presumptively based on a body of social and ethical standards whereby our civilization would differentiate itself from what it regards as lesser breeds outside the law. If this ethnocentric standpoint is now regarded as an instance of hemispheric provinciality, if modern anthropologists study the Easter Islanders no less conscientiously than the humanists once studied the classics, if underdeveloped countries are represented in the councils of the United Nations today, we must thank Montaigne for his pioneering attitude. The impression he gathered from his servant who had been in Brazil was that "there is nothing in that nation, that is either barbarous or savage, unlesse men call that barbarisme which is not common to them." Our sole criterion, as it is formulated by Montaigne and Englished by John Florio, cannot be other than "the example and *Idea* of the opinions and customes of the countrie we live in." Judged in their own light, the Brazilians have achieved "perfect religion, perfect policie, perfect and compleat use of all things." The argument progresses more smoothly in French, inasmuch as *sauvage* means both savage and wild. Since the folkways of the savages have grown up naturally, like wild-flowers, might not the adjective be applied more pertinently to our habits, which have been bastardized by artifice?

Plato is then cited to the effect that, as a formative influence, nature is much more important than art. Montaigne regrets that Plato and Lycurgus did not live to witness and discuss this empirical fulfilment of classic ideals:

for me seemeth that what in those nations we see by experience, doth not only exceed all the pictures wherewith licentious Poesie hath proudly imbellished the golden age, and all her quaint inventions to faine a happy condition of man, but also the conception and desire of Philosophy.

Yet neither Plato, whose republic stands in such rigorous contrast, nor Lycurgus, whose regime at Sparta was even more austere, could have foreseen a society maintaining itself in so utterly pure and simple a form.

It is a nation, would I answer *Plato*, that hath no kinde of traffike, no knowledge of Letters, no intelligence of numbers, no name of magistrate, nor of politike superioritie; no use of service, of riches or of povertie; no contracts, no successions, no partitions, no occupation but idle; no respect of kinred, but common, no apparell but naturall, no manuring of lands, no use of wine, corne, or mettle. The very words that import lying, falshood, treason, dissimulations, covetousnes, envie, detraction, and pardon, were never heard of amongst them.

While Montaigne is conducting his imaginary dialogue with Plato, his Brazilian particulars seem to be merging with the Ovidian commonplaces. (Ovid is not mentioned in the essay, though it includes cross-references to Vergil's *Georgics* and Seneca's *Ninetieth Epistle*.) The savages are endowed, by their healthy environment and their natural resources, with the negative gifts of the golden age. But, the more the ethnic details accumulate, the farther we find ourselves from the unbounded pleasures of Tasso's anarchy. Leisure is pleasantly spent in dancing and hunting, to be sure, and the moral code is simply stated: "First, valour against their enemies, then lovingnesse unto their wives." Marriage is not so much of a responsibility as it might seem, inasmuch as the husbands practice polygamy, and it is the wives' duty not merely to serve them their wine but to abet them in procuring additional wives. Families, as well as goods, are enjoyed in common. It is warfare that spoils the euphoric picture, as it did for some of the voyagers. Montaigne extenuates this pattern of behavior somewhat; the Brazilians fight, using wooden weapons, for glory rather than spoils; and, although they behead their enemies, they roast and eat them in common. "I am not sorie we note the barbarous horror of such an action," he comments, "but grieved, that prying so narrowly into their faults we are so blinded in ours."

He is not defending the virtues of savagery; he is attacking the vices of occidental culture. Voltaire, since he did not share Montaigne's belief in the nobility of some wars, could push the attack much farther, arguing that the morality of the cannibals was superior to that of the Europeans because they slaughtered for their sustenance and did not let the carnage go to waste. "We may then well call them barbarous, in regard of reasons rules," allowed Montaigne, "but not in respect of us that exceed them in all kinde of barbarisme." *Des cannibales*, like Montaigne's other inquiries, comes back to the inquirer, having incidentally toured the world. Its reflexive answer could be summed up in Melville's rhetorical question: "Cannibals? Who is not a cannibal?" The last page brings about a double reversal. Having accompanied the youthful Charles IX to Rouen, Montaigne records his conversation with the three cannibals at large, who have braved cisatlantic corruption. Typically, he is dissatisfied with their interpreter, but moved by the naive penetration of his interlocutors. The New World is by no means overawed by the pomp of the Old. Applying their own criteria, they have two criticisms to make—there was a third, but Montaigne has somehow forgotten it. First, it is very strange to see grown men, such as the fine tall Swiss guard, submitting to the command of that mere boy who happens to be king. Second, and even stranger, is the sight of rich men gorging themselves with commodities while others, emaciated with hunger, beg at their gates. How long will the poor suffer such injustice, without grabbing the masters by the throat and burning down their houses?

The tables are turned again on the final page, when the train of meditation breaks off in a parting shrug. All this does not sound too bad (*"Tout cela ne va pas trop mal"*). But, after all, these informants wear no trousers (*"mais quoy, ils ne portent point de haut de chausses*"). How can they be taken seriously, under the circumstances? Yet the concluding expression, *haut-de-chausses*, reverberates to provoke an afterthought; the comparative nakedness of the Amerindians is juxtaposed to the ridiculous foppery of the breeches and hose then worn by French courtiers; and it is quite uncertain which has the last laugh, America or Europe. A loincloth might have seemed a clearer token of modesty than the flamboyant codpiece glorified by Panurge. The fashionable small-clothes of the eighteenth century were to be discarded by the revolutionary *sansculottes*. With Montaigne, the trial has been essayed, the experiment has teetered to an equilibrium, and the ambiguity remains two-sided. "For if my fortune had beene to have lived among those nations, which yet are said to live under the sweet liberty of Natures first and uncorrupted laws," he has confided in his prefatory note to the reader, "I would most willingly have pourtrayed my selfe fully [*tout entier*] and naked [*tout nud*]." The self-portrayal is complete enough to attain a certain objectivity, since the artist is so willing to reflect everything in his mirror. The adage about emulating the Romans when in Rome has its corollary in doing as the Barbarians do when in Barbary. It was a triumph for Latin humanism that one of its ripest products—by putting himself on the outside, so to speak—broke through the limitations of ethnocentricity and achieved a relativistic world-view.

In a later essay, *Des coches*, it is not the naïveté of the American primitives so much as the grandeur of the pre-Columbian empires that engages Montaigne's sympathy, and diverts his contemplation from imperial luxuries in general to the Spanish conquest of Mexico and Peru. Vividly he adopts the point of view of the Aztecs or the Incas, who had welcomed the strangers in good faith. Indignantly he contrasts the innate morality of these subjugated peoples, who have so dearly bought "our opinions, our new-fangles and our arts," with the hypocritical brutality of their conquerors. Such ignoble victories are obtained by pressing vulgarly commercial and technological stratagems: "*Mechaniques victoires*." The Romans or the Macedonians would have proceeded more humanely and without such chicanery. The consequent feeling is that history has been taking a wrong turn, that both hemispheres have missed a great opportunity. And Montaigne seems ready to share the Aztecs' conviction that the ages have run through their predestined sequence and we are nearing the end of the world. Elsewhere, in *De l'expérience*, he has a kinder word for Spanish policy, on the specific grounds that King Ferdinand forbade the migration of jurisconsults to his Indian colonies. This proviso is in keeping with the Platonic distrust of lawyers and physicians, as well as with the avoidance of legalism during the golden age. As for the proscription of medicine, Montaigne turns to that in his essay on fathers and children, pointing out that lives were longer and healthier in the best and happiest ages, before there were any doctors.

Thus Montaigne has earned his reputation as a primitivist of sorts, and his *Essais* have been a primary source for the stream of primitivistic thought that was to become a major current of the romantic movement. With the proclamation and dissemination of the idea itself, we are accustomed to credit or discredit Jean-Jacques Rousseau. Yet Rousseau's crucial discourse on the origins of inequality was characterized by Chateaubriand as "nothing but an eloquent paraphrase" of Montaigne's essay on the cannibals. It is more than that, as we shall be noting; and it is less uncritical in its cult of *le bon sauvage* than writers like Chateaubriand were to be; but it is sentimental enough to overweigh the delicate equipoise of *Des cannibales*. The underside has come to predominate, while the hard-headedness of the critique has been softened. For Montaigne the savage is not absolutely noble, he is relatively nobler than the European in some particular respects. Whether he fits Montaigne's or Rousseau's description, whether the uncivilized races of today actually correspond to the ancestral generations of humanity, is a problem which the man of letters may well refer to the anthropologist. Claude Lévi-Strauss reports that, on an expedition into the jungles of the Amazon, he elicited the same responses from a native chief that Montaigne had heard from his Brazilians at Rouen four centuries ago. And M. Lévi-Strauss comments that more civilized countries do not witness such persistence in their political thinking.

This evidence, from a twentieth-century thinker who is well qualified by his range of perception to be a commentator on Montaigne, offers corroboration to some extent. Yet persistence is not a political virtue under every conceivable circumstance. The tribe of the Matto Grosso that Lévi-Strauss was investigating had preserved the most elemental forms of social organization, which had badly equipped it for survival into the modern world. It was not a burgeoning but an agonizing society, no closer to the golden age than our Indian reservations are to the happy hunting-grounds. If we put the blame on civilization for the falling off of these wayside cultures which cannot keep up with its march, then the debate continues and the balance kicks the beam again. In the *Apologie de Raymond Sebonde* the apparition of the New World rises once more to reproach the Old World for its bureaucratic complexities; curiosity, subtlety, and knowledge are weighed against the simpler qualities that make life pleasant and sociable. The *Apologie* is a treatise rather than an essay, and rather more of a diatribe than an apology. The rationalism of the Spanish doctor, whose work on natural theology he had translated, brought out Montaigne's skeptical capacity for seeing the other side. Against the all too human conception of an anthropomorphic deity and an anthropocentric universe, he postulates that the animals must conceive of their gods in their own images.

For why may not a Goose say thus? All parts of the world behold me, the earth serveth me to tread upon, the Sunne to give me light, the starres to inspire me with influence: this commoditie I have of the winds, and this benefit of the waters; there is nothing that this worlds-vault doth so favorably looke upon as me selfe; I am the favorite of nature; is it not man that careth for me, that keepeth me, lodgeth me, and serveth me? For me it is he soweth, reapeth and grindeth: If he eat me, so doth man feede on his fellow, and so doe I on the wormes, that consume and eate him.

If this is a reduction to animality for man's higher aspirations and vanities, it is likewise an apotheosis for the goose. Previously, in a memorable sentence of the *Apologie*, Montaigne has wondered: "When I am playing with my Cat, who knowes whether she have more sport in dallying with me than I have in gaming with her?" The very next sentence recalls the dictum of Plato that the men of the golden age had the advantage of communicating with the beasts. Versions of the *topos* stressed the advantages that the animal kingdom itself enjoyed, in the days when beasts of burden went unyoked. Men could naturally coexist on better terms with snakes that had no venom and wolves that had no fangs. Poets like Lorenzo de' Medici conducted their readers through a menagerie, which was harmless and friendly as well as colorful. Theriophily, a fondness for animals, is a normal human inclination which finds its congenial outlet in household pets; but it has taken stranger shapes when tribes have worshipped totems, or when the misanthropy of Swift exalted the Houyhnymns at the expense of the Yahoos. From the assumption that man is happier in a state of nature, it follows that the beast could be his exemplar of the good life—a doctrine which has been categorized as animalitarianism. Hence Nietzsche could define a human being as a sick animal, seeking compensation for physical weakness in mental activity; D. H. Lawrence could develop a mystique of the healthy animal, inverting the Christian subjection of the senses to the intellect; and, through an animalitarian ethic, primitivism could reach its ultimate phase.

Traditionally man debased himself by descending to the animal plane, as the followers of Ulysses had done when they yielded to the sensual allurements of Circe, who transformed them into swine. Ulysses withstood the lure and broke the enchantment; but there is an instructive fragment of Plutarch in which a former mariner refuses to be disenchanted; a certain Gryllus prefers to go on living the life of a hog. This sardonic conceit persisted into the era of Darwin, when it became a theme for Peacock's *Gryll Grange*.

In the mid-sixteenth century, it was elaborated into ten dialogues by the Florentine academician, Giovanni Battista Gelli, *Circe*. There Ulysses strives vainly to convince his former crew that man's lot is preferable to beast's. One by one, the members of Circe's bestiary extol the benefits of their present condition. The oyster is better off now than when he was a fisherman. The hare prefers herd instinct to civilized frustration. Though the mole agrees that the golden age is a fable, he is happy burrowing in the earth. The goat persuades Ulysses to admit that the distinction between *mine* and *thine* has done much mischief. No one but the elephant, at the end, thinks it worth his while to rejoin the human race. Spenser has incorporated the situation into his legend of temperance, the Second Book of *The Faerie Queene*, where Sir Guyon invades the Bower of Bliss, puts down the enchantress Acrasia, and delivers her former lovers from their beastly predicament. One of them, Grill by name, objects to relinquishing his "hoggish forme" as the episode concludes.

> *Said Guyon, See the mind of beastly man,*
> *That hath so soone forgot the excellence*
> *Of his creation, when he life began,*
> *That now he chooseth, with vile difference*
> *To be a beast, and lacke intelligence.*
> *To whom the Palmer thus, The donghill kinde*
> *Delightes in filth and foule incontinence:*
> *Let Grill be Grill, and have his hoggish minde,*
> *But let us hence depart, whilest wether serves and winde.*

Platonist though he be, Spenser is fascinated by the gradations in the chain of being from the carnal stage upward. Several of them are subsumed in the person of the fierce Sir Satyrane, illegitimate scion of a lady raped by a satyr, who rescues the fair Una and conveys her to the house of Holiness; later, conducting a tournament in honor of Florimel, he is finally overthrown by Sir Artegall, disguised in rustic armor and bearing the motto, "*Salvagesse sans finesse.*" At a lower level of nature's hierarchy is the Salvage Man,

—or rather, there are two savage men, and one of them is an ugly creature who combines rape with cannibalism. The other, though unblest with speech or clothes or arms, proves to be of gentle blood and mild humanity, and his instinctive helpfulness is invaluable to the more courtly characters on the trail of vulgar calumny, the Blatant Beast. Such wild men, or woodwoses, peep through the foliated tracery on the margins of medieval art and literature, darting in and out to reassert the often neglected claims and skills of nature. Sometimes they voiced an honest plaint against an untrustworthy civilization, as in Hans Sachs's *Klag der Wilden Holzleut über die Ungetrewe Welt*. The Peasant of the Danube, whose uncouth integrity showed up the oppressive rule of hypersophisticated Rome, was a variant of the species, lent eloquence by Guevera and LaFontaine. Spenser, as he demonstrated in Ireland, had no ear for the voice of the outsider, and his wild man remains significantly mute. His golden age is thrice removed, though it now invites us to revisit it, since it lies on the other side of the Middle Ages and of Fairyland. Montaigne's golden age was on the opposite side of the ocean. It was populated by cannibals, with whom he had freely conversed; for, though he had no illusions, he had horizons.

[IV]

FICTIONS

"WE HAVE FEW good pastorals in the language," conceded William Hazlitt. "Our manners are not Arcadian; our climate is not an eternal spring; our age is not the age of gold." Hazlitt's age, from which he himself maintained a crisp independence, was what we retrospectively term the romantic period, chiefly in honor of its poets. As the nineteenth century settled in, they were voicing a reaction against its more prosaic tendencies—commerce, industry, urbanization, cant—and in favor of a reversion to nature. This could no longer be expressed through Arcadianism; that, for Hazlitt, was "not nature but art, and the worst sort of art, which thinks it can do better than nature." Pastoral, as an exercise in wish-fulfilment, would continue to cast its potent spell; but, as a neoclassical genre, it had worn out its welcome when Dr. Johnson chose to deprecate *Lycidas*. As for the golden age, its original designation in England had been "the golden world." The Oxford English Dictionary cites this epithet in a theological context by William Tyndall and from a political chronicle by Edward Hall. A belated upholder of "olde antiquitie," Stephen Hawes, justifies his adherence by explaining that then

> ... *the golden worlde had dominacion,*
> *And nature, hyghe in her aucthoritie,*
> *More stronger had her operacion*
> *Than she had nowe in her digression.*

Looking back from the bloody reign of Mary to the accession of Henry VIII, George Cavendish tells us that England was "called than the golden world, such grace of plenty reigned then within this realm." There may be some significance for us in the unaccustomed noun, which puts the emphasis on topography rather than chronology; for England, as an island and as the seat of an empire, solved a good many of its temporal problems in the spatial dimension. Another world seems somewhat more accessible than another age—or, at any rate, more of a stimulus to free enterprise. But the old meaning of *world* could either encompass all human existence or designate some period thereof.

The adjective has its own effulgence in English poetry, particularly when we turn to the writings of the Elizabethans. We think of Shakespeare's "golden lads and girls" or of Dekker's "golden slumbers." Even Wordsworth, reminiscing of childhood, is not beyond a classical metaphor:

> *I had approached, like other youths, the shield*
> *Of human nature from the golden side,*
> *And would have fought even to the death to attest*
> *The quality of the metal which I saw.*

But the sense of a lost world associated with one's own youth or with the unspoiled springtide of civilization, for the Englishman, had more associations with greenery than with gold. Hence it could be rediscovered, if not recaptured, by a trip to the country. A climate whose distinguishing feature was rain, rather than the Mediterranean sun, nurtured a differing set of esthetic norms. The preoccupation with what Keats called "the green world," which is so salient an aspect of England's literature, was intensified by the poetic recoil from its industrial development. Its counterpart for Rome's Saturnalia was not urban but sylvan in character, rather more like the Roman feast of Flora. The merrymakers took to the woods as foresters, returning thence with the May Pole. A King and Queen of the Forest, or Lord and Lady of May, were chosen to impersonate Robin Hood and Maid Marion. This couple, who presided over the pastimes on the village green, owed their existence to balladry rather than history, and could point to courtly ante-cedents in the French *pastourelle*, notably the thirteenth-century *Jeu de Robin et Marion* by Adam de la Halle. The sports—the archery contests, bouts at quarterstaff, wrestling for the ram—culminated in a ritual of initiation. To join the band of merry men and to wear Lincoln green was to renew one's contact with nature. To give a lass "a green gown" was to tumble her in the grass. The may-games, with their morris-dances and hobby-horses, could be not only rough but frankly carnal. When they were repressed by the Puritans, they were popularly lamented:

> *Happy the age, and harmelesse were the dayes,*
> *For then true love and amity was found,*
> *When every village did a May Pole raise,*
> *And Whitson-ales and* MAY-GAMES *did abound.*

There had been a time when Londoners raised a may-pole in the Strand, and one occasion when Henry VIII and Katherine of Aragon were entertained by a visit from Robin Hood and two hundred archers dressed in Kendall green. Nationally celebrated, May Day was the most gladsome festival of the seasons, a veritable *sacre du printemps*. More intimately, it was an annual reminder that the best time for love was passing all too quickly, and Robert Herrick could but embellish what Richard Edwards had caroled:

> *Use May while that ye may, for May hath but his time;*
> *When all the fruit is gone it is too late the tree to climb.*

The poignance of missed opportunity is heightened by a nostalgia for the halcyon epoch now foreclosed with the abolition of Maying and, beyond that, for an eternal return to the greensward and all that it connotes. The green world has its echo in Hamlet's catch-word: "For oh, for oh, the hobby-horse is forgot." And Shakespeare links the legend of the forest to the myth of the golden world, when Robin Hood is mentioned in *As You Like It.*

Some notion of retreating from the noxious city to a greener world had already been entertained in some quarters under the early Tudors. A dialogue written by the King's Chaplain, Thomas Starkey, during the actual reign of Henry VIII, takes a much grimmer view of it than Cavendish would take from the retrospect of an even more turbulent era. The humanist Thomas Lupset is represented trying to persuade the learned ecclesiastic, Cardinal Pole, that his talents should be applied to the public needs.

> Therefore yf thys be cyvyle lyfe *and* ordur, to lyve in cytes *and* townys wyth so much vyce *and* mysordur, me seme ma*n* schold not be borne thereto, but rather to lyfe in the wyld forest, ther more folowyng the study of vertue, as hyt is sayd me*n* dyd in the golden age, where in ma*n* lyvyd accordyng to hys natural dygnyte.

The purpose of the discussion is to face the issues, not to flee from them, although one well might flinch before Starkey's panorama of depopulation and unemployment, profit-seeking and poverty, the law's delays and the abuses of power, discontent and dissension among the clergy and the nobility. The worst single cause of complaint is the enclosure of the open fields for pasturage. Hitherto available for cultivation by the villagers, the commons were now being claimed and fenced off by the landowners, who were making large fortunes by raising sheep for the booming textile trade. That was pastoralism with a vengeance; Arcadia must have seemed very far away. The ideal of holding land in common had been no mere whim of the golden age, but a tenet of the Christian Fathers, medieval popes, and doctors of the church. Saint Ambrose held that the sense of property was a consequence of the Fall. An egalitarian state of nature is one of the premises for Gratian's *Decretum*, the basic text for the study of canon law. Gregory the Great based a plea for alms on the assumption that "the soil is common to all men; when we give the necessities of life to the poor, we restore to them what is already theirs." John Wycliffe, in his Latin treatise on civil dominion, worked out the following syllogism:

> First, that all the good things of God ought to be common. The proof as follows: every man ought to be in a state of grace, and if he

is in a state of grace he is lord of the world and all that it contains; therefore every man ought to be lord of all. This will not work for the majority of men unless they hold all things in common. Therefore all things ought to be common.

The phrase became a socialistic slogan, called forth by a concern for the inequities of the later Middle Ages, and falling from the lips of Wycliffite preachers or social critics who would be increasingly regarded as radicals, if not as heretics. The rebel priest, John Ball, harangued the restless peasantry in the market-place after mass: "O ye good people, the maters gothe nat well to passe in Englande, nor shall nat do tyll every thyng be common." According to the homiletic dialogue of *Dives and Pauper*, the tenet that "all thynge is common" had the sanction of both God's law and nature's ("the lawe of kynde"). William Langland was more conservative in this regard, and Piers Plowman associates radicalism with book-learning when he protests

> *het freres go to scole,*
> *And lern logic and lawe / and eke contemplacion,*
> *And preche men of Plato / and proven hit by Seneca,*
> *That alle thynge under hevene / ouhte to bee in comune.*

The prudent husbandman, Thomas Tusser, would argue for the advantages of "severall" or enclosed farms over "Champion countrie" or commonage:

> *Where all thing in common doth rest,*
> * corne field with the pasture and meade,*
> *Though common ye doo for the best,*
> * yet what doth it stand ye in steade?*

The communistic rallying-cry had gone up for Jack Cade's rebellion in the fifteenth century; but when Shakespeare came to dramatize that event, in the Second Part of *Henry VI*, the royal authority had been securely established, together with an unshakeable respect for private property. Accordingly, his treatment of Cade is a caricature, and Cade's political platform is a Land of Cockaigne:

There shall be in England seven halfpenny loaves sold for a penny. The three-hoop'd pot shall have ten hoops, and I will make it felony to drink small beer. All the realm shall be in common, and in Cheapside shall my palfrey go to grass . . .

Meanwhile the Tudor regime had been supported by a body of political theory which was anti-communistic and hierarchical. Sir Thomas Elyot began his book of *The Governor* with a distinction between *res publica* and its usual translation, *commonweal*, bolstering an aristocratic preference for the word *public* as opposed to *common*. It was contrary to reason, he argued, to believe "that every thinge shulde be to all men in commune, without discrepance of any estate or condition." With the homilies appointed to be read in churches during the sixteenth and seventeenth centuries, the original doctrine of primitive Christianity has become a subversion of the established order:

Take away Kings, Princes, Rulers, Magistrates, Judges, and such estates of GODs order, no man shall ride or go by the high way unrobbed, no man shall sleepe in his owne house or bed unkilled, no man shall keepe his wife, children, and possession in quietnesse, all things shall bee common, and there must neede follow all mischiefe and utter destruction both of soules, bodyes, goods, and Commonwealths.

Shortly afterward, during what is known as the Commonwealth period, kings and princes actually would be taken away, and some of the more subversive questions about the ownership of property would be arising again.

Communism had been a recessive trait of the classical golden age, introduced by Ovid into his *topos* when he was explaining the subdivision of the soil during the iron age. Reinforced by the Christianized precept of *omnia communia*, it became the major premise for one of the most provocative books that was ever conceived. We should be contradicted by More's own terms, if we spoke of his *Utopia* as an affirmation, since this great good place is designated as no place, nowhere. *Nusquama* is the Latin synonym applied to it by its humanistic creator; we might well call it Never-Never-Land. J. W. Allen has characterized it as "the saddest of fairy tales, . . . an indictment of humanity almost as terrible as *Gulliver's Travels.*" It is all but unalloyed in its vision of happiness —if anything, perhaps too sage and bland. Yet the title proclaims the unlikelihood of the hypothesis from which it all proceeds:

> that no equal and just distribution of things can be made, nor that perfect wealth shall ever be among men, unless this propriety [property] be exiled and banished. But so long as it shall continue, so long shall remain among the most and best parts of men the heavy and inevitable burden of poverty and wretchedness; which, as I grant that it may be somewhat eased, so I utterly deny that it can wholly be taken away.

This is the opinion of the traveler who has visited Utopia, Raphael Hythlodaeus, with whom the skeptical More himself engages in argument: "But I am of a contrary opinion, quoth I; for methinketh that men shall never there live wealthily, where all things be in common." Yet these opposing positions are partially reconciled by the report that some Utopians were converted to Christianity after hearing "that Christ instytuted amonge hys all thynges commen." That such a proposition should be entertained by a lawyer of lawyers, who would soon become Lord Chancellor, was as ironic as the provisions allowing Utopia to have no lawyers and as few laws as possible. But irony was the essence of More's career, which took him from his woolsack to execution, martyrdom, and sainthood, and yet permitted him to envision an ideal commonwealth whose inhabitants were not even Christians. The argument is brought home to the reader *a fortiori*, both by the Latin gloss and by Ralph Robynson's English translation: "*O sanctam rempublicam, et vel Christianis imitandum* ("O holy Commonwealth, and indeed worthy of imitation by Christians)!"

Sir or Saint Thomas More, however you take him, offers admonition to the believer, on the one hand, and encouragement to the revolutionist on the other. It was inevitable that he should be claimed by both the neo-orthodox and the Marxists, and that—as a master ironist—he should resist them both. As a projector of ideals, he was firmly grounded in the harsh realities of his time. The personal dialogue that prefaces his traveler's tale, and was probably written somewhat later, is as realistic as Thomas Starkey's would be in its castigation of rents and enclosures, crimes and punishments, as well as in its plea for a recognition of public responsibilities on the part of the humanist. The charter of Utopia is a protest against the condition of England. Its basic suspicion of those who were then engaged in contriving and extending the networks of modern capitalism becomes explicit when More indicts the conspiracy of the rich ("*conspiratio divitum*"). The peroration of Hythlodaeus reinforces the running contrast:

> Heere nowe woulde I see yf anye man dare be so bolde, as to compare with thys equytie the justice of other nations. Among whom, I forsake God, if I can fynde any signe or token of equitie and justice . . . Is not thys an unjust and an unkynd publyque weale, whyche gyveth great fees and rewardes to gentlemen, as they call them, and to goldsmythes, and to suche other, whiche be other ydell persones or els onlye flatterers, and devysers of vayne pleasures; and, of the contrary parte, maketh no gentle provision for poore plowmen, coliars, laborers, carters, yronsmythes, and carpenters; without whome no commen wealth can continewe? But when it hath abused the laboures oft heire lusty and flowringe age, at the laste, when they be oppressed with old age and syckenes, being nedye, poore, and indigent of all thynges; then, forgettynge theire so many paynfull watchynges, not remembrynge theire so many and so great benefytes; recompenseth and acquyteth them moste unkyndly with myserable death.

Erasmus has testified about his friend's indifference to money, and More himself attests his scornful attitude toward my Lady Pecunia. In his meditation on *The Four Last Things*, he describes the illusory possession of riches as "a very gay golden dream," one that will immediately vanish when we are awakened by death. The economic system of Utopia, which imports its iron and limits its exports, is based upon not only the abolition of property but the devaluation of gold. Indeed the Utopians demonstrate their contempt for this metal daily, since it is the substance from which they manufacture their chamber-pots. Soviet Russia has yet to fulfil its ambivalent promise of introducing golden latrines.

Though the tradition of the *Utopia* goes back to Plato and the lost Atlantis, its narration has been quickened by the recent accounts of the transatlantic voyagers. Specific reference is made to the explorations of Vespucci, whose comment on the inherent Epicureanism of the South American Indians may have had some influence upon the ethical stance of More's natives. There is a touch of Stoicism, marginally signalized, in their definition of virtue: "Lyfe ordered accordying to the prescrypt of nature." The basic formula (*"secundum naturam vivere"*) could be an echo from Seneca's *Ninetieth Epistle* (*"sequere naturam"*). In candidly defining the object of their lives as the pursuit of pleasure, More commits his islanders to the practice of an enlightened hedonism. His criterion of *"honesta voluptas* (harmless pleasure),"* is perfectly compatible with Tasso's *"onesto piacere"*—if not with the more problematic golden law of Aminta—and likewise with the conventual rule of Rabelais, who would be More's reader and admirer. It is reassuring that, for the Utopians, liberty of mind is the highest felicity; their society, for all its permissiveness, may not always seem to us completely open in its material arrangements. They are forward-looking in such areas as eugenics, women's rights, and religious toleration; and if they look backward when they view their island as one big family, that patriarchal view is not without its attraction. Somewhat less appealing, for readers who have been pampered by the indulgences of post-Renaissance individualism, are the communal meals, the uniform clothes, and the *esprit de géometrie* of the city-planning.

But More was not pretending to be a social planner or a human engineer; he was a social critic, a whimsical moralist, a prophet of unacknowledged legislation. His example has engendered a large and uneven corpus of literature, utopiography, whose systematic daydreams and wayward blueprints have tended toward a regimented monotony, disappointingly reminiscent of barracks or boarding-school—if not of beehive or ant-hill. That should not obscure the originality of More's own insights or their hopeful impact upon his contemporaries. Guillaume Budé wrote to Thomas Lupset that Astraea had now redescended from heaven to earth, and that another golden age would be reared upon three divine institutions: equality, peace, and scorn for gold and silver. At this point we are prompted to remember that, when the *Utopia* was being published, through the good offices of Budé and others, Machiavelli had just written *The Prince*; although it would not see publication for a number of years, it gave a more incisive expression to the spirit of sixteenth-century politics. Yet, if old Europe was no Utopia, there was still the New World, which had helped to inspire the dream and would witness many attempts toward its realization. In Spanish Mexico, Vasco de Quiroga, the humane bishop of Michoacán who had translated the *Utopia*, tried to use it as a practical basis for the rules and regulations of his Indian colonies. Those *pueblos* were expected to live "in the manner of the apostles"—and concurrently in the manner of the golden age, which Quiroga had solemnly absorbed through his reading of Lucian's jocular *Saturnalia* in the Latin translation of More and Erasmus.

For not in vain [Don Vasco wrote back to Spain, in the very year when More was tried and condemned and beheaded] but with much cause and reason is this called the New World, not because it is newly found, but because it is in its people and in almost everything as were the first and golden ages.

Much of the Renaissance is a record of truths outdistancing fictions. Sir Philip Sidney's life could be retrospectively described, in his own phrase, as an absolute heroical poem. Yet the facts of life, whenever we apprehend them from the past, are likely to have been filtered through literary conventions. When Sidney fell in love with Penelope Rich, he addressed his sonnet sequence to her under the name of Stella, the Anglo-Latin equivalent of the Greco-Roman

Astraea, while the poet was the star-lover, Astrophel. When he spun a fantasy for his sister, the Countess of Pembroke, he was tempted by the theme of King Arthur and his knights; but he left it for Spenser to devise some extraordinary variations thereon. Sidney headed back instead to the heartland of pastoral tradition, Arcadia. The Vergilian setting, the grassy valleys framed by craggy mountains, had been repainted by Sannazaro, who had unified his eclogues with a semi-autobiographical continuity in prose. Sidney elaborated his narrative into a romance along the adventurous lines of the post-classical *Daphnis and Chloe*, or the *Ethiopic History*, in a meandering prose which palpably contrasts with the highly structured verse of his Arcadian singing-matches and lyrical interludes. He dismissed the whole effort as "a trifle, and that triflinglie handled," a cultivated amusement for the Countess and her circle in her country house at Wilton or Ivychurch. Nonetheless he had carefully revised slightly more than half of his manuscript at the time of his premature death, so that she was able to join the fragments together and supervise them through the press. The general effect is a transposition of romance to the key of epic: serious, didactic, and even political, as contrasted with the single-minded amorousness of the Spanish pastoral romances.

In his *Apology for Poetry*, Sidney had embraced the Horatian maxim: "A speaking Picture, with this end to teach and delight." Poets, "looking but for fiction," manage to "use the narration but as an imaginative ground plat of a profitable invention." Since he was on the defensive in his critical treatise, he may have been overprotesting; he knew as well as any genuine poet that the delight must precede the profit; and any comparison of the two versions of the *Arcadia* will show how he began by amusing his select audience and continued by loading the rifts with instruction. The plot, with all its entanglements, is more interesting than the characterization, which provides little more than a series of mouthpieces for a varied display of bravura rhetoric. If the reader does not sympathize with the characters as deeply as he might in a modern novel, then he empathizes; he puts himself in their place; he undergoes their adventures vicariously; he suffers their anxieties when they are menaced by wild beasts or lustful ravishers or rebellious traitors, and he shares their unique exhilaration when they are inevitably rescued or make their escape. Escape is the main attraction, as it was in the medieval romances that bemused Don Quixote, and as it would be in the cliff-hanging serials of the early cinema or pulp-fiction. The quality of the experience is determined not simply by whence one is escaping but whither. To those who long for the green world or the golden age, Arcady is—of all places—the most wished-for landscape, the *Wunschlandschaft* or *locus amoenissimus*.

Arcadia, we are told at the outset of the original version, enjoys its "singuler reputation, partly for the sweetnes of the Aire and other naturall benefittes: But, principally, for the moderate and well tempered myndes of the people." The shepherds are happy, "wanting litle, because they desire not much," a later touch adds. But they are merely a chorus in the background, while the foreground is occupied by temporary sojourners whose desires and wants are more sophisticated. The heroes, shipwrecked as the revision opens *in medias res*, are a brace of wandering princes, Musidorus from Thessaly and Pyrocles from Macedon. The latter, struck at once by "the pleasauntnes of this place," tries to reassure his homesick traveling companion. "Do not these stately trees seeme to maintaine theyre florishing olde age with the onely happines of their seat, being clothed with a continuall spring, because no beautie here should ever fade?" This classic response has been prompted by a *locus amoenus* which is a show-piece of Elizabethan craftsmanship. The trees are pavillions; the rivers are silver; the meadows are enamelled with flowers; the birds are well-tuned as if they were instruments; the bleating of the lambs is oratory; the shepherd-boy pipes "as though he should never be old." Hazlitt had such descriptions in mind when he complained of art trying to outdo nature, and accused Sidney of interposing himself between the scenery and the onlooker. Artifice is aided by the pathetic fallacy when he self-consciously sets the scene for "the shepherdish pastimes." The brook is both arresting and soporific; the field is blushing; the sun is menacing; and all these gestures seem to be taking place in some sort of Elizabethan playhouse.

> It was indeed a place of delight; for thorow the middest of it, there ran a sweete brooke, which did both hold the eye with her azure streams, yet seeke to close the eie with the purling noise it made upon the piebble stones it ran over: the field it self being set in some places with roses and in al the rest constantly pressing a florishing greene; the Roses added such a ruddy show unto it, as though the field were bashfull at his own beautie: about it (as if it had bene to enclose a *Theater*) grew such a sort of trees as eyther excellency of fruit, statelines of grouth, continuall greennes, or poeticall fancies have made at any time famous. In most part of which there had been framed by art such pleasant arbors, that (one tree to tree, answering another) they became a gallery aloft from almost round about, which below gave a perfect shadow, a pleasant refuge from the cholericke look of *Phoebus*.

The adjective *pleasant*, conveying no visual image, addresses itself to our general sense of well-being. Its reiteration would convince us, if we held any doubts, that what we are being invited to envisage is a pleasance: that is to say, a projection of pleasure on to the landscape. As such it forms a perfect backdrop for pastoral drama, wherein whatever pleases is permitted. Utopia, however, seems to lie in another direction from Arcadia, for there what is permitted seems to please. The central habitation of Sidney's story, located in the midst of "a pleasant picture of nature, with lovely lightsomenes and artificiall shadowes," is the retreat of Basilius, "truely a place for pleasantnes, not unfitte to flatter solitarinesse." One of those oracles whose ambiguous workings end by revealing the design of fate, or the hand of the author, has affrighted Duke or Prince Basilius—actually the king, as his Greek name indicates—into moving from court to cottage incognito with his womanly queen, Gynecia, and their two daughters, Philoclea and Pamela. If this isolation seems rustic, it is "a civil wildnes" and "an accompanable solitarines." It strikes a sympathetic chord in Pyrocles, whose own solitariness is nourished by contemplations and by "the conceites of the Poets." Ultimately, after threading the maze of intrigue, the princes errant are destined to achieve a *solitude à quatre* with the two princesses. The solitudes of Sidney, like the *Soledades* of Góngora, are haunted with reverberations from polite society. One of Sidney's metrical experiments, interpolated into his earlier draft, brings the flight from court along into the woodland by its negative enumeration:

> *O sweete woodes the Delighte of Solitarynes?*
> *O howe much do I like your solitarynes,*
> *Here, no treason ys hidd vailed in Innocency,*
> *Nor Envyes snaky eye fynds any harboure here,*
> *Nor Flaterers venymous Insinuations,*
> *Nor Conning Humoristes pudled opinyons.*
> *Nor Courteous Ruyning of proffered usury,*
> *Nor Tyme prattled away, Cradle of Ignorance,*
> *Nor tryffling Tytle of vanity daseleth us.*
> *Nor golden Manackles, stand for a Paradyse,*
> *Here wronges name ys unhearde, Sclaunder a Monster ys,*
> > *Keep thy Spirite from abuse, here no abuse dothe haunte,*
> > *What Man graftes in a Tree dissimulation.*

Unfortunately Arcadia, as it turns out, is by no means free from such vices. Pyrocles, forced to assume the guise of an Amazon, finds himself in a quadrangular situation, wooed by both the father and the mother of his beloved. It is a "stage play of Love," as Sidney admits, and a bedroom farce at that. Not for nothing are the five books of the *Old Arcadia* listed alternatively as acts. Nor is it surprising that so many Elizabethan and Jacobean playwrights delved into Sidney's romance as a mine for plots. One of his protagonists is self-consciously lamented: "*Arcadia, Arcadia* was the place prepared to bee the stage of his endles overthrowe." And, at the news of another's death, the very pleasance becomes a setting for "universall Complaynte":

Why shulde wee spare oure voyce from endles waylinge?
Who Justly make oure hartes the seates of Sorowe,
In such a Case, where yt apeares that Nature,
Dothe add her force unto the stinge of Fortune,
   Chosing alas, this oure Theater publique,
    Where they woulde Leave Tropheys *of cruell Damage.*

This bucolic realm is intermittently raised to tragic levels by its foreign and domestic troubles. It is confronted by a war with neighboring Laconia, an uprising of downtrodden helots, and a state trial which nearly culminates in a miscarriage of justice. Pastoral fiction is disciplined by what Sidney calls "intermitted historiologie." Inasmuch as he is writing about an imaginary regime, he can go farther than More and Starkey went in criticizing England:

> The daungerous division of mens mindes, the ruinous renting of all estates, had nowe brought *Arcadia* to feele the pangs of uttermost perill (such convulsions never comming but that the life of that government drawes neere his necessarye periode. . .).

We gain a glimpse of revolution, and even of an Arcadian republic, before order is restored and the political object-lesson completes itself. *Et in Arcadia ego* . . . Erwin Panofsky has taught us the meaning of that inscription, and of the tomb in the idyllic painting by Poussin. Even in Arcadia there is no way of avoiding the intervention of death—nor, in the long run, of excluding the harsher aspects of life. Goethe's Faust anticipates an Arcadian existence of freedom and happiness together with Helena: *"Arkadisch frei sei unser Glück!"* But the best of his humanitarian plans, his project for reclaiming land from the sea, ruthlessly destroys the idyll of Philemon and Baukis. "All arcadian cults of carnal perfection"—to subjoin a paradoxical line from W. H. Auden—are precluded from achieving perfection by the circumstances of their carnality. The fact that Arcadia was the code-name for a Washington conference on joint strategy with Winston Churchill and his staff, when the United States entered the Second World War, might serve as a clinching illustration of the truism that men cannot escape from history.

Among the Never-Never-Lands of fiction, Arcadia is oriented toward the immemorial past as Utopia is oriented toward the inscrutable future. Since *never* can be said with more assurance about the past than about the future, Arcadianism represents a purer state of escapism. It was a favorite playground for the Elizabethan fancy. The facile Robert Greene could turn out Arcadian romances with one hand and journalistic exposures of the London underworld with the other. On a larger scale, all Englishmen found themselves engaged in a collective romance, since their sovereign was not merely a woman but a notorious virgin, whose courtiers acted out the rituals of courtship and made a mystique of her virginity. If Diana was her patron goddess, she herself was patroness and godmother of colonial Virginia. It is not surprising that those melodious fanfares which greeted Queen Elizabeth I, wherever she went, should be attuned to the harmonics of the golden age. William Camden began his annals of her reign with the proper citation from Vergil's *Fourth Eclogue*. A play she witnessed at the Inns of Court, *The Misfortunes of Arthur*, linked her with a prophecy involving the descent of Virgo. George Peele made her the heroine of a Lord Mayor's pageant, *Descensus Astraeae*, in which she was personified as a shepherdess, surrounded by shepherds and virtues. Sir John Davies adulated her in acrostic hymns, whose lines spelled out ELIZABETHA REGINA. Sidney contrived an entertainment, or happening, which waylaid her in a private garden and encircled her with the festivities of May Day.

None of the ceremonial parts she was called upon to play had been more magnificently idealized than the title role of *The Faerie Queene*. Strictly speaking, it cannot be said that the titular character really appears in the poem. Gloriana remains an offstage presence, emanating virtue from her capital at Cleopolis, where the several exploits of her knightly champions are scheduled to converge. Her viceroy among them is Prince Arthur, who figures as the *deus ex machina* if not the most active protagonist of the work; and she has her surrogates among the heroines of the separate episodes, not so much the damsels in distress as the Amazonian types like Britomart and Belphoebe. It is hard to imagine what *The Faerie Queene* would be like if Spenser had completed the second half. Clearly he could not have arranged a marriage between Gloriana and Arthur, though he might plausibly have staged a flirtation in the grand style of Leicester or of Essex. Spenser's besetting problem was that his symmetrical framework, with its plan for twelve interrelated allegories, pressed him to repeat the same story twelve times. Working within these self-imposed limitations, he displayed much ingenuity in varying the particulars of each quest, and it was enough of an achievement to have brought six books to such ornate completion, with each of the seventy-four cantos summarized in a ballad stanza. It is the Virgin Queen who endows them with unity, since each book is heralded by a salute and a rededication to her, most spectacularly and at greatest length the Fifth Book, where she is identified with her counterpart in the Zodiac. Sir Artegall, the knight of justice, is Astraea's protégé, to whom she has given a sword and bequeathed a groom, the iron man Talus.

The departure of "the righteous Maide" was the starting-point of *Mother Hubberds Tale*, where the Fox recalls the scorn for gold in Saturn's age, along with its unconcern for *mine* and *thine*. In the Fifth Book of *The Faerie Queene*, when a wicked giant proposes to restore "all things to an equall," he is much admired by "fooles, women, and boys." But his speech on equality does not square with Artegall's, or Spenser's, feudal conception of right and wrong; so Talus hurls the giant to destruction and routs the egalitarian multitude with his iron flail. The proem, like all of the others but more explicitly, draws an invidious comparison between the "state of present time" and the "image of the antique world." Men have been hardening since then, and growing worse every day, worse than iron.

> For from the golden age, that first was named,
> It's now at earst become a stonie one.

Customarily, a royal eulogy praises both the monarch and the moment. Spenser's praise of Elizabeth is somewhat qualified by his distrust of their stony age, which he flatteringly trusts his "Dread Sovereyne Goddesse" to amend. But the innate conservatism of Artegall ("All change is perillous, and all chaunce unsound") would seem to be at odds with any hope for the better or endeavor to set matters right. The case for modernity can only be stated by spokesmen who are suspect, such as Mammon, who revels in the economic expansiveness of "later times" and disparages "the rudenesse of that antique age." Sir Guyon has no hesitation in spurning the temptations of Mammon's treasure and evoking the time-honored curse against the sacrilege of digging for metals in the womb of grandmother earth. Spenser's positive values are located, like Ariosto's, in the age of chivalry, in the great goodness of the ancient knights: "*O gran bontà di cavalieri antichi!*" To the surquedry or insolence of contemporary usage, Spenser is constantly opposing the medieval code of honor:

> *O goodly usage of those antique tymes,*
> *In which the sword was servaunt unto right;*
> *When not for malice and contentious crimes,*
> *But all for praise, and proofe of manly might,*
> *The martiall brood accustomed to fight:*
> *Then honour was the meed of victorie,*
> *And yet the vanquished had no despight:*
> *Let later age that noble use envie,*
> *Vile rancor to avoid and cruell surquedrie.*

If we are sympathetic, we may pause to heave a nostalgic sigh, but Spenser is downright quixotic in his allegiance to the obsolete. He holds up an ideal Middle Ages as an object-lesson for a decadent Renaissance. His chivalric paragons have frequent reason to deplore the pitfalls and atrocities of their own epoch; whenever it may have been, it could not have been Wycliffe's England; and one may doubt whether any regression to a non-hierarchical state of affairs would have satisfied Spenser's views about the distribution of property. Yet Edwin Greenlaw went so far as to assert that "the golden age doctrine is the *Faerie Queene's* fundamental principle." The recurrence of the word *antique* is an index to Spenser's ethical loyalties, as well as to his stylistic canons. His construction of a special language, archaistic rather than archaic and more idiosyncratic than traditional, is as uniquely Spenserian as his improvisation of a private mythology, eclectically pieced together from a wealth of inherited lore, both erudite and popular. The Italian romancers scarcely allowed a freer rein to Charlemagne's paladins than Spenser does to Arthur's knights. When the British prince visits the house of Alma, he reads a book entitled *Briton moniments*, which traces his ascendants back to the legendary Roman founder of the British monarchy, Brut. Eftsoons his companion, Sir Guyon, scans a parallel volume, *Antiquitie of Faerie lond*, where the lineage of Gloriana is traced back to the creation of the elfin race by Prometheus. The synthesis is characteristic: two fictitious heroes, one the product of a historical legend, the other a figment of the poetic imagination, consulting the scholarly authorities to authenticate their own existence.

Just as the temporal perspective is doubled by reverting from the age of chivalry to the golden age, so the spatial distance is prolonged indefinitely by moving from history to legend, from legend to myth, and from myth to folklore. That the final redaction should be a fairy tale is not so thin-spun an assumption as it might seem to us; for the Elizabethans, even when they ceased to believe in fairies, had a homelier and sturdier impression of them than we have been able to retain. They had belonged to Merry England and the green world and the festive customs that were put down with the old religion, as Richard Corbet would lament in his "Farewell to the Fairies." Anticipating a geographical question,

> *Where is that happy land of Faery,*
> *Which I so much do vaunt, yet no where show,*
> *But vouch antiquities, which no body can know,*

Spenser deflects the reader's curiosity by pointing out that Peru, the Amazon River, and "fruitfullest Virginia" had existed long before their late discovery. Here, where he comes closest to the New World, he seems more intent upon substantiating illusion than upon discovering reality with Montaigne. The terrain of Fairyland is vastly more diversified than that of Arcadia; it seems to number Eden among its tributary kingdoms; and many a prospect owes its picturesqueness to its moral significance. Readily we call to mind Spenser's pleasances, his lush depictions of flowery meads and inviting bowers. But even as "blisse" is turned to "balefulnesse" when Acrasia's bower is destroyed, so the pictorial allegory zigzags between contrasting extremes of loveliness and loathsomeness, dancing grace and clashing violence. Medievalist that Spenser is, he intersperses his landscapes with outcroppings of grotesquerie; he has a sneaking fondness for ugly hags and gruesome caves. He exhibits the other side of his idealism when he reduces the epic of Troy to the *fabliau* of Hellenore, Paridell, and Malbecco. There may be more of a moral than he intended, in breaking off his seventh book, since the legend of constancy survives only through the two cantos on mutability.

Much of the reader's vicarious satisfaction depends, as in Sidney's romance, on ambushes circumvented or hairbreadth scapes from overhanging menaces. Yet there is a welcome lull when chivalric exertion gives way to a pastoral interlude, significantly near the end of Book Six. The subject of this legend, courtesy, is central to Spenser's design of mirroring the complete gentleman, the perfect courtier. "Of Court it seemes, men Courtesie doe call." The hero, Sir Calidore, is sometimes thought to have been modelled on Sidney. In his long and labyrinthine chase of the Blatant Beast, he stoutly imposes his courtesies on whomever he encounters. Falling among shepherds, he finds himself envying "this safe retyre / Of life" within the sheepfold, and is impressed by the rural wisdom of Melibee, who rejects his proffered gold: "That mucky masse, the cause of mens decay." But alas, the wise old shepherd is slain by brigands, who kidnap the foundling shepherdess Pastorella; and before Calidore has rescued her, won her hand, and learned about her noble descent, they have left the sheepfold for the more dangerous precincts of Fairyland outside. Fascinated with the state of nature, Spenser is continually approaching and backing away from it. Its purest, most elemental, not to say archetypal, manifestation is the Garden of Adonis in Book Three. That is nothing less than the seed-bed of life itself, the matrix of all forms and kinds, which grow "of their owne accord." If this prelapsarian garden must— like all other gardens—sooner or later be a witness of death, it is also a scene of regeneration, as prefigured in the cycle of its eponymous hero, the dying god. Not the least of its glories is the delicately feminine Amoret, who grew up there in all innocence, enjoying the climate of the golden age and the foliage of the earthly paradise.

> *There is continuall spring, and harvest there*
> *Continuall, both meeting at one tyme.*

Spenser goes on to describe "a pleasant arbour, not by art / But of the trees owne inclination made." Such naturalness and spontaneity stand in striking contradistinction to the deliberate artificiality and the ultimate duplicity of the Bower of Bliss, where a similar arbor is framed by "art, striving to compaire / With nature." The questionable morality of the place is insinuated by its pleasance,

> *whose faire grassy grownd*
> *Mantled with greene, and goodly beautifide*
> *With all the ornaments of Floraes pride,*
> *Wherewith her mother Art, as halfe in scorne*
> *Of niggard Nature, like a pompous bride*
> *Did decke her, and too lavishly adorne,*
> *When forth from virgin bowre she comes in th'early morne.*

The curious implication seems to be that, while grass is natural, somehow flowers are artificial. The reduction of landscape-gardening to a genre-picture of an overdressed bride and an over-solicitous mother introduces a twist of bourgeois comedy into these purlieus of eroticism. Art is viewed as an ingenious and ambiguous rival of nature, which succeeds when it conceals itself, or—better still— when it enters into harmonious collaboration with nature. (Polonius may have been right in objecting to Hamlet's key-word *beautified*, with its cosmetic innuendo, as "a vile phrase.")

> *One would have thought (so cunningly the rude,*
>   *And scorned parts were mingled with the fine,)*
> *That nature had for wantonesse ensude*
> *Art, and that Art at nature did repine;*
> *So striving each th'other to undermine,*
> *Each did the others worke more beautifie;*
> *So diff'ring both in willes, agreed in fine:*
> *So all agreed, through sweet diversity,*
> *This Gardin to adorne with all varietie.*

The siege of this garden, as a matter of emphasis, occupies by far the longest canto in *The Faerie Queene*. Its "sensuall delights" are characteristically intermingled with a "thousand dangers, and ten thousand magick mights." Its presiding siren Acrasia, the very spirit of intemperance, dwells in a palace of pleasure; illicit pleasure is Spenser's dyslogistic conception of bliss. Pleasure itself is amoral, and will be personified by the daughter of Cupid and Psyche who grows up with Amoret in the Garden of Adonis. But bliss is immoral, and the classic appeal to gather roses—quite unlike Herrick's *carpe diem*, and much more sternly than Tasso's—is stigmatized as the voice of paganism:

> *Gather the Rose of love, whilest yet is time,*
> *Whilest loving thou mayst loved be with equall crime.*

Knights who heed such ambivalent lures come to grief through "pleasures poisoned baytes." Beauty itself, in the corruption of innocence since the golden age, has become "the baite of bestiall delight."

The dichotomy of art versus nature, coexisting on equal terms, was a commonplace which presupposed the assumptions that the world was made for man and that human ingenuity was more or less in control of its physical environment. The augmented understanding of nature that developed with experimental science was to disturb this neatly balanced relationship. The most eloquent spokesman for natural philosophy, Francis Bacon, observed that art was man's supplement to nature—that, furthermore, like all created things, it was an integral part of nature. In his monumental *De dignitate et augmentis scientiarum,* he considered the arts as products of imagination, in distinction from the two other mental faculties, reason and memory, which respectively functioned through philosophy and history. Imaginative literature (*poesis*) might be looked upon as fabulous history (*historia conficta*); it is not the same thing as experience, in a literal sense; in its attempt to imitate nature, it can go beyond nature, for better or for worse. "Poesy seems to bestow upon human nature those things which history denies to it; and to satisfy the mind with the shadows of things when the substance cannot be obtained (*atque animo umbris rerum utcumque satisfacere, cum solida habere non possint*)." This is gratifying in its way, and it accounts for much of the pleasure we take in reading fiction, but fiction is synonymous with false-hood from a rigorously empirical point of view. With poetry, as with religion, Bacon leans over backward to give the counter-argument its due.

> For if the matter be attentively considered, a sound argument may be drawn from Poesy, to show that there is agreeable to the spirit of man a more ample greatness, a more perfect order, and a more beautiful variety than it can anywhere (since the Fall) find in nature. And therefore, since the acts and events which are the subjects of real history are not of sufficient grandeur to satisfy the human mind, Poesy is at hand to feign acts more heroical; since the successes and issues of actions related in true history are far from being agreeable to the merits of virtue and vice, Poesy corrects it, exhibiting events and fortunes as according to merit and the law of providence; since true history wearies the mind with satiety of ordinary events, one like another, Poesy refreshes it by reciting things unexpected and full of vicissitudes. So that this Poesy conduces not only to delight but also to magnaminity and morality. Whence it may be fairly thought to partake somewhat of a divine nature; because it raises the mind and carries it aloft, accomodating the shows of things to the

desires of the mind [*rerum simulacra ad animi desideria*], not (like reason and history) buckling and bowing down the mind to the nature of things.

Bacon's lawyerlike defense of poesy, his stress upon its didactic aims and its exemplary effect, might well have instanced *The Faerie Queene*, for this accords with some of Spenser's points in his explanatory epistle to Sir Walter Ralegh. The argument that the poet may improve upon history by rearranging it to suit his beliefs and wishes, by superimposing what critics might condemn as poetic justice, is a weak point, as Bacon knew if Spenser did not. Elizabethan England could hardly have nurtured two more divergent minds. Bacon was a philosopher and a historian, not a poet, after all. For all his literary skills and imaginative resources, he was the exponent of scientific inquiry, which demanded—as he says for himself in his *Aphorisms*—the submission of the mind to things ("*ingenium rebus submittentem*"). To accomodate the shows of things to the desires of the mind is to give way to sheer fantasy, with consequences which can be illusory, impractical, and—worst of all—untrue. The Baconian analysis foreshadows the Freudian attitude toward poetry, regarding it as a process of wishful thinking or daydreaming, an indulgence in the pleasure principle which may and must be corrected by confrontations with reality. Sidney, reviving a Platonic distinction, had maintained that poetry should be *icastic*, "feigning forth good things," rather than *phantastic*, "which doth contrariwise infect the fancie with unworthy objects"—in other words, idealistic rather than realistic. It seemed morally superior to feign good things rather than bad, but in either case the poet was feigning. If their poems were fictitious, were the poets liars?

To that question, which crossed many minds during the Renaissance, including Shakespeare's, Sidney gave a resounding disavowal in his *Defence of Poesie* by bluntly distinguishing between esthetic and empirical truth. "Now for the *Poet*, he nothing affirmeth, and therefore never lieth." He is offering neither testimony nor evidence but ideas and sentiments, albeit these are presented in concrete guise. They are "not Affirmatively but Allegorically and figuratively written," so that a pastoral writer "under the prettie tales of Woolves and sheepe, can enclude the whole considerations of wrong doing and patience." Since he makes no pretence of reporting facts, the poet is "not laboring to tel you what is, or is not, but what should, or should not be." Poetry employs the optative mood; and Sidney is even willing, with slight reservations, to accept More's *Utopia* as a poem: "for that Way of patterning a Common-wealth was most absolute though he perchaunce hath not so absolutely performed it." In the age-old quarrel between the poets and the philosophers, Aristotle had responded to Plato's objections by arguing that poetry is more philosophical than history, insofar as it universalizes its subject-matter. Conversely, Sidney would add that poetry is more historical than philosophy, insofar as it might be said to concretize its universals. Unlike the other arts or the sciences or the professions, it is not dependent on preconceived rules or given materials.

> Onely the Poet disdeining to be tied to any such subjection, lifted up with the vigor of his own invention, doth grow in effect into an other nature: in making things either better than nature bringeth foorth, or quite a new, formes such as never were in nature: as the *Heroes, Demigods, Cyclops, Chymeras, Furies,* and such like; so as he goeth hand in hand with nature, not enclosed within the narrow warrant of his gifts, but freely raunging within the Zodiack of his owne wit. Nature never set foorth the earth in so rich Tapistry as diverse Poets have done, neither with so pleasaunt rivers, fruitfull trees, sweete smelling flowers, nor whatsoever els may make the too much loved earth more lovely: her world is brasen, the Poets only deliver a golden.

This could be an apologia for the tapestried landscapes of Arcadia, as they have been set forth by Sidney himself. Yet it goes much farther in declaring the autonomy of poetic creation. Here it reaffirms the critical doctrine of the Renaissance, enunciated by Scaliger, that poetry creates another world, a heterocosm, and that its creator must be a demiurge, a second God. Sidney does not make quite so lofty a claim; he reasons that, if the poet is a maker, then God must be the maker of that maker; and thus his art belongs within God's cosmos. The poem may well be an amelioration or an enlargement of what the poet has experienced therein—or, for that matter, an invention or a discovery which might reshape the patterns of experience. By implication he is likened to an alchemist, transmuting the baser metals of actuality into the golden world of art. Bacon would not have used the alchemical metaphor, and he would by temperament prefer the immediate worlds of history and philosophy to the other world of imagination. But he does not differ widely from Sidney in his awareness of the idealizing function of poetry. As a realist and a utilitarian, he was interested in useful metals. "Iron commands gold," was one of his proverbs, and he might have learned it from More's Utopians. Speaking in the House of Commons on the naturalization of Scotland, he derided the Spaniards' endeavors to build an empire on their exploitation of the Indian gold-mines. Their rival, Britain, if it united its kingdoms and forgot its "reckonings and audits, and *meum* and *tuum*, and I cannot tell what," could count upon "the best iron in the world," its manpower as a military potential.

The Baconian metaphor has proved to be prophetic, for Britain's future lay not so much in the green or the golden world as in industry and technology, shipping and steel. Bacon's own speculations pointed the way. His *New Atlantis*, with its greenhouses and high-rise buildings, its laboratories and observatories, its expeditions and projects, was much more specialized and professionalized than the *Utopia*. The "lanthorn of this kingdom" was Salomon's House, prototype of the Royal Society and precursor of the scientific foundations and research institutes that set our sights today. Whether these have flourished at the expense of the arts is a question frequently raised by the artists themselves. Critics, from Hegel to Edmund Wilson, have assumed an inverse correlation between material progress and poetic accomplishment. "We think that, as civilization advances, poetry almost necessarily declines," wrote Lord Macaulay. The romantic movement was, among other things, a protest on the part of the mythological as against the rationalistic outlook. Poets could not be expected to assent tamely to the allegation that their art had reached a stage of technological obsolescence. The most direct attack was all the sharper because the witty assailant was something of a poet himself. Thomas Love Peacock, who had mused upon "the lamentable progress of degeneracy and decay" in his satirical novel, *Headlong Hall*, utilized the Hesiodic scheme as a paradigm for literary criticism in *The Four Ages of Poetry*. Though he juggled the sequence of ages to some extent, he took the present iron age for granted, and looked upon the surviving poet as a displaced primitive.

> A poet in our times is a semi-barbarian in a civilized community. He lives in the days that are past. His ideas, thoughts, feelings, associations, are all with barbarous manners, obsolete customs, and exploded superstitions. The march of his intellect is like that of a crab, backward . . . [Poetry] cannot claim the slightest share in any one of the comforts and utilities of life of which we have witnessed so many and so rapid advances.

Peacock's mockery was successful in provoking a rejoinder from among his romantic friends, and Shelley was never more serious than in his *Defence of Poetry*, which he seems to have dashed off at white heat. Sidney had defended poetry against the moralistic critique of the Puritans by taking higher moral ground. Shelley's defense, against a utilitarian critique, was to contend that the social need for the poet was greater now than ever before. The conscience that he brought with him from "the infancy of society" authorized him to speak out at a time which was conspicuously deficient in acknowledged legislators or recognized prophets. Shelley's trope spans a limitless interval when he announces: "All high poetry is infinite; it is as the first acorn, which contained all oaks potentially." Believing in "the eventual omnipotence of mind over matter," as he professed in a letter, "my golden age is when the present potence will become omnipotence." As an idealist, his attention was centered not on the Arcadian past but on the Utopian future. His lyrical drama, *Hellas*, sought to draw back "the curtain of futurity," and to foresee a triumphant outcome for the contemporaneous Greek Revolution. His incentive was his discontent with the reactionary Europe of the Holy Alliance, as well as his reverence for the Hellenic tradition. In *A Defence of Poetry* he affirms that ancient Greece was "the image of the divinity in man." In *Hellas* the despotic Turkish Sultan, Mahmud, is warned by the Wandering Jew, Ahasuerus:

> *The coming age is shadowed on the Past*
> *As on a glass.*

The valedictory ode of the chorus looks into that glass. It is a prophecy, as Mrs. Shelley comments, "such as poets love to dwell upon, the Regeneration of Mankind." Shelley's own note refers to the prophecies of Isaiah and Vergil.

> *The world's great age begins anew,*
> *The golden years return . . .*

Soon a brighter Hellas will rearise, along with another Athens, and a new race of heroes will outstrip the Argonauts. But the poet turns aside from the saddening tale of Troy and the spectacle of recurrent war to call for the return of Saturn and Love.

> *The world is weary of the past,*
> *Oh, might it die or rest at last!*

The Vergilian convention, as we are all too well aware, has been flourished many times to flatter a ruler. Here we see it pressed into the service of revolution. The *topos* persists unchanged because it is fiction. The application changes, revealing the change through nuances that catch our attention, because it responds to the urgencies and contingencies of the hard facts.

[V]

PAGEANTRY

If we trusted the panegyrics of the courtly poets, we should
have little doubt that the golden age had been reborn in the Renaissance. There would be some disagreement among them, however,
as to whether that rebirth had taken place under the Medici or the
Valois or the Tudors or the dynasty of Spain and Austria. Who-
ever happened to ascend the throne at the moment, of course, was
always the new Saturn or Astraea; but it would have been tactless
to assume that, with his or her demise, the golden age had passed on.
On the other hand, a plethora of golden ages, vying with one another at short intervals, was confusing—and not less so because few
of them lived up to the predictions of their panegyrists. Alas,
Charles I was not destined to restore the Saturnian reign in Albion,
as William Drummond of Hawthornden had predicted. (He had
made the same prediction for James I.) The single event that did
most to support the revival of the myth, the opening of the western
hemisphere, offered a glimpse of an anthropological golden age
perpetuating the origins of mankind. There, too, the brightness of
the original vision shaded off into silver or brass, if not iron. If it
were attainable, then by definition it would no longer be golden.
Freedom from specific wants and constraints could be envisioned
through a variety of socio-economic schemes; these, when they
took political shape, ranged from Utopian regimentation to Arcadian anarchy; and neither alternative, luckily, seemed ready for
the test of immediate realization. The moral of the renovated fable,

at all events, registered a change in the ethical climate; it was a direct acknowledgment of pleasure as a value in its own right and a closer acclimatization of man to nature.

In a period of such artistic flowering, we might well expect the painters to join the poets in their celebration of so timely a theme. Undoubtedly they felt inspired to do so, and their paintings abound in motifs that are vernal, youthful, idyllic, mythological, and more or less germane. But the iconology of the golden age itself is difficult to trace, because the concept is so general; rather than tell a story, it projects a mood. It has only two *dramatis personae*, and they seem quite unrelated to one another. Moreover, the jocund Saturn of ancient days has become less familiar by now than the melancholy influence of his tutelary planet, while Astraea's sheaf seems less appropriate as a symbol of justice than the scales of Themis. The *topos* is essentially literary, as the Florentine pageant-masters must have realized when they garlanded their *tableaux* with inscriptions and put allusive lyrics into the mouths of their singers. To be sure, our myth has one inseparable emblem, but the rudimentary acorn is rather limited in its pictorial possibilities. Since so much is negatively described, the result might be said to resemble Trinculo's picture of nobody; the absence of weapons is not, in itself, a distinctive feature. To show an ox grazing unyoked, or a field unplowed and unfenced, is merely to exhibit another banal landscape. Whether the verdure grows spontaneously, or whether the verdant season lasts through the year, cannot be depicted within two or three dimensions. As for leisure, it is almost the precondition of sitting for a painting, and most sitters try to look as cheerful as possible. Nor is it any novelty to present half-naked models pairing off beneath the trees: even here there are limits in the way of presentation.

The graphic treatment of the golden age tends to coalesce with a much broader category, the illustration of pastoral themes, and to mellow into the elegiac vistas of the baroque masters, Poussin and Claude Lorrain: *Arcades ambo*, in the Vergilian terms. We have noted a similar coalescence in the pastoral drama of Tasso and

Guarini. Because the myth had even less plot than characterization, it could not be regarded as dramatic material in itself. It had certain catchwords and connotations which could drape a spectacle of state, particularly when the royal protagonist was qualified by sex and temperament to enact the role of Astraea. Consequently, it has a fixed position in the Elizabethan frame of reference; it is so well established a convention that most of the Elizabethans touch upon it in one context or another. Much of their interplay with it is too conventional to warrant repetition. Sometimes it is twisted into an individual conceit, as when Thomas Nashe magnified a Roman banqueting-house in *The Unfortunate Traveler*, or when Christopher Marlowe invented a wry apologue to explain why scholars are poor in *Hero and Leander*, or when John Donne mourned Elizabeth Drury: "in all she did / Some figure of the Golden times was hid." It is a perennial gambit for satirists like Joseph Hall:

> *Then farewell, fairest age, the world's best days;*
> *Thriving in ill, as it in age decays.*

The usual point of departure is made explicit in a satirical poem, *The Massacre of Money*, by an unidentified T. A.:

> *England, thou art Pleasures-presenting stage,*
> *The perfect patterne of the golden age.*

The couplet, taken literally, represents the official view, as it surrounded the person of the monarch with pomps and ceremonies. But inasmuch as the trope was aimed at society and not at the court, it becomes ironic. A more settled conviction seems to prevail that this is the iron age—and Donne crowned insult with injury by adding that the iron was rusty, at that.

> *O Age of rusty iron! Some better wit*
> *Call it some worse name, if ought equall it;*
> *The iron Age that was, when justice was sold; now*
> *Injustice is sold dearer farre.*

These imputations are classic grounds of complaint, and so are those of Thomas Howell, who Anglicized the Ovidian quip that the golden world is not past, since "now all things may for Golde be had." What is worse, because it was unexampled among all previous ages, is the development of artillery, deplored by the epigrammatist, Thomas Bastard:

> *We have invented engines to shed blood,*
> *Such as no age did ever know before.*

This penitent strain is an undertone among the more exuberant notes in the Elizabethan diapason. After the death of the Queen, with the accession of the Stuart line, it swelled to its deepest resonance. Not that the chorus of flattery was any less vocal for King James than for his predecessor; if his ministers lived up to him—according to one of them, Bacon—"it were enough to make a golden time." The British Solomon, as he liked to conceive himself, was at once more generous and more influential in his patronage of the arts than Elizabeth had been; witness James's sponsorship of Shakespeare's theatrical company, as well as the magnificent translation of the Bible that bears his name. Jacobean literature is a continuation of, and a climax to, the preceding work of Shakespeare and the other writers who spanned both reigns. If the conscious tone is more critical and introspective, that makes for more incisive satire and more searching tragedy. The pathos of retrospection was intensified when poets could look back not simply to a dim golden age but also to the vivid age of Elizabeth, Sidney, and Spenser. Drayton tried to shrug it off in an eclogue:

> *Well, shepheard, well, the golden age is gone,*
> *wishes may not revoke that which is past:*
> *It were no wit to make two griefes of one,*
> *our proverb sayth, Nothing can alwayes last.*

Spenserians like Phineas Fletcher and William Browne made natural use of the topic as a vehicle for their nostalgia. Abraham Cowley would voice his regrets in "A Dream of Elysium," from which the precocious poet is awakened by the crowing of a cock. Fulke Greville interwove the pattern of decline from gold to brass into his versified "Treatise of Monarchy." An anonymous political pamphlet from the crucial year 1648 is entitled *The Four Ages of England, or The Iron Age.* A broadside ballad, "The Golden Age; or, An Age of Plain-Dealing," is in a lighter vein, but its irony is heavy:

> *Base dealing is banisht,*
> *and women growne chaste,*
> *And by their owne Husbands*
> *will scarce be embrac'd,*
> *And will not their times*
> *in idlenesse waste,*
> *For fear in their carriage*
> *They should be disgrac'd:*
> *O this is an honest Age,*
> *O this is a hopefull Age.*

The nadir may have been reached when Drummond's "Urania," lamenting the "haplesse Hap" of being born in "these unhappy Times," insinuates that Astraea herself is no longer a virgin but has become a "Whoure prostitute for gold." More touching is the reminiscence in *The Compleat Angler,* where a pretty milkmaid sings Marlowe's lyrical invitation, "Come live with me and be my love." Whereupon her buxom mother, who had learned that song at her daughter's age, her own "golden age," now joins in with Ralegh's autumnal and uncomplying response. And Isaak Walton's interlocutor comments: "I now see it was not without cause that our good Queen Elizabeth did so often wish herself a Milkmaid all the month of May, because they are not troubled with fears and cares, but sing sweetly all the day, and sleep securely all the night . . ."

The lack of anything like a scenario did not keep the dramatists from exploiting the golden age. One of the most prolific, Thomas Heywood, boasted that he and his colleagues had dramatized every segment of British history from the prehistoric Brut to the reign of James. Having done more than his share to exhaust the chronicles, Heywood turned to classical mythology. His poetic genealogy, *Troia Britanica*, traced the Stuarts back to the Old Testament via the line of Brut and the legend of Troy, starting from "the Worlde's Child-hood, . . . I mean the golden world." For the theater he jumbled a medley of Greek myths into a sequence of five plays purporting to deal with the four ages. The first play, *The Golden Age: or the Lives of Jupiter and Saturne with the deifying of the Heathen Gods*, has little or nothing to do with the era of pristine felicity; it treats the struggle between the Titans and the Olympians in the fashion of the more episodic histories. It is introduced by Homer as prologue, taking a lofty line with Heywood's popular audience:

> O then suffer me,
> You that are in the worlds decrepit Age,
> When it is neere his universall grave,
> To sing an old song; and in this Iron Age
> Shew you the state of that first golden world,
> I was the Muses Patron, learnings spring
> And you shall once more heare blinde Homer sing.

Oddly enough, although he continues his choric interventions through the irrelevant gallimaufries of *The Silver Age* and *The Brazen Age*, Homer drops out of sight in *The Iron Age*, the last two extravaganzas which cover the Trojan War. The golden age more pertinently figures, in the work of other playwrights, as a source of precept and allusion. Seneca had invoked it in his choruses, where it sets a moral standard for judging his tragic atrocities. He was imitated most assiduously, in this respect as in others, by the mournful William Alexander, Earl of Stirling. Alexander's *Alexandrean Tragedy*, which is not about himself but about the last days of the Macedonian Empire, is therefore Alexandrian in three senses. A chorus contrasts the aggressiveness and the acquisitiveness of his characters with their peaceable ancestors, who

> *could no kinde of want bemone,*
> *For, craving nought, they had all things:*
> *And since none sought the regall Throne,*
> *Whil'st none were Subjects, all were Kings:*
> *O! to true blisse their course was set,*
> *Who got to live, not liv'd to get.*

George Chapman, who professed the same Stoic philosophy, made more of an attempt to put it in action through his tragedies. It underlines the individualistic code of his eloquent adventurer, Bussy D'Ambois:

> *Who to himself is law, no law doth need,*
> *Offends no law, and is a king indeed.*

Such a man is likely to have his detractors and, sooner or later, mortal enemies. In the King himself, however, Bussy has a magnanimous defender with something of his own eloquence. The royal eulogy harks back to an image of "Man in his native noblesse" before the fall, before there was any need for monarchy.

> *Kings had never borne*
> *Such boundless empire over other men*
> *Had all maintain'd the spirit and state of D'Ambois;*
> *Nor had the full impartial hand of Nature*
> *That all things gave in her original,*
> *Without those definite terms of Mine and Thine,*
> *Been turn'd unjustly to the hand of Fortune,*
> *Had all preserv'd her in her prime, like D'Ambois;*
> *No envy, no disjunction had dissolv'd*
> *Or pluck'd one stick out of the golden faggot*
> *In which the world of Saturn bound our lives,*
> *Had all been held together with the nerves,*
> *The genius and th' ingenuous soul of D'Ambois.*

The characterization may strike us as somewhat above the level of the hero's conduct in *Bussy D'Ambois*, which displays arrogance, violence, opportunism, and a penchant for intrigue and adultery. Yet, for Chapman, all is redeemed by Bussy's professions of Stoicism, his resolution to act as a law unto himself and to set the gifts of nature above the tricks of fortune. That, at any rate, is an energetic conception of how to preserve the golden age, and it is appropriately symbolized by the golden faggot, a bundle of fasces. Chapman employs more traditional imagery elsewhere in this connection: with determined obscurity in his poem, "The Shadow of Night." But he winds up his comedy, *All Fools*, with a cynical tirade burlesquing the succession of ages; gold, silver, brass, and iron are followed by lead and wood; and the present is the hornèd age, whose universal touchstone is cuckoldry. He made a fresher approach to the comic spirit when he collaborated with Ben Jonson and John Marston on *Eastward Ho*. This London parable of idleness and industry mounts an expedition to the New World. "Come boys," roars Captain Seagull to his tavern companions, "Virginia longs till we share the rest of her maidenhead." His most lavish promise is that gold will be as plentiful as copper among the Indians, and the Utopian gesture of contempt becomes an enticement when he elaborates: "Why, man, all their dripping-pans and their chamber-pots are pure gold." The Virginian voyage gets no farther than the Isle of Dogs, a garbage dump in the Thames, where it runs aground in sundry disillusionments. The title, a familiar cry among ferrymen on the Thames, indicates a reversal of direction: not westward but home again.

Chapman's *Masque of the Middle Temple* arrives at a romanticized Virginia, whose Indian priests engage in solar rites to celebrate "the milk-and-honey age" with "golden dreams." Neither this pretty picture nor Captain Seagull's prospectus faces the actual hardships and mishaps then being suffered by the settlers of the Jamestown colony. Moreover, there were those in England who would take a decidedly unromantic attitude toward the colonists. When a toast is proposed to "this seat of majesty," Virginia, in *The City Madam* by Philip Massinger, Lady Frugal objects:

> *How*, Virginia!
> *High Heaven forbid. Remember Sir, I beseech you,*
> *What creatures are shipp'd thither.*

Her daughter amplifies:

> *Condemn'd wretches,*
> *Forfeited to the law.*

Her other daughter is even more specific:

> *Strumpets and bawds,*
> *For the abomination of their life,*
> *Spew'd out of their own Country.*

It is interesting to hear contemporary testimony regarding some of the first families of Virginia. Arcadia may well have been a safer backdrop for drama, since the fantasies it inspired could not be spoiled by returning travelers. Six or eight dramas were based upon *The Countess of Pembroke's Arcadia*, most of them falling within the domain of pastoral tragicomedy. A resourceful variation on the formula was devised by Samuel Daniel in *The Queen's Arcadia*. There a quacksalver and a pettifogger, unworthy representatives of the two professions that Montaigne would have proscribed, somehow gain admittance into the happy land, and proceed to undermine its happiness by teaching the Arcadians the distinction between *mine* and *thine* and other motives for discontent. Though they are ultimately banished, their question has a ringing pertinacity:

> *Is't possible that a societie*
> *Can with so little noyse and sweat subsist?*

Among the dramatizations of episodes from the *Arcadia*, only one is of major importance, and that is one of Shakespeare's most unlikely transmutations. He was in the habit of reinforcing his plot with a parallel underplot; but he never made a bolder use of this structural device than when he connected the legend of King Lear and his three daughters with the tale of the blind King of Paphlagonia and his two sons, who became the Earl of Gloucester and Edgar and Edmund in the play. We are justified in our suspicion that Arcadia has its lurking dangers when we realize that the cruelest scene in the Shakespearean repertory, the blinding of Gloucester, was derived from Sidney's pastoral romance, where it figures very indirectly. The tragedy of Lear himself is scarcely pastoral; yet the old king moves across the heath, in a Stoic regression, from the realm of fortune to the state of nature; and the storm, which strips away the superfluities of courtliness, reduces him to the quivering nakedness of "unaccomodated man," like Edgar in his simulated madness.

It would be strange if the golden age were not among the all but limitless resources of Shakespeare's diction. Formally and rather conventionally, it ornaments his poems. The young friend of the poet, in the *Sonnets*, is enjoying his "golden time." The silver cheeks of Lucrece are gilded with "Beauty's red, / Which Virtue gave the Golden Age"—the shift from red to gold was frequent with the Elizabethans. When Titus Andronicus cries out against injustice, he quotes directly from the proper passage in Ovid's *Metamorphoses*, as Shakespeare had learned it at school: "*Terras Astraea reliquit.*" Amid the dynastic conflicts of the earlier histories, the "golden days" of certain rulers are signalized invidiously. When Henry IV is succeeded by Prince Hal, Ancient Pistol trumpets the glad tidings of "lucky joys / And golden times." The funereal love-song of the Clown in *Twelfth Night* is pronounced by the Duke to be simple truth:

> *It is silly sooth,*
> *And dallies with the innocence of love,*
> *Like the old age.*

All of Shakespeare's comedies are romantic in their engagement with this innocent dalliance. It is menaced by the adverse pressures of experience, in the guise of intrigues and complots, though the pleasure principle is calculated to win out in the long run: *All's Well That Ends Well*. Shakespeare deferred to the golden rule of the Abbey of Thélème in the very title of *As You Like It* and again in the subtitle of *Twelfth Night, or What You Will*. Ben Jonson, less concerned to gratify the spectators, told them flatly in the last line of the epilogue to *Cynthia's Revels*: "By [God], 'tis good, and if you like 't, you may." But Shakespeare consistently manifested the audience-consciousness of the professional entertainer, which Samuel Johnson was to sum up in his shrewd couplet:

> *The drama's laws, the drama's patrons give,*
> *For we that live to please, must please to live.*

When Rosalind invites Orlando to rehearse his wooing, in *As You Like It*, she tells him that she is now "in a holiday humour, and like enough to consent." This holiday humor continually enlivens the atmosphere of what C. L. Barber has aptly characterized as Shakespeare's festive comedy. *Twelfth Night* marked the height of the Christmas festivities, and was sometimes celebrated at court with a holiday performance from Shakespeare's troop. *Midsummer Night* is suffused with the folklore of May Day when Shakespeare brings his fairy queen on the stage. Seasonal customs are observed in the sheep-shearing pastimes of *The Winter's Tale* or the harvest festival of *The Tempest*. The banished Duke of *As You Like It* holds his court in a retreat described by the wrestler Charles:

> They say he is already in the Forest of Arden, and a many merry men with him; and there they live like the old Robin Hood of England. They say many young gentlemen flock to him every day, and fleet the time carelessly as they did in the golden world.

This Arcadia is not readily identified with the Ardennes, since it has lions and palm trees in it; yet it cannot be too far away from Stratford, where the Ardens were Shakespeare's mother's family. When Rosalind and Celia take to the forest, they go "To liberty and not to banishment," because they are going "from Fortune's office to Nature's," where classical shepherds will serve as amorous models for rusticating courtiers. The basic antithesis between the court and the countryside is sharpened by the antagonism between the saturnine moralist Jacques, who cannot live with society nor without it, and the adaptable jester Touchstone, who will even go so far as to marry in his emulation of "the country copulatives." Jacques' theatrical set-piece on the seven ages of man has its parody in Touchstone's prose monologue on the seven pretexts for a duel. Shakespeare himself becomes a denizen of the golden age, when we recall that he probably created the part of old Adam, that faithful retainer who exemplifies—in a quasi-Spenserian phrase—"The constant service of the antique world." His aboriginal godfather is evoked when the Duke Senior holds forth on the uses of adversity; the only disadvantage of life in the forest is that it involves an exposure to the difference of the seasons, which was man's penalty for Adam's fall; and even the winter wind, as a later song chimes in, is "not so unkind / As man's ingratitude." The Duke's much-echoed conclusion suggests that communion with nature may be an education in itself.

> *And this our life exempt from public haunt*
> *Finds tongues in trees, books in the running brooks,*
> *Sermons in stones, and good in everything.*

Since these lines can be misread as a deprecation of literacy, we can well understand why they appeal so strongly to Marshall McLuhan. "Here is the image of the golden age," he comments in *Understanding Media*, "as one of complete metamorphoses or translations of nature into human art, that stands ready of access to our electric age." Thanks to the audiovisual revolution, the materials of the natural world can be programmed and played back. "We are now in a position to go beyond that and to transfer the entire show to the memory of a computer." Mr. McLuhan's obsessive mode of argument is to turn common sense upside down, a procedure which can be heuristic but which risks the statistical odds of being wrong much more often than being right. How he manages to get from his intuitive premises to his mechanistic conclusions is as much of a *non sequitur* as the path from the Forest of Arden to the electronic millennium.

The characters of Shakespearean comedy are translated, but in Bottom's sense rather than Mr. McLuhan's, whenever they leave the town and repair to the woods. Even Falstaff is purified, in a mock-ceremonial by pseudo-fairies, under Herne's oak in *The Merry Wives of Windsor*. The pattern is adumbrated in *The Two Gentlemen of Verona*, where the route from the city to the court leads through the greenwood; Silvia traverses it with a chivalrous escort, Sir Eglamor, and Valentine hastens the dénouement by joining a band of outlaws—who, in the manner of Robin Hood, practise "an honourable kind of thievery." *The Merchant of Venice* solves its dilemmas by shifting back and forth from the bustling Rialto or the acrimonious courtroom to a gracious garden for lovers in Belmont, and the two plots are interlinked by the message within the golden casket: "All that glisters is not gold." Flowering gardens are the recurrent symbol for all that is wholesome and normal in Shakespeare's imagery, just as weeds and ranker growths betoken the opposite. *The Winter's Tale*, beginning as a tragedy of the Sicilian court, takes a leap in time and space to engender a romance in a Bohemian sheepcote. The shepherdess Perdita, a devotee of pure nature, is distrustful of flowers produced by grafting; but if that is an art, as King Polixenes explains to her, it is still part of nature, since the artisan is. "Nature is made better by no mean / But nature makes that mean." And what is the ultimate maker (*"deus"*) if not, in Ovidian epithet, a better nature (*"melior natura"*)? Polixenes, as defender of hybridization, is not entirely consistent in regarding Perdita's betrothal to his son Florizel as a misalliance. Yet nature makes its final embracement of art when the statue of Hermione, attributed to Giulio Romano, comes to life and proves to be the resurrected queen.

The emphasis on stage effects, on recognition scenes, on voyages to remote and wonderful places, and menaces averted by happy endings is characteristic of those later tragicomedies which we more usually classify as Shakespeare's romances. These, however, merely accentuate certain characteristics which shaped the structure of his comedies from the outset, and which were the *donnée* of Arcadian romance: above all, the withdrawal to a greener world, which brings about a renewal of energies and a resolution of problems. *The Tempest* is the ultimate crystallization of this design, a calming of the storm that raged through *King Lear* and the tragedies. Here the restorative terrain is "an uninhabited island," according to the Shakespearean designation, presumably somewhere in the Mediterranean Sea. Yet the tempest itself seems to have been conjured up by dewdrops from the Bermudas, and the shipwreck seems to have been suggested by a recent misadventure of the Virginia Company's fleet off American shores. A touch of social criticism is brought home to the English audience with Trinculo's remark: "When they will not give a doit to relieve a lame beggar, they will lay out ten to see a dead Indian." Frequently Shakespeare underlines the ideal from which his dramatic realities deviate with an exhortation or parable from a *raisonneur*, such as the deathbed prophecy of John of Gaunt in *Richard II*, the exposition of order and degree by Ulysses in *Troilus and Cressida*, or Menenius Agrippa's tale of the belly and the members in *Coriolanus*. Here it is the honest old councillor, Gonzalo, who endeavors to cheer up the shipwrecked King of Naples by playing the childish game of "If I were king." His jest is that he has been given "plantation of this isle," the same right to colonize that King James gave to the Virginia Company.

From the very beginning Gonzalo recognizes the antipodal nature of the wish-dream, its inversion of European mores.

> *I' the commonwealth I would by contraries*
> *Execute all things; for no kind of traffic*
> *Would I admit, no name of magistrate.*

Most of his exclusions follow Montaigne's list in the essay "On the Cannibals," echoing the phraseology of Florio's translation: no letters, riches, poverty, use of service, bound of land, tilth, metal, corn, or wine. Since Gonzalo is a Christian, he does not exclude family relationships, as Montaigne's Indians apparently did: "no respect of kindred, but common." He is amplifying Montaigne slightly when he stipulates:

> *No occupation; all men idle, all;*
> *And women too, but innocent and pure.*

Since he has said nothing about marriage, he is rallied by his supercilious critics. Sebastian will ask, "No marrying 'mong his subjects?" And Antonio will reply, equating idleness with frivolity, "None, man—all idle, whores and knaves." Gonzalo has also gone beyond Montaigne with the sweeping stipulation, "No sovereignty," and the two Machiavellian courtiers have picked him up upon the contradiction. "Yet he would be king on't," jeers Sebastian. "The latter end of his commonwealth forgets the beginning," sneers Antonio. This is the inherent flaw in the logic of all Utopias. Perhaps we may call it Gonzalo's paradox, though due credit for pointing it out should go to his fault-finders. How could an ideal commonwealth ever come into existence? If not by bloody revolutions, which would thwart its own aims, then by edict from some founding lawgiver in the dark backward of time, the fiat of a Lycurgus. It takes a benevolent despotism to legislate against laws. The government of More's Utopia is reported to have been the creation of an ancient king, Utopus, and there is a revealing letter from More to Erasmus in which the former confesses that he has dreamed of himself as the ruler of his model kingdom. The crux in the problem of anarchy is that someone must take office. Responsibility presupposes authority; authority imposes responsibility.

But the optimistic Gonzalo continues unruffled, and his discourse mounts beyond Montaigne to some of the classic features of the *topos*, contrasting nature's spontaneous fruitfulness with man's destructive ingenuity:

> *All things in common nature should produce*
> *Without sweat or endeavour. Treason, felony,*

Sword, pike, knife, gun, or need of any engine
Would I not have; but nature should bring forth,
Of it own kind, all foison, all abundance,
To feed my innocent people.

As he concludes, his insular majesty is hailed with derisive cheers; but King Alonso, whom he has been addressing, and who could well have profited from the lesson, has not been listening. If Gonzalo's mock-reign outdoes Saturn's, that is because it is even farther away, because actualities have been deliberately replaced by their contraries.

I would with such perfection govern, sir,
T' excel the golden age.

Arthur Lovejoy has designated Montaigne's "famous passage on the superiority of wild fruits and savage men over those that have been 'bastardized' by art" as "the *locus classicus* of primitivism in modern literature," and has suggested that Shakespeare "wrote two replies to it—a humorous one in *The Tempest*, a serious and profound one in *The Winter's Tale*." Whether or not he felt an "extreme antipathy" to Montaigne's position, or whether or not Montaigne can fairly be said to have taken a position, Shakespeare was clearly not a primitivist, though Gonzalo may well have been. It was Shakespeare's gift to envisage many viewpoints, to endow conflicting purposes with words. Taken in dramatic context, Gonzalo's soaring ideals are accompanied by a ground-bass of scurrilous banter from Sebastian and Antonio, who are about to hatch a murderous plot against Alonso. This runs parallel to the plot that has dethroned Prospero and exiled him from his dukedom of Milan, where he had preferred his library to the responsibilities of ruling. Circumstance has sent him back to nature, on this nameless and enchanted island, where the season's difference is virtually unknown:

Spring come to you at the farthest
In the very end of harvest!

The natural condition in all its native rawness and brutality, nature without nurture, is incarnate in the person of the single indigene, the bestial Caliban, who has attempted to ravish the virginal Miranda and now figures in a third conspiracy, a comic underplot against Prospero. Caliban's name, with a letter or two displaced, constitutes another link with Montaigne's essay on the cannibals; but he seems a much cruder creature than those exemplary primitives, and extremely anti-social by comparison with the tame wild man in Spenser's legend of courtesy. Still, as a child of nature, Caliban has something to teach Prospero about "the qualities o' th' isle," where the fresh water or nourishing herbs can be found, and "how / To snare the nimble marmoset." His master compounds such lore with his own book-knowledge, and with the command of the ethereal forces that are personified by the spritely Ariel. The consequence is the fully pondered art of Prospero, which exerts its control over the physical world in the form of natural magic, but which is also related through his pageantry to the dramatic art of Shakespeare himself. Since Prospero has incidentally learned to be a good ruler, the reconciliation envisages a suitably prosperous ending in his duchy on the mainland. The cycle of exile and return has been acted out again; society has been refreshed by recourse to the norms of nature, with art functioning as the mediator between them. Ferdinand has won Miranda's hand by serving her father, piling logs and eating "husks / Wherein the acorn cradled." When she first beholds the King and his courtiers, her exclamation naively echoes the meaning of her name:

> *O wonder!*
> *How many goodly creatures are there here!*
> *How beauteous mankind is! O brave new world*
> *That has such people in 't!*

Such people as Antonio and Sebastian or, for that matter, Alonso? Prospero is a master of disenchantment as well as enchantment, and his comment is a gentle sigh of worldly wisdom: " 'Tis new to thee." Miranda's brave new world will turn out, ironically, to be the same old one. But if the golden age ever existed or ever will exist, it can only be in the sense of wonder, the freshness of outlook, and the continually renewed expectations of youth.

Shakespeare has not been allowed to say the last word for or against the figure of Caliban, which has exerted a peculiar fascination over modern writers—possibly because he could have been Shakespeare's contribution to the Darwinian quest for the missing link in the great chain of being. Caliban's subsequent roles extend from the revolutionary hero of a philosophical drama by Ernest Renan to an unconscious theologian in a poetic monologue by Robert Browning, while W. H. Auden has let him speak a soliloquy in the most polished style of Henry James. Shakespeare's ever-critical contemporary, Ben Jonson, was less impressed; he prided himself on observing a classical canon against the artistic fabrication of monsters; and in the induction to *Bartholomew Fair* he gibes at rival playwrights who beget such creatures in their "*Tales, Tempests*, and such like *Drolleries*." Yet Shakespeare is kinder to animals than Jonson is to men and women. While Shakespearean romance could lead its personages to self-realization on desert islands or in faraway retreats, Jonsonian satire cramped them within the dwarfing perspective of city streets and brought out the monstrous propensities of human nature. Compare the wise and kindly Prospero with the raffish swindler Subtle, whose pretensions to sorcery amount to no more than another confidence-game. Gold, as a means of social corruption, is the mainspring for the motivation of Jonson's comedies; but it is no more than a hoax in *The Alchemist*; it is fool's gold. The terminology of pseudo-science is exploited to dazzle the gulls into enlarging the fortunes of their deceivers.

Whereas the deceits of *Volpone* are even more sinister, there the treasure is dazzlingly genuine. It is amassed and dangled before us as an intrinsic part of the luxury and the lechery of the Venetian setting, in contradistinction to the petty chicaneries of the makeshift household in Blackfriars. Volpone, the grand voluptuary, begins his day with orisons at his chest of gold, the shrine of his saint.

Well did wise Poets, by thy glorious name
Title that age, which they would have the best.
Thou being the best of things . . .

His single-minded scheme of values subverts all human relations, as it does religion. The satisfaction he derives from not earning his wealth, but gaining it through fraud and enjoying it in idleness, is his personal subversion of the golden age.

> *I use no trade, no venter's,*
> *I wound no earth with plow-shares; fat no beasts*
> *To feede the shambles; have no mills for yron,*
> *Oyle, corne, or men, to grind 'hem into pouldre.*

Volpone's hymn to gold is a credo of immorality, and Jonson takes no chance on our misunderstanding. Similarly, when Volpone is urging the naive Celia to commit adultery with him, the rhetoric of enticement is heavily charged with perverse and decadent overtones. His song is a graceful adaptation from that very lyric of Catullus which Tasso had echoed in the golden-age chorus of his *Aminta*. But the healthy sensualism of Catullus and Tasso, confronted with the Jonsonian situation, acquires an aftertaste of dust and ashes.

> *Sunnes, that set, may rise againe:*
> *But if, once, we lose this light,*
> *'Tis with us perpetuall night.*

It takes not one but two trials to superimpose poetic justice upon *Volpone*, and the moralization tends to outdo the dramaturgy in Jonson's fifth act. *The Alchemist*, perhaps because of its seamy London background, is more realistic in its characterization and more easy-going in its morality. There are no good characters to confuse the reckoning; there are simply knaves and fools; and the reversals come about when knavery stoops to folly. The two male cheaters, Subtle and Face, are reminded by their female confederate that they have agreed to share "All things in common." Her name,

Doll Common, is a reminder that she is one of the things they are privileged to share. It is a sordid reduction of Elizabethan grandeur when she is called upon to impersonate the Faerie Queene. For the arch-speculator Sir Epicure Mammon, to enter the alchemist's den is to set foot "in *novo orbe*, . . . the rich *Peru*." He talks—and he is not less conversant than Volpone with the vocabulary of libidinous blandishment—"all in gold." But it is all talk. "If his dreame last," declares Subtle, "hee'll turne the age, to gold." But Subtle knows, better than anyone else, that the projection for the Philosophers' Stone will go up in smoke. Mammon's designs on a more achievable object, the favors of Doll Common, will be balked by a sham mad-scene. The prostitute will babble prophecies of the five monarchies as foretold by Daniel. The epicurean will react by vowing to turn Puritan and to "preach / The end o' the world."

Both as a satirist and as a classicist, Jonson rings the traditional changes upon our theme. One of his epigrams distinguishes between the golden age, the time of Astraea, and the age of gold, the present commercialism. The declination from the one to the other is measured by a loss of respect for poetry and learning. Verse, he writes in an epistle to the Countess of Rutland,

> *was once of more esteeme*
> *Than this, our guilt, nor golden age can deeme,*
> *When gold was made no weapon to cut throtes*
> *Or put to flight* Astrea, *when her ingots*
> *Were yet unfound, and better placed in earth,*
> *Then, here, to give pride fame, and peasants birth.*

The positive side of the allusion comes to the fore when Jonson is addressing complimentary verses to his cultivated and aristocratic friends; a visit to them at their country houses is an opportunity to relive "Saturnes raigne." Both as an inveterate Londoner and as a self-conscious craftsman, Jonson seldom comes near rural life; and when he does, his approach is Arcadian. It is not without significance that he left his one pastoral drama half-finished, or that from its very title, *The Sad Shepherd*, it continuously sounds an elegiac note. Jonson's stated aim was to naturalize the bucolic conventions, fashioning from English wool "a Fleece / To match, or those of *Sicily*, or *Greece*." Therefore he conflated the idyll of the sad Aeglamor, seeking vainly through the course of the fragment for his lost Earine, with the legend of Robin Hood. "The SCENE is Sher-wood. Consisting of a Landt-shape of Forrest, Hils, Vallies, Cottages, A Castle, A River, Pastures, Heards, Flocks, all full of Countrey simplicity." This might not look so simple to the scene-designer. The topographical nostalgia for a greener world is deep-ened by a chronological nostalgia for a happier day. Robin is warned that the sports of his merry men are now being denounced as "*Pagan* pastimes" by "the sowrer sort / Of Shepherds." In other and plainer words, the drama is under attack from the Puritans, who will be closing the theaters within a few years. Robin's lament becomes Jonson's elegy for Merry England.

> *I doe not know, what their sharpe sight may see*
> *Of late, but I should thinke it still might be*
> *(As 'twas) a happy age, when on the Plaines*
> *The Wood-men met the Damsells, and the Swaines,*
> *The neat'ards, Plow-men, and the Pipers loud,*
> *And each did dance, some to the Kit or Croud,*
> *Some to the Bag-pipe, some the Tabret mov'd,*
> *And all did either love, or were belov'd.*

Through the latter half of his career, Jonson had worked in some detachment from the public theater. Attached to the Stuart court as Poet Laureate, he was the chief purveyor of its pageants. Or rather, as he loudly complained, his learned and ingenious efforts were considerably less appreciated than the spectacular scenery designed by Inigo Jones—not to mention the contributions of the music-master, the dancing-master, and the cook. But insofar as the English masque is a literary genre, Jonson is its main practitioner; and he seems warranted in his regret for having put so much talent and craftsmanship into so evanescent a series of decorative occasions. The association had started, under the most fitting auspices, on the day of James's coronation, when the royal procession had been met at Temple Bar with Jonson's allegorical greeting: "REDEUNT SATURNIA REGNA. Out of Vergil, to show that now those golden times were returned againe." The motif could not have been avoided in an encomium at a tournament for the short-lived heir to the throne, Prince Henry: "The golden veine / Of SATURNES age is here broke out againe." *The Golden Age Restored* was the most obvious subject available for a masque at court, with Pallas quelling the tumult of the Iron Age and calling on Astraea to descend in the machine, while the older English poets—Chaucer, Gower, Lydgate, Spenser—make up a choir to accompany the benediction. None of the fabled blessings will be foregone.

> *Then earth unplough'd shall yeeld her crop,*
> *Pure honey from the oake shall drop,*
> *   The fountaine shall run milke:*
> *The thistle shall the lilly beare,*
> *And every bramble roses weare,*
> *   And every worme make silke.*

Saturn in person, as could have been foreseen, is the protagonist of *Time Vindicated*; and his Saturnalia overflow into some of the other masques, notably *Pleasure Reconciled to Virtue*. Here the antimasque, the grotesque expository dialogue that links the body of masque itself with the sphere of Jonsonian comedy, centers upon Comus, "the god of cheere, or the belly, riding in tryumph, his head crownd with roses, and other flowres; his haire curld." This Falstaffian figure, leading a drunken orgy, to the wild music of cymbals and tabors, is graphically saluted by the chorus:

> *haile, haile, plump Panch, o the founder of tast*
> *for freash meates or powlderd, or pickle, or paste.*
> *devourer of broild, bak'd, rosted, or sod,*
> *and emptier of cups, be they even, or od.*
> *All which have now made thee, so wide i' the waste*
> *as scarce with no pudding thou art to be lac'd:*

> *but eating and drinking, untill thou dost nod*
> *thou breakst all thy girdles, and breakst forth a god.*

As a mountain looms up from behind a vanishing ivy grove, the clownish Comus gives way to the real hero, Hercules, who takes no joy in intoxication: "Can this be pleasure, to extinguish man?" Since his victories over the giants and the pygmies are easy, there is not much conflict. Rather, there is to be, as Mercury announces, "a cessation of all jars / 'twixt vertue and hir noted opposite, / Pleasure." The mountain opens and these personifications appear, while Daedalus guides the labyrinthine mingling of the dancers. The truce seems a little uneasy. "You were sent," the masquers are told, ". . . to walke with Pleasure, not to dwell." They must finally return to their labors in the hill of Virtue, "she being hir owne reward." But Jonson's Pleasure, daughter of Venus though she be, is such a refinement upon the intemperance of his Comus that the sophisticated need have few fears about putting themselves in her hands:

> *Descend,*
> *descend,*
> *though pleasure lead,*
> *feare not to follow:*
> *they who are bred*
> *within the hill*
> *of skill,*
> *may safely tread*
> *what path they will.*

Though the personification falls somewhere short of apotheosis, the concept of pleasure is set on a high elevation—much higher than the place it occupied in the medieval scheme of values or, if we hold with a recent essay of Lionel Trilling's, in our own. The ethos of the Renaissance did not rest content with conjoining the *vita contemplativa* and the *vita activa*. Ficino also complimented Lorenzo de' Medici on his achievements within a third realm of being, the *vita voluptuosa*. There were three paths, classically symbolized by the Three Graces, as Edgar Wind has shown, which led the universal man toward triple felicity: wisdom, power, and pleasure. Tasso's vindication of pleasure was ultimately qualified when he came to reconcile it with honor (*Onesta Piacere*). Lorenzo Valla had dared to go much farther, arguing amid the epicurean pros and stoic contras of his dialogue *De voluptate*, that the *summum bonum* was *voluptas* rather than *honestas*. Though the golden age provided the usual exhibit for epicurean arguments in this vein, humanistic thinkers could point out that it had its Christian counterpart in the garden of Eden. In an essay on the poetic interrelationship between ancients and moderns, *Mythomystes*, Henry Reynolds would ask:

> What could they meane by their Golden-Age . . . But the state of Man before his Sin? and consequently, by their Iron age, but the worlds infelicity and miseries that succeeded his fall? . . . what can *Adonis horti* among the Poets meane other than *Moses* his *Eden*, or terrestrial Paradise,—the Hebrew Eden being *Voluptas* or *Delitiae*, whence the Greekes ἡδονή, or pleasure, seemes necessarily derived?

Without necessarily accepting the etymology, we must take note of the thematic connection: Adam and Eve, before the fall, were hedonists as well as Edenists. Reynolds, borrowing a formulation from Aulus Gellius, goes on to talk about a "*locus amoenissimus et voluptatis plenissimus.*" That superlative pleasance can be invoked to underline a reliance on pleasure as the basis of a naturalistic credo. Freud, and perhaps his interpreter Professor Trilling, might come to look *Beyond the Pleasure Principle*, but the principle itself has been central to the ethics of modern naturalism.

Persistently the golden age has embodied an ethic of hedonism, which has conflicted with postlapsarian notions of duty. Jonson was in the delicate position of providing entertainment for the court while accounting himself a better moralist than those who subjected it to their puritanical censure. They may well have felt that he was trying to keep his wine and drink it. In any case, his attempted reconcilement of pleasure and virtue has been overshadowed by a work it may have helped to stimulate, the masque of *Comus* sixteen years afterward. Milton's lifelong interest in the drama had previously rehearsed for a pastoral with the fragmentary *Arcades*. Strictly speaking, despite the music of Henry Lawes and the production at Ludlow Castle, *Comus* is less of a masque than a morality play. Furthermore, it is just as misleading to name the play after its villain—which Milton did not—as it is to consider Satan the hero of *Paradise Lost*. Milton's Comus, as opposed to the reeling belly-god of Jonson, is not without a certain seductive charm. His proposals to the Lady, as Douglas Bush has discerned, show us what Milton might have written like, had he chosen to become a Cavalier poet. Jonson's Comus seems to be wholly immersed in gluttony and inebriety; he offers nothing like the erotic enticements that Milton develops into so tense an *agon*. Temptation, from first to last, is the leading motive of Miltonic drama. The course of the Lady, lost in the tangled wood or transfixed in the stately palace, has a fairy-tale quality; and the spell is so potent that, although her two brothers can drive the rout away, she can only be rescued by Sabrina, the goddess in the machine. The Attendant Spirit points the moral:

> *Mortals that would follow me,*
> *Love vertue, she alone is free,*
> *She can teach ye how to clime*
> *Higher than the Spheary chime;*
> *Or if Vertue feeble were,*
> *Heav'n it self would stoop to her.*

It is paradoxical that Jonson could reconcile virtue with pleasure, for all the unattractiveness of his hedonistic spokesman, whereas Milton could give the devil his due, albeit he remains uncompromising in his allegiance to virtue. The Miltonic Comus is worthy of his name, κῶμος, the Greek for revelry. We are aware of his eponymous role in the history of comedy, when he marshals his unruly crew of revelers, with their glistering apparel and animal heads. Mythography makes him the offspring of Bacchus and Circe; iconology represents him as a drowsy but not uncomely youth, garlanded with roses and dangling an inverted torch. There can be no compromise, but there might be some ambivalence when the Lady is forced to summon up her "hidden strength," the secret weapon of chastity. She is climbing after virtue, not treading the path of pleasure. It may be a little more than coincidence that, when she speaks of "the sage / And serious doctrine of Virginity," she repeats the very epithets that Milton applied to Spenser. Milton is at one with Spenser—and with Guarini and ethical orthodoxy—in his belief that pleasures are firmly bounded by eternal laws. He is at a far remove from Tasso or Rabelais—or even, to some extent, More—in their naturalistic assumption that pleasure has laws of its own.

It follows that, although Milton absorbed the whole of classical mythology into his worldview, the golden age itself has a marginal place in that spacious prospect. When *Comus* ends at nearby Ludlow Town, the Attendent Spirit departs for the remotest Hesperides, where "eternal Summer dwels." This perdurable fancy, in its original Mediterranean version, "Eternal Spring," is one of those Hesperian fables which come true when Milton is describing the garden of Eden. The location of the earthly paradise, at the center of his cosmos in *Paradise Lost*, explains why there is so little room for our myth. Concentrating upon the Christian dogma of the fall, Milton had to be clear-cut in his rejection of its pagan analogue, like Dante and his other medieval predecessors. Having been so, he was then at liberty to adorn his resplendent garden with blooms transplanted from the garden of Adonis or from the vegetation of the golden age:

> *Flours worthy of Paradise which not nice Art*
> *In Beds and curious Knots, but Nature boon*
> *Powrd forth profuse on Hill and Dale and Plaine.*

This heaven on earth was the perfect milieu for the sexual union of Adam and Eve. Milton's account of that, with his attack on shame, that "honor dishonorable," which

> *banisht from mans life his happiest life,*
> *Simplicitie and spotless innocence,*

comes surprisingly close to Tasso in its yearning for a prelapsarian serenity in the absence of shame. But love could not be free in Eden, given the lack of choice. The one circumscription of freedom is Milton's doctrine of "wedded love" as the only claim of private property:

> *sole proprietie,*
> *In Paradise of all things common else.*

The mores of Milton's Eden have their counterpart in Campanella's utopian *City of the Sun*, where—by patristic injunction—wives are the sole exception to the rule of *omnia communia*. Milton, professing an orthodox scorn for money, is consistent in his pejorative employment of the noun *gold*. Conversely, his use of the adjective *golden* has favorable implications, after the broad Elizabethan usage. Christ feels the power of such ancient empires as Nineveh, "Of that first golden monarchy the seat," even while he is rejecting them in *Paradise Regained*. In *Paradise Lost* it is the Almighty who looks ahead, past tribulations and holocausts, to "golden days, fruitful of golden deeds." Between religious reformation and political revolution, the millennium seemed near at hand in the seventeenth century. The idea of the golden age as a lost paradise, in the anticipation of that advent, became a paradise to be regained, either in the next world or alternatively in this one. The scene shifts from the immemorial past to the chiliastic future.

[VI]

HISTORIOGRAPHY

"HAPPY THE PEOPLE whose annals are blank in history-books."
Carlyle, attributing the aphorism to Montesquieu, throws a dry
light on the fabulous happiness of the golden age, which by definition stands outside of history. Nevertheless we are able to take
a historical view of what it has meant to various ages of recorded
time. One of its principal attractions for them has been that it is
anti-temporal and ahistorical, out of time and thus sequestered
from the pressure of events. If we assume that it happened in the
distant past, nothing can recapture it, short of the time-machines
invented by science-fiction. If we believe in recurrence and in-
dulge in hopeful prognostics, we may expect it to happen sooner
or later again, as is predestined in Brahman lore. To speculate about
the future is a custom of civilization, as distinguished from a more
primitive condition, especially when speculation centers not upon
the eschatological future of the individual but upon the planned
survival of the race. The historical outlook presupposes accumu-
lated culture, disputable tradition, and an ensuing sense of the
fullness of time, such as that which followed the Renaissance and
the Reformation. Men who are in the habit of looking before and
after are not likely to think of their own epoch as absolutely
unique or indisputably preeminent. Our involvement with the
present gives us daily reasons for disquietude, even while it prompts
us to idealize the past or to pin our hopes upon futurity. We live
on the White Queen's regimen for Alice: "Jam tomorrow and jam

yesterday—but never jam *today*." Shakespeare put it more portentously: "Past, and to come, seems best: things present, worst."

Ordinarily a commitment to the past has a quietistic effect upon human behavior; men are more commonly aroused to action in the name of the future. Spenser and Ariosto could but sigh melodiously for the idealized world of medieval romance. Cervantes created the modern novel by exploding that fantasy. Don Quixote, most heroic of anti-heroes, by attempting to restore the golden age single-handed, has left his name as a byword for the good fight on behalf of a lost cause. Even though he did not succeed, he arrived, like all great figures, at the right conjunction of time and place. His century was to breed a succession of obsessed and embattled champions who looked upon themselves in the light of Messiahs. His country, then potentially the foremost in the world, was to base its policies on turning back the clock, and to preserve the spirit of the Middle Ages through and well beyond the Renaissance. The realism of Cervantes, hard won through the actualities of warfare and imprisonment and life along the road as a tax-collector, parodies the artificial forms in which he had tried to write, as well as the literary conventions of the books that bemused his knight. Cervantes had unsuccessfully experimented with pastoral in his first printed work, the long-drawn-out yet unfinished *Galatea*. Commenting upon it, when the Curate and the Barber are holding their inquisition over Don Quixote's library, the priest remarks that his poor friend the author is better versed in misfortunes than in verses (*"más versado en desdichas que en versos"*). The inquisitors deal mercifully with it, as they do with the *Dianas* of Montemayor and Gil Polo and certain other pastoral romances.

When Don Quixote finally retires from knight-errantry, he dallies—as his niece has feared he would—with the notion of taking up the pastoral way of life; he would be the shepherd Quijotiz and Sancho Panza would become the shepherd Pancino. That quixotic opportunity for exposing the absurdities of pastoralism to the test of common sense would be taken up by Charles Sorel in his anti-romance, *The Wayward Shepherd* (*Le Berger extravagant*). But one of Cervantes' canine witnesses, in *The Colloquy of the Dogs*, emphasizes the workaday requirements of herding sheep under masters named Pablo and Domingo, who are not Arcadian shepherds and who court no Galateas or Amaryllises out of Vergil. Echoes from bucolics are intermingled with the many echoes from the romances in *Don Quixote*. Defending the vicarious pleasures of reading fiction against the classical strictures of the Canon of Toledo, the hero sketches a whole romance in miniature. Its setting is a perfect *locus amoenus*, an imaginary garden laid out by nature collaborating with art in a disorderly order ("*ordén desordeñada*"). No such oasis lightens his own pilgrimage. He has no doubts whatsoever about his knightly mission: "I was borne by the disposition of Heaven, in this our age of iron, to resuscitate in it that of golde, or the golden world, as it is called." (So Thomas Shelton Anglicizes the synonym). And his proud vaunt to Sancho is rounded out by his promise to revive the Nine Worthies, the Twelve Paladins, and the order of the Table Round. He has just been challenging a noise in the dark, which daylight reveals to be the industrial sound of fulling-mills rather than the growling menace of giants or monsters as he had apprehended. Whereupon he is mocked and mimicked by Sancho, who repeats the apostolic boast; but the sad-faced Don would not be himself if he saw the joke or admitted the existence of anything so prosaic as a machine.

The contrast between the *edad moderna* and the *edad dorada* comes out most expressively during his second sally into the outer world. Having been bashed in the head through a typical encounter, he is offered the modest hospitality of a group of goatherds, not shepherds. With elaborate condescension, and with some hesitation on the part of Sancho Panza, that reluctant democrat, the knight insists that his squire must sit and eat with them, since chivalry—like love—makes all things equal. As the meal concludes, he casually takes up a handful of acorns by way of dessert, and an obvious quirk of mental association inspires him to a discourse:

"Happy time, and fortunate ages were those, whereon our Ancestors bestowed the title of Goulden! not because Gold (so much prized in this our yron age) was gotten in that happy time, without any labours, but because those which lived in that time, knew not those two words, *thine* and *mine*. In that holy age all things were in common: no man needed, for his ordinarie sustenance to doe ought else then lift up his hand, and take it from the strong Oke, which did liberally invite them to gather his sweete and savory fruit . . ."

The rest is eloquent but all too familiar, though Cervantes makes us notice that we are in Spain when he mentions cork-trees, and his mention of shepherdesses prepares us for the entrance of the unapproachable Marcela and the episode of her lover's suicide. The goatherds are confirmed in their suspicion of Don Quixote's madness. Again and again, in praising the happiest time ("*el felicísmo tiempo*"), he endeavors to reckon up what knighthood has accomplished when it was in the field. While dispraising the modern age ("*la depravada edad nuestra*"), he lauds the antique institution for taking upon itself the defense of the realm, the protection of damsels and orphans, the punishment of the proud, the rewarding of the humble, and the redressing of all wrongs.

"But now sloth triumphs upon industry, idlenesse on labour, vice on vertue, presumption on valour, the Theorie on the Practice of Armes, which onely lived and shined in those golden Ages and in those Knights Errant."

The chivalric principles embrace nothing less than the distribution of justice among men, both distributive and commutative. Practice is attended by such embarrassments as that which overtook Don Quixote's first sally, when his championship of the peasant boy Andrés gained him only another beating from his rich master. Sancho Panza manages to impose a kind of rough justice upon the island of Barataria, which significantly proves to be part of the mainland; and his wife Teresa acknowledges their debt to the Duchess by a touching gift of acorns, which she wishes had been gold; but Sancho's abdication comes much too quickly after his accession as governor. Possibly the saddest rebuff of the many that

Don Quixote receives is his meeting, after his very last discom-
fiture, with the highwayman Roque Guinart; for here is a Cata-
lonian Robin Hood, whose hands "have more compassion than
cruelty in them." Roque and his forty brigands, courteously engaging in a more equable redistribution of wealth, seem to be successfully living the doctrines that Don Quixote has been professing
so ineffectually.

Cervantes' outburst, pursuing an interest he has elsewhere expressed, and following the amplified and high-spirited prose ver-
sion of the *Metamorphoses* by Jorge de Bustamente, marks the
culmination of a voluble concern for the golden age which, in
Spain, was coextensive with the extraction of gold from the New
World. In the year of discovery, 1492, when a child was born to
Ferdinand and Isabella, it had been greeted by the poet Juan del
Encina with an adaptation of Vergil's *Fourth Eclogue*. Ten years
before, on the final page of a historical manual dedicated to her
Catholic Majesty, the chronicler Diego de Valera had hailed the
invention of printing as a miraculous means of recovering the
golden ages. Ariosto paused in the midst of an epic catalogue to
salute Charles V as the heir of Charlemagne and the favorite of
Astraea, though in fact that Austro-Spanish monarch was to preside over the disintegration of the Holy Roman Empire. Bernardo
de Valbuena, the Bishop of Puerto Rico who had discovered
eternal spring for himself in Mexico, wrote a sequence of eclogues
in the manner of Sannazaro, *Siglo de oro en las selvas de Erífile*.
He was more sanguine than most Arcadians in actually believing
that the richness of a living golden age had survived intact under
the secluded circumstances of this lovely place (*"este ameno sitio"*),
a wooded Spanish valley surrounding the fountain of a nymph,
albeit he regretted that the shepherds' songs had lost something of
their old simplicity and plainness.

> *Dulce es la historia de la vida nuestra;*
> *Aquí se muestra vivo il Siglo de Oro,*
> *Rico tesoro à pocos descubierto.*

It is poignant to recall that Lope de Vega, on the day before his death, completed a poem entitled *El Siglo de Oro*. This is a "moral sylva," rehearsing the *topos* with a few baroque embellishments and some embittered applications. Nature, resembling a woman, is most beautiful in her early youth, when her beauty is unadulterated by cosmetics or prostitution. The golden age has now become a touchstone for undeception, for recognizing the deceit, the perfidy, and the ignobility of life as Lope renounces it.

> ¡Oh siglo de oro,
> de nuestra humana vida desengaño,
> si vieras tanto engaño,
> tan poco fe, tan bárbaro decoro!

The irony is that the period of Lope and Cervantes and so many of Spain's major writers, would be known in the annals of literature as the Golden Age, *el siglo de oro*. But that is a retrospective designation, evidently conferred upon it in 1827 by the romantic poet and liberal statesman, Francisco Martínez de la Rosa. Exiled to Paris, he was writing his *Poética* and retracing the history of Spanish poetry. Its climax had been reached when, while still cherishing the divine echoes of Greece and Rome, the illustrious Castilian bard challenged Italy for the laurels, and the Muses signalized his victory with this title of honor:

> Así el divino coro
> de tanto ilustre vato dió renombre
> a aquella edad feliz de siglo de oro.

From our century it is easy enough to stand back and admire the Renaissance as one of the world's greatest epochs of art and thought. Many of its notable minds, though they were self-critical enough to harbor their misgivings and reservations, were by no means unaware of its greatness. Some of their commendations need to be qualified, since these often sprang from the exigencies of patronage; but the phraseology seems warranted by the occasion when Erasmus, who dedicated his edition of the Vulgate to Leo X, congratulated the pope on turning a worse than iron age into a golden one; and this particular association proved to be so widespread and long-lasting that Bishop Berkeley could still refer to the golden age of Pope Leo. If we had any doubt of Erasmus' sincerity, we could cite his private letter to the preacher Capito, where he longs to be young again so that he might enjoy more fully the blessings of peace, polite letters, and scholarship that Leo and Francis I are now conferring on Europe. More pragmatically, in an epistle to Cardinal Wolsey, Erasmus implies that princes must be inspired by scholars. Less secularly the mystical humanist, Guillaume Postel, prognosticated a religious revival and a French golden age in which women, like Joan of Arc, would have a prominent share. The conception of a Renaissance itself, the metaphor of renascence, was derived from the evangelical doctrine of rebirth and had its harbingers in Dante and Petrarch. It came into its own when it was blended with the Vergilian rhetoric of congratulation at the Medici courts. Vasari seems to have been responsible for introducing it into the vernacular when he spoke of the revival in the fine arts as a *rinascita.* Their pride at taking part in a restoration of classical learning was profusely attested by the humanists—though their testimony has been ignored by certain latter-day scholars, predisposed to blur the historic distinctions between the Middle Ages and the Renaissance.

Rabelais is a magniloquent witness when he symbolizes the transition in his paternal letter from the Gothic giant, Gargantua, to the humanistic giant, Pantagruel. *"Maintenant toutes disciplines sont restituées . . ."* Now, in the very moment of your matriculation at the University of Paris, all the disciplines have been restored. Moreover, divers exciting new studies have been opened up through geographical exploration and scientific investigation. Gargantua is both traditional and far-seeing enough to warn his son that there may be hazard as well as promise ahead—above all, the danger of science without conscience (*"science sans conscience"*). If the printing press was invented through divine inspiration, conversely the invention of artillery was prompted by diabolical suggestion. Gunpowder, it would be widely agreed, had been doing more than anything else to turn the present into an iron age. Don Quixote's reversion to the chivalric stance was a one-man protest against the very forces that had foredoomed it to ineffectuality. The sequel to his eulogy of the golden age is another set-piece on a classic *topos*, his discourse on arms and letters, which is similarly devoted to setting forth his ideals. He has been moved by books to leave his study and adopt the soldier's profession, with the object of securing the greatest good that men can desire in this life, the end of war, namely peace. One of his listeners is a former captive from Algiers, whose own contribution to the discussion will be a tale of military hardship and Turkish slavery, based in part upon the actual experience of Cervantes himself.

His encomium on *las armas y las letras*, like his praise of the golden age, has many literary counterparts, since it voices the aspiration of the Renaissance to combine the active with the contemplative life. Models of courtesy, such as the ideal courtier of Castiglione, were expected to be equally adroit with sword and pen. Sir Walter Ralegh was not the only Renaissance man who adopted the heraldic motto, *Tam Marti, quam Mercurio*, thereby placing himself under the double aegis of the god of prowess and the god of ingenuity. Leonardo da Vinci, along with his paintings and pageants and anatomical sketches, worked out plans for fortifications and martial engines. Louis Le Roy (or Regius) went so far as to devise a comprehensive and progressive philosophy of history, in his treatise *De vicissitudine*, which took "the concurrence of Armes and Learning" as its main criterion for measuring a culture, arguing that "the restitution of the tongues, and of all sciences" coincided with advances in the art of war, and that the modern era could be dated from the emergence of Tamburlaine at the end of the fourteenth century. This was more humanistic than humane, and it sorted ill with the conviction that golden ages brought peace—unless one is ready to follow the circular reasoning of Don Quixote, or some of our recent strategists of deterrence. Montaigne would have pounded his desk and protested: "Mechanical victories!" Technology had been taking the personal glory out of battle and making heroics as obsolete as Don Quixote's armor. Even the Don could see this:

"Those blessed ages were fortunate, which wanted the dreadfull furie of the divelish and murdering peeces of Ordenance, to whose inventor I am verily perswaded that they render in hell an eternall guerdon for his Diabolicall invention; by which he hath given power to an infamous, base, vile, and dastardly arme, to bereave the most valorous Knight of life . . . it grieves me to have ever undertaken the exercise of a Knight Errant in this our detestable age, for although no danger can affright me, yet notwithstanding I live in jealousie to thinke how powder and Lead might deprive me of the power to make my selfe famous and renouned by the strength of mine arme, and edge of my sword throughout the face of the earth."

One of Tamburlaine's Western European contemporaries, the French ecclesiastic and statesman, Jean de Montreuil, addressed a remarkable letter to an English commander, appealing for peace in the name of the golden age. The resulting truce was an early episode in what turned out to be the Hundred Years' War, wherein Jean lost his life. If the concord of Christendom was "the source and parent of piety and erudition," as Erasmus wrote to Leo X, then even Leo's dazzling pontificate could not be precisely described as an apogee. It lasted for less than a decade; it was notorious for its nepotism; its Medicean generosity was financed by simony and almost led to bankruptcy; its sale of indulgences contributed to the rise of the Church's harshest critic, Martin Luther; it saw the invasion of Italy by armies from France and the Empire; in short, it is generally instanced by historians to mark the close of the high Renaissance. The erudite Gyraldus, who had lived through it, preferred to look back far beyond it to the natural golden age before the arts and sciences existed. His invective against letters and men of letters, *Progymnasa adversus literas et literatos*, though admittedly a rhetorical exercise, presents a scathing indictment of scholarly vices and vanities. The pioneering printer and learned editor, Henri Estienne, capped his edition of Herodotus with a heavy-handed satirical apologia, undertaking to demonstrate that there were stranger anomalies in the sixteenth-century than in ancient Greek history. Citing and discussing classical texts on the golden age, he ironically links it with the second childhood of the present age:

> It seems to me that what happens to the age of men is happening to the age of the world. For if we closely consider the modes of conduct today, who would not say—if I may so express myself—that the world talks nonsense [*le monde radotte*]? Now if it talks nonsense, then it truly holds fast to the time of the good old man Saturn, and can drape itself in that fine title of the Saturnian reign.

Sir Walter Ralegh, in his *Historie of the World*, draws more serious inferences from this kind of parallel. Though his starting-point is the simplicity of the primal state, he does not consider it uniquely golden. "For good and golden Kings make good and golden Ages; and all times have brought forth of both sorts." As for the supposition that ours is the iron age, we are simply the subjective creatures of our own encroaching senility.

> For our younger yeares are our golden Age; which being eaten up by time, we praise those seasons which our youth accompanied: and (indeede) the grievous alternations in our selves, and the paines and diseases which never part from us but at the grave, make the times seeme so differing and displeasing: especially the qualitie of mans nature being also such, as it adoreth and extolleth the passages of the former, and condemneth the present state how just soever.

For others, the four ages were comparable to the four seasons, with winter now approaching. If the self-same period can seem the best of times to some contemporaries, while it seems the worst of times to others, the clue to the problem must reside in the viewpoint of the observer. Yet the growth of historical consciousness in the sixteenth and seventeenth centuries encouraged the mood of lateness, particularly when confronted with the change of dynasties in England and the *fin-de-siècle* preoccupation with melancholy and mutability. Sir Thomas Browne thought of his own day as "this setting part of time." For Robert Burton it was "this iron age wherein we live, where love is cold, *et iam terras Astraea reliquit . . .*" If antiquity was the youth of the world ("*Antiquitas mundi juventus saeculi*"), as Bacon pointed out, then the later generations were the true elders. It was for them to rejoice in the accumulations of knowledge, and to correct their failing eyesight with those up-to-date spectacles of science, the telescope and the microscope. Scholars, with John Selden, "preferring truth before what dulling custom hath too deeply rooted in them," would be "not unwilling to change their old akorns for better meat." Conflicting opinions were polarized in a debate between two weighty volumes by English clerics: *The Fall of Man, or the Corruption of Nature*, by Godfrey Goodman, and *An Apologie of the Power and Providence of God in the Government of the World*, by George Hakewill. Goodman's argument, as his alternating titles imply, shifts uneasily from the moral falling-off to a biological degeneration.

> when I observe the course of things, the severall actions and inclinations of men; when I consider the diseases of these times, together with all the signes, tokens, and symptomes; alas, I feare a relapse, I feare a relapse, lest the world in her doting age, should now againe turn infidell, and that the end of us be worse than the beginning.

Hakewill's sturdy answer, which carried the day with most readers, blames such lamentations upon "the *morosity* and crooked disposition of old men, always complaining of the hardnesse of the present times, together with an excessive admiration of *Antiquity*." Evidence that the world has been decaying is to be found not in the hard facts of nature but in the sentimental fictions of the poets. "But above all, that *pretty invention* of the *foure Ages* of the World, compared to foure mettals, Gold, Silver, Brasse, and Iron, hath wrought such an impression in mens mindes, that it can hardly bee rooted out."

Hakewill's part in this controversy had been somewhat anticipated by an Italian polemic which was even more spirited in its message of reassurance, *L'Hoggidì* by Secondo Lancelloti, Abbot of Perugia. The title and subtitle are readily translated: *Nowadays, or The World no Worse nor more Calamitous than the Past.* But the expression that Lancelloti coined for those he was counter-attacking resists translation; he called them *Hoggidiani*, the sort of people for whom the plaintive abverb *nowadays* is the opening note of a lament upon the deterioration of everything; in order to be dis-praisers of the present, they are *laudatores temporis acti.* Each of Lancelloti's fifty chapters is a *disinganno*, a refutation of some received opinion of theirs, such as the presumption that the acorn was the original food of mankind. One of the liveliest and most substantial of these *disinganni* shows "the golden age refuted as vain and false." The futility of the *Hoggidiani* had been chided by Ecclesiastes many centuries before: "Say not thou, What is the cause that the former days were better than these? for thou dost not enquire wisely concerning this." Such inquiries would not be decreasing with the increase of the centuries, and the discussion pro and contra will probably never be altogether resolved. None-theless it took its most decisive form, during the seventeenth cen-tury, in the celebrated quarrel of the Ancients and the Moderns. The Moderns were bound to win, if only because they had the advantage of fighting on their own terrain—a watershed between the Renaissance, with its passionate cult of the classics, and the Enlightenment, with its urbane neoclassicism.

Any significant writer, even when he does not align himself with the modernists, always maintains a vital relationship with his own time. It is characteristic of Milton, and it foreshadows his immer-sion in the political and theological currents of the Common-wealth, that one of his Latin exercises should vigorously affirm: "*Naturam non pati senium* (that nature does not suffer from old age)." Ben Jonson, characteristically, was not quite so affirmative; nature might not be in decay ("*Natura non effoeta*"), he allowed, but men and studies were. Were the arts advancing or declining? If these were years of superannuation, they would not be less event-ful for that reason. The old age of the world would mean that doomsday was at hand. Messianic reformers dramatized their strug-gles in the imagery of the Apocalypse: Rome was Babylon, the

Pope was Antichrist, and each sect had its own schedule for the second coming, the last judgment, and the kingdom of God on earth. Gradually, as religious movements were secularized, and as their respective doomsdays were inevitably postponed, millennarian prospects became utopian programs, and the golden age was definitively transferred from the past to the future. The millennium, Isaiah had prophesied, would replace iron and brass with silver and gold. The prophecies of Daniel were endlessly scanned and meticulously reinterpreted, in the hope that his metallic idol would provide some key to historic events. If gold represented the Babylonian monarchy, silver the Persian, brass the Greek, and iron the Roman, what then was portended by the clay? So fine a scientific intellect as Isaac Newton's pondered the enigma.

The simplest outline of occidental history is the triad projected in the twelfth century by the monkish prophet, Joachim of Fiore. Its three successive ages conform to a Trinitarian pattern. First comes the age of the Father and of the law, the Old Testament, then the age of the Son and of the gospel, the New Testament, to be followed by the age of the Holy Spirit and the Everlasting Gospel. Though the ideological content of the prophecy has continually changed, the same triadic framework has been used again and again. Auguste Comte, for all his claims to science, could think of no better scheme to forward them than a sequence moving from the religious through the philosophical to the scientific age. Russians long expected the mystical advent of a third realm, as Tolstoy reminds us in *War and Peace*, and Germans were perverting the Joachite vision when they invoked its sanction for their Third Reich. In the seminal *New Science* (*Scienza nuova*) of Giambattista Vico, the three successive epochs are the divine, the heroic, and the civil, and they recur continuously in upward-spiralling cycles. In his attempt to develop a historical method for interpreting mythology or for extracting history from myths, Vico was incidentally seeking a rational explanation for the fabulous gold of the golden age. He conjectured that it had really been grain, which constituted the basic source of wealth. Despite some poetic assertions to the contrary, the age was noteworthy for the first tillage of the soil. Witness its tutelary allegiance to Saturn, god of planting, and to Astraea, with her wheaten sheaf. As for its innocence, that was a superstitious conceit.

Standing at an eighteenth-century midpoint between the Renaissance and ourselves, Vico was ambivalently concerned with the historicity of our myth. We have seen the golden age displaced by the Judeo-Christian paradise or else fitted into syncretic legends which could only pass current before historiography had acquired more rigorous standards. The enterprising forger, Johannes Annius of Viterbo, had tried to find a place for the golden age in his apocryphal chronologies of the world, but he does not seem to have made up his mind whether it came before or after the flood. The Anglican theologian, Thomas Burnet, sought to impose his theology on cosmology with his *Sacred Theory of the Earth*, a work which puts him forcefully on the side of those who lamented nature's decline. He assumes that the golden age was "common to all the earth" at the beginning, though some parts of it were "more Golden, if I may so say, than the rest." Why, he thereupon inquires, do we no longer enjoy the perpetual spring, the spontaneous fertility, the longevity, and the other paradisal benefits? He is begging the question, of course, with his very hypothesis. It is all very well for priests and poets to talk of a golden age "which preceded the present state of vice and misery," according to the skeptical David Hume, but when philosophers—"who pretend to neglect authority, and to cultivate reason"—tell the same tales, we have the right to challenge their deductions. And if we accept Thomas Fuller's aphorism, "The golden age was never the present age," we are bound to conclude that it was nonexistent. The enlightened citizens of Campanella's City of the Sun do not believe in it, since they have achieved their Utopia.

Seneca, who had utilized the myth as a Stoic parable, was well aware that, in the last analysis, it amounted to nothing more nor less than a chronological value judgment. "Whatever age the poets wish to be viewed as the best, they call golden." Seneca's own age has gone down, in the history of Latin literature, as the Silver Age. "With Ovid ended the golden age of the Roman tongue," says Dryden, summing up the consensus of critics. No one, except for Peacock, has taken the trouble to discern a brass or iron age of *belles lettres*; and silver, after all, is the next best evaluation to gold. In this context, it seems to betoken something more than a fine-spun series of linguistic and stylistic differences. To move on from Ovid toward Seneca is to move out of the triumphant Augustan principate into the turbulent and corrupting regimes of the Roman emperors. Rome, as our central model for historical conceptualization, has set the most striking examples of both grandeur and decadence. The concept of a golden age, to be sure, is implicitly decadent in its consequences, insofar as it must indicate a downward curve from a higher point in the past to our own situation. But insofar as the thinking of the Renaissance grew in self-confidence, insofar as it took a more critical attitude toward the remoter past, it could reverse the inclination of that curve; and if the trend was rising instead of falling as it approached the present, the idea of decadence was yielding to the idea of progress. Gabriel Harvey, unlike his correspondent Spenser, espoused the more optimistic cause:

> You suppose the first age was the gold age. It is nothing so. Bodin defendeth the gold age to flourish now, and our first grandfathers to have rubbed through in the iron and brazen age at the beginning when all things were rude and unperfect in comparison or the exquisite fineness and delicacy that we have grown into in these days.

Harvey was adventurous in adopting the ideas of more original minds. Jean Bodin, the French jurisconsult and political theorist, had subjected the interpretations of Daniel's prophecy to an incisive questioning in his *Method for the Easy Understanding of History*. He had gone on to argue that the primitive period, if it were to be realistically compared with the sixteenth century, would be seen as an iron age of lawlessness and disorder. He was confident that living men had as many virtues as the ancients, and that certain disciplines were improving, since nature was now revealing more of her secrets. Those who felt that humanity was deteriorating, as other spokesmen for the moderns would also suggest, were old men sighing for the loss of youth.

> As if returning from a long voyage, they talk about the golden century—their golden age—to young men. But then it happens to them as to those who emerge from the harbor into the sea; they think that the houses and the towns are departing from them. Thus they believe that delight, good behavior, and justice have flown to heaven and deserted the earth.

The Advancement of Learning, Bacon's monument to the idea of scientific progress, in briefly surveying the background of the advance, again recognizes three ages. This is not quite the threefold continuity of the Joachites, since there had presumably been intervening periods unworthy of such recognition, such as the Middle Ages, Petrarch's Dark Ages. These are the high points, the visitations of knowledge: Greece and Rome and now the contemporaneous visitation. By the time that Voltaire was addressing himself to the problem of historical periodization, he was ready to accept Bacon's categories and to single out a fourth epoch of intellectual flowering: Greece, Rome, the Renaissance, and the century of Louis XIV—which was being continued into the eighteenth century by whom but Voltaire himself? A generation earlier Fénelon, who was truly a figure of France's *grand siècle*, was far from regarding it as a golden age. The pedagogical voyage of his Télémaque led to some realms not unworthy of Astraea's patronage, notably the pastoral dominion of Bétique and the model city-state of Salente. But these vistas of perfection ended by alerting him to the imperfections of his compatriots. "We regard the behavior of these people as a beautiful fable, and they must regard ours as a monstrous dream."

The eighteenth century was less self-critical than the seventeenth. Endeavoring to fill in the grand outlines laid down by Bacon, its *Encyclopédie* looked upon the Enlightenment ("*la lumière renait de toutes parts"*) as the consequence and continuation of *"la renaissance des lettres."* Voltaire, in his bland and sybaritic monologue, "The Man of the World (*Le Mondain*)," fairly revels in the comforts and conveniences of modernity. Let him who will regret the good old days, he exults.

> *Regrettera qui veut le bon vieux temps,*
> *Et l'âge d'or, et le règne d'Astrée ...*

Life is well worth living in this iron age. Our metropolitan capitals have become terrestrial paradises, especially Paris, what with its boulevards and cafés, its carriages and shops, its perfumes and sparkling wines, its operas by Rameau and paintings by Poussin. In spite of all that the Stoics have preached, superfluity has become a necessity, as the old world has been enriched by the exploitation of the new world and adorned by the importation of luxuries.

> *O le bon temps que ce siècle de fer!*
> *Le superflu, chose très nécessaire,*
> *A réuni l'un et l'autre hémisphère.*

Criticized for his candid enjoyment of luxury, Voltaire was to become its most vocal apologist. Not for him the long and dirty fingernails or the tousled hair or the dingy nakedness of our first parents, who subsisted like a pair of monkeys on water, grain, and acorns, ignorant of the capitalistic delights of gold and silk and *le mien* and *le tien*. If they were willing to share all things, it was because they had nothing. This worldly descendant of theirs, so urban in his urbanity, would have been ill at ease in the garden of Eden—or, as he himself specifies, in the realms of Télémaque. Why should a Parisian ever travel? The worldling is thoroughly comfortable where he is: it is indeed the earthly paradise. *"Le paradis terrestre est où je suis."*

This elegant complacency was shattered by the Lisbon earthquake of 1755, which provoked not only Voltaire's self-searching poem on the disaster but likewise his satire on the philosophy of optimism in *Candide*. Much of the ingenuous hero's quest for the best of possible worlds is conducted in South America, where he is brought close to the golden age on one or two tantalizing occasions. He concludes that "pure nature is good," because the cannibals refrain from eating him, when they realize that he is not a Jesuit. The Jesuit colony of Paraguay is not exactly a Utopia; "it is the masterpiece of reason and justice" because "the fathers have everything and the people nothing." Just as Candide is about to decide that one hemisphere is as bad as the other, he chances to stumble into the aureate land of Eldorado, which Europeans had sought for so long and never discovered before. Its rocky isolation in the Andes, protecting it from Spanish depradations, has preserved its innocence and its felicity. The Utopian precondition for both is the overabundance, and hence the devaluation, of gold. Children play at quoits with it; modest houses are panelled with it; the King cannot understand the European taste for "our yellow mud." He prefers to expound the enlightened institutions of his kingdom: its absence of law-courts, its palace of the sciences. Travel has been broadening, and rewarding in more ways than one. Candide and his Indian servant take their departure after loading a herd of sheep with easy riches, most of which are lost in the precipitous descent.

Eldorado has not been rediscovered since, and its memory remains the bright exception among all the inequities and the calamities, in Candide's disillusioning tour of the world. When he finally settles down to cultivate his garden in Asia Minor, he has learned the lesson of industry, Voltaire's recipe for the good life. Even in Eldorado there was no leisure, although the land was cultivated "more for pleasure than for need." What is pleasing, for Voltaire, is what is useful: "*partout l'utile était agréable.*" Commenting on the book of Genesis and on the cultivation of Adam's garden, in the *Philosophical Dictionary*, Voltaire discusses

the notion which men had, and still have, that the earliest times were better than the latest. Men have always bewailed the present and lauded the past. Overburdened by their labors, they have fixed their happiness on idleness, not realizing that the worst condition is that of a man who has nothing to do . . . Hence the notion of the golden age . . . and all those old wives' tales.

As a hard-working utilitarian who had little use for simplicity, Voltaire was unlikely to be charmed by the vogue of the noble savage. His reaction to the manifesto that spread that vogue, Rousseau's *Discourse on the Origins of Inequality*, is recorded in an ironic letter to his philosophical rival. Though he has been all but carried away, Voltaire confides to Rousseau, he is too old to get down on all fours. From his opposite pole, the latter took the keenest delight in the kind of subjective meditation stimulated by woodland solitude. To Malesherbes he would write:

> I created a golden age in my fantasy, and filled those beautiful days with all the scenes of my life that had left me pleasant memories, and all those which my heart could still desire; I was moved to the point of tears over the true pleasures of humanity, pleasures so delicious and so pure and nowadays so far away from men. Oh, if some notion of Paris, of my epoch, or of my petty vanity as an author came to disturb my reveries in those moments, with what scorn I dismissed it at once, in order to give myself up without distraction to the exquisite sentiments with which my soul was filled!

In reverting to the myth of the golden age, and in reviving the ambivalent speculations of Montaigne, Rousseau's *Second Discourse* was advancing more or less historically toward that critique of civilization which he would make explicit in *The Social Contract* and that idyll of nature which would suffuse his more personal writings. Properly speaking, his golden age is not the happy primitive state but the demoralizing stage that comes afterward, brought about by the introduction of metallurgy and agriculture. "For the poet it was gold and silver, but for the philosopher it was iron and corn which first civilized men and ruined humanity."

Clearly, this is postulated upon the old dream of ease and the inherited distrust of technology—postulates which were dismissed as nonsense by Voltaire, who in turn must have outraged Rousseau by glorying in the urbanization of the iron age. The crux of the argument, which would lead via *The Social Contract* to *The Communist Manifesto*, is that the organization of agricultural and industrial labor had been grounded upon the ownership of property.

> The first man who, having enclosed a plot of ground, thought of saying "This is mine," and found people simple enough to believe him, was the real founder of civil society. How many crimes, wars, murders, how many miseries and horrors would that man have spared the human race who, pulling up the stakes and filling in the ditch, had cried out to his fellows: "Beware of listening to that impostor; you are undone if you forget that the fruits of the earth belong to everybody, and the earth itself to nobody."

This last suggestion is what we mean by Uchronia: that is to say, the idealization of history, the mythical event that should have taken place when circumstance was taking the wrong turn. It confirms the position of Rousseau as the middle man between our images of the golden age and the slogans of modern revolution. As if he were taken aback by the radicalism of his own rhetoric, he appended certain afterthoughts to his discourse in which he neutralized his criticisms by transposing them into rhetorical questions. What should then be done? Should societies be totally abolished? Could the fatal distinction between *meum* and *tuum* be wiped out at this stage? Could men go back to the forests again and live among the beasts? When life is no longer simple, the very process of simplification becomes extremely complicated. Institutions are at least as tenacious as they are corrupt. As for himself, Jean-Jacques admits, he does not care for acorns. The argument for reversion had been reduced to absurdity by Prudentius long before, in lines which Hakewill had approvingly translated:

> *If we must still embrace, and ne're refuse,*
> *What th' infant world in ruder times did use:*
> *Let us each age then, step by step recall,*
> *And damne in order even to th' originall*
> *What after by succeeding use was found.*
> *In the first world no Rusticks ear'd the ground,*

What meane the ploughs then? what the needlesse care
Of harrowes? akornes yeeld sufficient fare.

During these thematic excursions, we must have gathered several handfuls of nuts; we might almost claim, in the jargon of recent criticism, to have sketched a phenomenology of the acorn. With this gesture of understandable inconsistency on the part of Rousseau, we may take our leave of that meager yet meaningful emblem.

In a programmatic lecture which reverberated in other minds, J. G. Fichte announced: "*Before* us lies what Rousseau, in the name of the state of nature, and every poet, under the appellation of the golden age, have located *behind* us." Rousseau had played his part in that relocation through the generation of revolutionary thinkers that grew up as his readers; he had shifted the poet's gaze, as Schiller put it, from Arcadia to Elysium—to a new, if visionary, order. One of the projectors of socialism, the Comte de Saint-Simon, affirmed in 1814:

> The imagination of the poets has placed the golden age in the cradle of the human race, amid the ignorance and crudity of primitive times. It was rather the iron age that should have been abandoned there. The golden age of mankind is not behind us; it is ahead; it is in the perfection of the social order. Our fathers have not seen it; our children will get there one day; and it is for us to open the way for them.

The reversal of the two ages was no great novelty in itself; it had been suggested by Bodin on purely historical grounds; and, even with the golden age in the future, patient men could conceivably wait for it as the Brahmans did. Where Saint-Simon outdistanced his predecessors was in calling for an immediate effort to shape the future. His call had loud and wide reverberations, which echo in Emerson's *Journals* and in Carlyle's *Sartor Resartus*. Edward Bellamy, after devising his New England Utopia in *Looking Backward*, added an explanatory postscript looking forward to the golden age: ". . . Our children will surely see it, and we, too, who are already men and women, if we deserve it by our faith, and by our works." As usual, the object seemed closer at hand in the New

World. Indeed an article in the *Scientific American*, as of the year 1849, proclaims that the golden age is now. But, since its essence is timelessness rather than timeliness, since any given date is destined to fade more and more dimly into the past, it is a comfort to think of the golden age as a continuing futurity—like the concept of posterity. So Whittier apostrophizes it:

> *O golden age, whose light is of the dream*
> *And not the sunset, forward, not behind . . .*

If modern poetry has dealt charily with the theme, this is partly because it had been so richly treated before, partly because the classical frame of reference had become less universally applicable, but mainly because the golden age had been taken over by the ideologues. Shelley tried to combine the two commitments, and to make his poems the vehicles of social regeneration. Byron, though he was active in both areas, registered the tensions of their inter-relationship:

> *O for old Saturn's reign of sugar-candy!*
> *Meantime I drink to your return in brandy.*

The issue narrowed, for Robert Frost, into a choice between "the golden line / Of lyric" and "the golden light" of ideology:

> *. . . to live ungolden with the poor,*
> *Enduring what the ungolden must endure,*
> *This has been poetry's great anti-lure.*

For John Berryman, the myth is a half-forgotten toy of childhood:

> *It was only a small dream of the Golden World,*
> *now you trot off to bed.*

William Blake had been held back by romantic suspicions of the classics, as well as by his Christian reservations against pagan myths. "Such is the mighty difference between Allegoric Fable and Spiritual Mystery." Impelled by his chiliastic ambitions, he could formulate his mythographic or iconological intentions in *A Vision of the*

Last Judgment: "The Nature of my Work is Visionary or Imaginative; it is an Endeavour to Restore what the Ancients call'd the Golden Age." But, though his protests against the rationalistic materialism of the Enlightenment have aided us to understand the deeper uses of mythology, his own myths were too eclectic and idiosyncratic to bring about that restoration. The nineteenth century had better reason than any of the preceding centuries—its factories, its railroads, its artillery—for identifying itself with the iron age. That identification became explicit in both the Hegelian and the Marxist dialectic. Such crusading novelists as Zola saw in human affairs an endless struggle between the opposing forces of *le mien* and *le tien*. Forsaking the domain of poetics, our *topos* aligned itself with the rhetoric of social controversy.

Even while lamenting the gods of Greece, the romanticists had acquiesced in their eclipse. Great Pan had expired. The first line of the first poem in *The Collected Poems of William Butler Yeats* re-affirms: "The woods of Arcady are dead." That was merely another country, for the poet whose heart was divided between Eire and Byzantium. The laureate of modern nostalgia, Flaubert, had expressed his sentiment of *autrefois* through the mouth of Saturn in *The Temptation of Saint Anthony*: "Lost age which will return no more, when action followed instinct, while human life, closely attached to the reality of the soil, turned undeviatingly around a fixed point, like the shadow on a sun-dial!" Flaubert removed this passage from his final text, possibly because his time-telling metaphor sounded rather awkward and made existence in the golden age sound—as it may well have struck us from time to time—rather monotonous. Yet the speech excised reveals the unspoken premise for his temporal dissatisfactions. Similarly Baudelaire, in a fanciful portrait of Poe, attributes the poet's alienation from his bourgeois environment to his "regrets for the golden age and the lost Eden." That this pattern of motivation has affected men of letters in the twentieth century is evinced by the recently published diaries of the gifted and unhappy Cesare Pavese. "Your worst enemy," he admonishes himself, "is the belief in a happy prehistoric time, in

Eden, in the golden age, and the belief that everything essential
has been said by the first thinkers. The two things are a single one."
The burden of the past can become a writer's block. But, as Pavese
noted five years later, writing is primarily an effort to reclaim the
past. "The first great manifestation of 'literature' and indeed its
archetypal origin are accompanied by the myth of a golden age,
of an ivory tower (Vergilian Arcadia)."

The novelist for whom the golden age held the most urgent
meaning was Dostoevsky. His obsession with it should not surprise
us, if we consider it as the dialectical counterpart of his concern
for the spiritual malaise, the miseries, and the indignities that insult
and injure the human psyche. The recurrent dream that pervades
his fiction was not his, to begin with; it was a wish-dream of the
Crystal Palace, a figment of propaganda for technological perfecti-
bility, in a utopian novel by the socialist Chernishevsky, to which
Dostoevsky had scornfully responded through his *Notes from
Underground*. The inspiration that stimulated his divergent fantasy
was a painting of Acis and Galatea by Claude Lorrain, which had
fascinated him in the Dresden Gallery. There the nymph and her
swain are depicted embracing, against the Arcadian landscape of
an island in a Greek archipelago, bathed in the luminosity of a
setting sun. The childish cupid at their feet may have lent a domestic touch to the picture; and Dostoevsky ignores the jealous cy-
clops, Polyphemus, poised upon a crag to hurl a rock and slay his
rival; but the mood of perfect bliss is momentary; the sun will set
and Acis will be slain. Dostoevsky's glimpse of the golden age is
gained at the moment preceding its expiration.

> "A marvellous dream, mankind's highest delusion! the golden age,
> the most improbable of all dreams that ever existed, but the one for
> which men gave their lives and all their strength, for which prophets
> died and were slain, without which peoples do not wish to live and
> cannot even die!"

Such is the exclamation of Versilov, the irresponsible yet ultra-
Russian wanderer in *A Raw Youth*, confessing to his illegitimate

son. For Versilov the dream was a cosmopolitan vision, and the reality to which he awakened—western Europe torn by nationalism and revolution—is the last sunset of humanity. Here the dream recurs from the excluded section of *The Possessed* known as "Stavrogin's Confession," where it was dreamed by the demonic protagonist. There it functioned as a symbolic commentary upon the corruptness of Stavrogin and the innocence of the eight-year-old Matryosha, whom he has violated and who has hanged herself. Dostoevsky's fullest elaboration is *The Dream of a Ridiculous Man*, where the dreamer is the half-mad narrator, who has just rebuffed an appeal for help from an eight-year-old girl on a rainy street, and who is now on the point of committing suicide himself. He dreams that, having done so, he is resurrected on a faraway planet, whose scenery is similar to Claude's Arcadian isle. The inhabitants of this terrestrial paradise are children of the sun, who live in ease and love as one happy family. It is the ridiculous man who corrupts them, who introduces lying, shame, crime, war, slavery—and science, which rationalizes the other evils and recapitulates man's unhappy history. No longer believing in the original happiness from which they have fallen, they make a religious cult of it, a dream within a dream. The narrator awakens resolving to find the little girl, and to preach redemption in the face of corruption.

A dream? What is a dream? Isn't our life a dream? I'll say more: suppose that this will never come to pass and there never will be a paradise—that at least I understand—even so I shall still preach. And in the mean while it is all so simple; in one day, *in one hour*, everything would be settled at once. The main thing is—love others as you love yourself—that is the main thing. And this is all, not a thing more is needed. Right away you will find out what to do.

Thus the golden age is summed up in the golden rule, not Tasso's but Christ's. Whether that consideration brings it any nearer to our day is a problematic matter, upon which Dostoevsky has given his comment in "The Legend of the Grand Inquisitor." Men talk and dream a good deal about happier days in the future; they visualize themselves running and chasing after a happy golden objective, poetized Schiller. The world grows old and again grows young, yet man always hopes for the amelioration of his lot.

> *Die Welt wird alt und wird wieder jung,*
> *Doch der Mensch hofft immer Verbesserung.*

Dreams of the future, unlike those of the past, can have a melioristic effect. The main perspective for man's achievements, between the Renaissance and the twentieth century, has been the idea of progress; and progress, in the maxim of Oscar Wilde, is the realization of utopias. Yet utopia, by definition, remains as remote as the golden age. "Arcadias are dreams of an imaginary past, and utopias are the intellectualized concepts of an idealized society," writes an eminent biologist, René Dubos. "Different as they appear to be, both imply a static view of the world which is incompatible with reality, for the human condition has always been to move on." We cannot say that we have not been moving. Having watched predictions for brave new worlds become old-fashioned and commonplace, having come within conceivable sight of the ominous year 1984, having seen utopian plans materialize as dystopias under totalitarian domination, many among us have been entertaining second thoughts. Ineluctably, as we grow older, we think more about what has passed, and are tempted to shake our heads over what is passing or to come. Some of those case-histories of head-shaking which we have been reviewing may serve a purpose, if they warn us against the pitfalls of chronolatry or *passéisme*; for it is debilitating to believe too rigidly, with Charles Péguy, that the modern world debases ("*le monde moderne avilit*").

Sigmund Freud's approach to the problems of modernity, in *Civilization and its Discontents*, was much broader and saner: "It seems to be certain that our present-day civilization does not inspire in us a feeling of well-being; but it is very difficult to form an opinion whether in earlier times people felt any happier and what part their cultural conditions played in the question." Happiness may not be the *summum bonum*, after all. History offers little to confirm the naive assumption that the greatest men have been the happiest. Eudemonism, when it is not a philosophic abstraction, may be only a regression toward childishness, a self-deluding and ungraspable goal which is forever receding. To learn to live with frustrations and disquietudes, to weather and sublimate them, to transform them on occasion into accomplishments, may well be a precondition of maturity. Historical knowledge, as opposed to poetic speculation, offers a corrective for our depressive fantasies about better days gone by. Though it may not elevate our total impression of human nature, it should help us to face the world, as the buoyant Lord Macaulay pointed out: "Those who compare the age on which their lot has fallen with a golden age which exists only in their imagination, may talk of degeneracy and decay: but no man who is correctly informed as to the past will be disposed to take a morose or desponding view of the present." If this seems too blandly Whiggish, it can be reformulated in the conservative phraseology of Edmund Burke's *Thoughts on the Course of the Present Discontents*:

> To complain of the age we live in, to murmur at the present possessors of power, to lament the past, to conceive extravagant hopes of the future, are the common dispositions of the greatest part of mankind; indeed the necessary effects of the ignorance and levity of the vulgar. Such complaints and humours have existed in all times; yet as all times have *not* been alike, true political sagacity manifests itself, in distinguishing that complaint which only characterizes the general infirmity of human nature, from those which are symptoms of the particular distemperature of our air and season.

The golden age is a mirage and a nuisance, for Friedrich Schlegel, "a modern disease, through which every nation must pass, like children through smallpox." Later nations, modelling their cultural style on the Roman adaptation of Hellenism, have prided themselves upon patronizing the Muses.

What happened under Augustus and Maecenas was a foretaste of sixteenth-century Italy. Louis XIV sought to impose the same springtime of the spirit upon France, while the English agreed to consider the taste of Queen Anne's period as the best, and henceforth no nation wanted to be without its golden age. Each successive one was more hollow and wretched than the preceding, and propriety of expression keeps me from characterizing more accurately what the Germans have conceived as golden.

We are confirmed in our historical relativism by the number of writers who have spoken of their own varying ages as the best, and by the questionable sincerity of many such testimonials. Abraham Cowley preferred a complacent ode "In Commemoration of the Time We Live in, under the reign of our Gracious King Charles II," wherein the poet compliments the sovereign on having attained the philosophers' stone and converted "The Iron Age of old / Into an Age of Gold." The Restoration was, at the very utmost, a silver age, as Dryden and others admitted. Can we take at face value, then, the litanies of praise that the Queen's own subjects bestowed on the age of Elizabeth? No, but we can respect them when they are reinforced by the later concurrence of disinterested judgments. The enthronement of the Elizabethan period in literary history was not acknowledged until 1764, when Bishop Hurd published his imaginary dialogues. Two of these are between a neo-classical Addison and a romantic-minded Dr. Arbuthnot. The latter holds that the most favorable time for the writing of poetry is one which combines an exuberance of fancy with the refinements of reason. Thomas Warton would concur with the premise and reach the same conclusion, when he styled the golden time of Elizabeth the most poetical age, in the path-breaking history of English poetry that he was to bring out in 1781. Rather more broadly, Hurd's spokesman contends: ". . . to express myself in the classical forms, you have seen by this view of their CONVIVIAL, GYMNASTICAL, and MUSICAL character, that the times of ELIZABETH may pass for golden, notwithstanding what a fondness for this age of baser metal may incline us to represent it."

Yet Hurd's Addison has other views; he is one of the arbiters of Queen Anne's Augustanism; and he is not the only dissident. In

Virginia Woolf's *Orlando* we are shown another fictitious literary portrait, that of a minor Elizabethan poet called Nick Greene, who can "say the finest things of books provided they were written three hundred years ago." Nowadays, he insistently believes, the art of poetry is dead in England. Splenetically and spitefully, he recalls an evening at a tavern, when Kit Marlowe was drunk enough to tell Shakespeare that they were all trembling on the verge of something big in English literature. "Poor foolish fellow," says Greene, "to go and say a thing like that. A great age, forsooth—the Elizabethan a great age!" The irony was not wasted on Mrs. Woolf's readers, many of whom were less than enthusiastic about the culture of the Nineteen-Twenties, which she herself did so much to adorn. Nick Greene, even if he had existed, would never have been among those who made his age great. True Elizabethans were not lacking who, with John Florio, deprecated their contemporaries and envied the classical ancients. "Oh golden age, when learnyng was sought for farre and neare: when wyt was exercised, and policie practised, and vertue honoured." So we are tempted to say in our turn, whenever we contemplate the Elizabethans. The truth is, as we may have been suspecting all along, that the golden age resides within us, like the kingdom of heaven, so far as we have any contact with either. If we believe, with Montaigne, that every man bears the whole pattern of the human condition within him, it is for us to choose between its weaknesses and its virtues.

[✿]

Appendices

[A]

PARADISES, HEAVENLY AND EARTHLY

THIS SUBJECT IS ONE for which I cannot profess to be qualified. So far as can be gathered, there does not seem to be much prospect that I shall ever come to know it at first hand. In fact it does not come, by definition, within the divinely specified limits of human observation. "Eye hath not seen, nor ear heard, neither have entered into the heart of man, the things which God hath prepared for them that love him," wrote the Apostle Paul to the Corinthians, echoing the prophecy of Isaiah. Yet where there is not a shred of evidence, there can be an endless amount of speculation. There exists a Shrovetide farce by Hans Sachs in which a wandering scholar tells a farmer's widow that he has recently been sojourning in Paris. The simple woman has never heard of the French metropolis; but she has heard a good deal about paradise, where she likes to think that her late husband abides; and she somehow confuses those two places, with a credulity which works out to the scholar's dishonest advantage. One could hold forth with more confidence about Paris, which has not the reputation of being such an ineffable locale or of having such Rhadamanthine entrance requirements. It is narrated that when Moses himself asked an angel about the nature of paradise, he was sternly warned that it was immeasurable, unfathomable, and innumerable. However, this injunction has not stayed the age-old effort to take its measure, fathom its range, and enumerate its attractions.

The flaming sword that guards the interdicted entrance continues to fascinate, as well as to put off, curiosity-seekers. The apocryphal Sir John Mandeville, whose fancies greatly outdistanced his famous travels, confessed: "Of paradys ne can I not speken propurly for I was not there; it is fer beyonde and that forthinketh me [I regret it]. And also I was not worthi. But as I have herd seye of wyse men beyonde, I schall telle you with gode will." And Mandeville went on, as so many others had done before and still others would do since, depending on hearsay, to describe the indescribable. Such descriptions, when we sort them out, testify with monotonous eloquence to the poverty of the human imagination, reminding us of the poor cockney dwarf in a novel by Dickens, who had been to the country once in his childhood and cherished a vague remembrance of a lot of grass and some swans. The radiance, the fragrance, the balmy climate, the spontaneous bounty, the twittering birds, all those lawns and terraces and fountains, those pavilions of so little else except crystal and jasper, that continual music in the background, the fruit so available and uniformly delicious that Eve grew fatally bored with it, the colorful verdure and kindly animals varying only with the flora and fauna known to the describer—there can hardly be another theme, among the universals of folklore, that has been sounded for so long and so widely with such a modicum of variation.

"If a man could pass through Paradise in a dream," mused the dreamy Coleridge in *Anima Poetae*, "and have a flower presented to him as a pledge that his soul had really been there, and if he found that flower in his hand when he awoke—Ay! and what then?" What then indeed? Perhaps our most appropriate answer to this rhetorical question, characteristically a self-interruption, would be to suggest that insofar as the floral memento was real, it would have been a poem. Mystics have presumably passed through paradise in their dreams, but their transport has not lent itself too palpably to verbal description, whereas the poets—fusing their private fantasies with racial memories—could bring that vision into the upper reaches of our experience. Therefore comparative literature rushes in where comparative religion fears to tread. The enraptured Elizabethans could sing, with Michael Drayton:

> *The poets paradice this is,*
> *To which but few can come;*
> *The muses onely bower of blisse*
> *Their deare Elizium.*

Yet, as these verses blithely hint, the initiation is rare. The poet who returns from it to tell his tale may envision himself, like Coleridge, as having drunk the milk of paradise. But since that particular rapture was actually stimulated by opium, it was what Baudelaire would call *un*

Appendix A

paradis artificiel, an expansion of consciousness promised today by those who experiment with psychedelic drugs. Moreover, Coleridge found himself unable to recapture his paradisiac dream of "Kubla Khan." His sunny pleasure-dome, his underground river, his incense-bearing trees, his caves of ice, though they will always tantalize our minds, are fragmentary glimpses of a realm that we shall never be enabled to visit.

All the more honor, then, to that greatest of poetic visionaries whose septicentennial we crossed a few years ago, and whose bust was then encircled with many garlands of scholarly asphodel! For, questionless, no dream vision has ever been so graphically rendered as Dante's; no single work of fiction has encompassed so vast a conception; no other dreamer, awakening from an immersion in the guiltiest anxieties and the most ecstatic hopes of mankind, has succeeded in framing them all within so architectonic a synthesis. Benedetto Croce, with an esthetic rigor which has proved to be untenable, tried to draw an oversharp distinction between the pure poetry and the didactic structure of *The Divine Comedy*. Happily, other critics have not pursued that endeavor to splinter its unique wholeness into fragments. Though it abounds in passages that could stand as poems by themselves or touches of detail that confer immediacy on seemingly distant matters, Dante's supreme imaginative achievement surely is to play the demiurge, the poet as maker who has made the framework of his poem coextensive with the cosmic system. Yet its very scale has hindered the common reader from appreciating its larger symmetries. He is likely to be more familiar with the excerpts that turn up in anthologies than with the context of supernal design. Setting out to accompany Dante, like Vergil, he may never get to paradise.

This propensity to fall by the wayside—or, at any rate, to linger in less exalted regions—is by no means limited to the faint-hearted, but represents a deep-seated aspect of the response to Dante, which his commentators and editors confirm. Thus the catalogue of the British Museum lists some five hundred titles under *Inferno*, as contrasted with a hundred and fifty under *Purgatorio* and about a hundred under *Paradiso*. Though there are fewer entries, the same discouraging proportions are roughly preserved in the Library of Congress, the Bibliothèque Nationale, and most other libraries. Thence a number of implications follow, least of all the naïve fact that more people start to read a big book than ever finish it. More profound is the hard-won wisdom of Vergil, who figures as Dante's guide because he has visited Hades in the *Aeneid* and has discovered that the way down is much easier than the way back: "*facilis descensus Averni*." The descending path seems also to be the more attractive, for those who do not take it personally as a matter of life and death. Hell and purgatory are more closely linked to the circumstances of mundane existence. "The greater part of those who have heretofore lived," Jonathan Edwards would preach, ". . . are now in hell." The threat of hellfire has been the main concern of Puritan sermons; Calvinism has stressed the damnation of sinners more than the salvation of the elect; and the repression of physical impulses, if less interesting, has seemed nobler than their indulgence.

Sin is more recognizable than grace, just as descent is less arduous than ascent. As in Plato's myth of Er, the soul, whatever the conditions of its journey through the afterlife, confronts the alternative of moving downwards or upwards. Heaven itself, as the homeland of souls, would scarcely be meaningful unless it were juxtaposed to the notion of hell— a complementary relationship which may have originated in Jung's collective unconscious, and which has been suggestively illustrated by Maud Bodkin's *Archetypal Patterns in Poetry* (London, 1934). The threat of infernal punishments, as it is invoked by the traditional doctrines of eschatology, seems to leave a stronger impression than the promise of heavenly rewards. Hell is regarded as matter, where heaven is pure form. One of Dante's most clear-headed critics, Francesco De Sanctis, commented upon the *Paradiso*: " Its adequate form is feeling, the eternal jubilation." Hence it cannot be too precisely described; the feeling is not merely subjective, it is supersensory; and the poet can best convey some sense of it, paradoxically, by dwelling upon the inadequacy of its means of expression. Its basic precondition, along with height, is light: "*prima luce, . . . pura luce, / luce intelletual, . . . somma luce, . . . luce eterna.*" Dante is dazzled, to the verge of blindness, again and again. This bedazzlement seems all the brighter in its contrast to the darkling air he has traversed. The general effect could be epitomized in a verse from the Scottish poet Sir David Lyndsay: "Evident brychtnes, but obscuritie."

Every culture harbors a longing of its own for a great good place, an island of the blest or happy valley, whose qualities are notable for their freedom from those ills to which that culture is ordinarily vulnerable. Consequently the concept of the next world flourishes most richly in situations that are by no means flourishing; conversely it tends to be played down where satisfaction is taken in the material things of this world. The *contemptus mundi* of the Middle Ages was the point of departure for a spectacular series of visions, such as the *Visio Pauli* or Saint Patrick's Purgatory, which Howard Rollin Patch has recounted in his fascinating survey, *The Other World according to Descriptions in*

Mediaeval Literature (Cambridge, Mass., 1950). An ascetic bleakness here below, in various religions of the East, seems to have promoted the most gorgeous expectations of the hereafter. In the United States it is the underprivileged Negro whose consolatory gospel has harped on the blessings stored up for him beyond the pearly gates. Our attempt to imagine heaven is bound to be an amelioration of the earth as we have experienced it. When—colloquializing a numinous phrase—we talk of being in the seventh heaven, we often mean no more than that we are indulging our vanity or satisfying our appetite. The voyager Maeldúin was greeted with good liquor when he explored the otherworldly isles. Possibly this was because he had set out from Ireland; yet we recollect that the Olympian gods prided themselves upon the ambrosia they served.

The fairylands of Celtic lore are far more imaginative than the Bauernhimmel, let us say, the peasants' heaven of Germanic popular tradition, which is single-minded in its devotion to creature comforts and riotous living. The daydream of another world becomes much earthier than our existing one when it takes the form of Schlaraffenland, or the Land of Cockaigne, as it has been pictured by Pieter Brueghel. There the cottage roofs are thatched with pies, the fences are composed of sausages, the streams overflow with wine, and little pigs already roasted—with knives and forks conveniently stuck into them—run about squealing: "Eat me! eat me!" Its denizens, who have eaten their way into it through a rice-pudding mountain, grossly snore unbraced and surfeited, the incarnations of sloth and gluttony. Its counterpart on the American scene would be the hobo's heaven, with its lakes of stew and whiskey too, and its Big Rock Candy Mountain. Here the idea of happiness is the removal of inhibitions ("All the cops have wooden legs"), as well as the gratification of the senses. A slightly more sophisticated tribute to the enjoyments of this unbuttoned *modus vivendi* is presented in a seventeenth-century English broadside ballad, "An Invitation to Lubberland":

> *There's nothing there but holy-days,*
> * with musick out of measure;*
> *Who can forbear to speak the praise*
> * of such a land of pleasure?*
> *There you may lead a lazy life,*
> * free from all kinds of labour,*
> *And he that is without a wife*
> * may borrow of his neighbor.*

Such heavens, from a more orthodox viewpoint, would obviously be hells. Yet they can be vehicles of religious ethics: the Middle English poem on the Land of Cockaigne is an ironic satire on the idleness, the luxury, and the lechery of the monastic establishments. And, though these all too anthropomorphic mock-heavens reduce the whole process to their own level of crude·burlesque, they remind us that man's heavenly ideals could not but be projected out of his earthly involvements. Indian huntsmen seek a happy hunting ground, Viking warriors a feast in Valhalla after the battle, Jews a family reunion in Abraham's bosom, and polygamous Moslems a dalliance attended by houris. Every man has his own self-centered definition of euphoria, and creates a heterocosm out of his unfulfilled desires.

But if there is a projection from the stuff of our daily lives to the image of a higher existence, there can likewise be a sublimation in the fullest sense of the term. Of this the shining exemplar is Dante's Beatrice, who began as an object of courtly poetizing and ends—prefiguring the Virgin Mary—as a principle of spiritual enlightenment. Even as she replaces Vergil in guiding Dante through his Paradiso, so an ethereal insight must transcend a mere corporeal perception. Significantly, the transition takes place in the Terrestrial Paradise; Dante rejoins his lost love, divinely transfigured though she be, in the very garden where Adam and Eve tasted forbidden fruit. Despite the refinement of Dante's symbolic overview, it still conceives the afterlife as an eternal prolongation of this life's happier moments, just as his Inferno transfixes its sinners in the unchanging postures of their sins. Differing views of the next world would emphasize its antitheses to this one, rather than its continuities. Many of Professor Patch's paradises cannot be described except by a string of negatives. The voyage of St. Brendan brings him to the Land of Promise, "where will be found health without sickness, pleasure without contention, union without quarrel," and so on. Felicity is the absence of such griefs as would seem to be man's usual lot, and Brendan's fabled land is a critique of what must have been a much grimmer actuality. Similarly, to praise the virtues of the Golden Age is to deplore the vices of subsequent ages, the deterioration of man and nature. One of the oldest Sumerian tablets celebrates the idyllic land of Dilmun, which is fabled to be free from sickness, old age, and death.

"Goodness is Heaven," said William Blake, abstracting the problem in accordance with his belief that all deities reside in the human breast. "Evil is Hell." If this disembodiment were heresy, it had been foreshadowed long before, when certain Fathers of the Church had propounded an allegorical interpretation. The Kingdom of God, if it was not of this world, must be within; paradise must then be a state of mind.

> *The mind is its own place, and in it self*
> *Can make a Heav'n of Hell, a Hell of Heav'n.*

But we ought not to repeat Milton's dictum without recalling that it is spoken by Satan, who has just failed to make a hell of heaven and who will now fail to make a heaven of hell. The mind may well be its own place, but Satan's mind is an anti-paradise: "Which way I flie is Hell; my self am Hell." Milton's predecessor, Hugo Grotius, in his play *Adamus exul*, allows his Satan to define heaven as the sole location of our hopes, with the corollary that anywhere else is a place of banishment for our ills:

> Quicquid est optabile
> Gratum in unum pariter adfluxit locum,
> Iusso exulare, quicquid est alibi, malo.

So long as goodness is opposed by evil, some men will go on believing in a literal heaven and hell. Emanuel Swedenborg, though qualified as an eighteenth-century scientist, claimed that his extraordinarily concrete account of both places had been dictated to him by an angel "from things heard and seen." Furthermore, he believed that humans could keep in touch with the celestial sphere through a network of correspondences. "In general," he had learned from his seraphic informant, "a garden corresponds to the intelligence and wisdom of heaven; and for that reason heaven is called the garden of God; and men call it the heavenly paradise." Swedenborg, in his metaphysical zeal, almost puts the signification ahead of the symbol. In the natural order, gardens come at the beginning, heavens loom at some distance, and—since the two conceptions have often coalesced—we must try to bear in mind the differentiation.

The parable of the garden is the *ur*-myth of mankind. Bacon recapitulated the original statement of Genesis when he opened his essay: "God Almightie first Planted a Garden." Voltaire, after extended philosophic inquiry, could make no better recommendation for happiness than the continuance of Adam's pursuit: to dress and keep, to cultivate, one's garden. Edgar Allan Poe, in one of his megalomaniac reveries, fancied himself playing God as a landscape gardener and rearranging the scenery of a large and luxuriant domain. The garden—perennial norm of Shakespearean values—is central to the human condition because it sustains a personal relation with the universe; it embraces man's adaptation to nature and nature's adaptation to man; it domesticates for him what would otherwise be an alien environment. Taking it for granted as we too readily do, we can barely surmise how much its shade and sustenance must have meant to nomadic tribes wandering through the sunbaked wastelands of the Middle East—all that Canaan, flowing with milk and honey, later meant to the Israelites in the wilderness, all that the land of Beulah would promise again, or Zion from the vantage point of Babylon. "By how much Adam exceeded all living men in perfection, by being the immediate workmanship of God," Sir Walter Ralegh would write in his magniloquent *Historie of the World,* "by so much did that chosen and particular garden exceed all parts of the universal world, in which God had planted . . . the trees of Life, of Knowledge; plants only proper, and becoming the Paradise and Garden of so great a Lord."

Ralegh devoted his third chapter, which cited Ovid and the pagan fabulists, to a question perennially moot, "Of the place of Paradise." Immemorially, the Garden of Eden had been the navel of the earth, the center of the cosmos, beyond the dawn; but where would that have been? Only one of its four rivers, the Euphrates, bore its modern name; the other three have been identified with the Tigris, the Ganges, and the Nile. Thence the speculative geographers shifted its locality to Asia or Africa or—as we shall be seeing—to the Americas, and beyond that to the North Pole, the stratosphere, or the moon. Those sites were "castles in the air" for Ralegh, who staunchly kept his feet on scriptural ground, and appended a map of Asia Minor to show that "eastward in Eden" designated the valley of the Euphrates. The second chapter of Genesis is the tersest of outlines; but it is greatly amplified in the hexaëmeral literature of the Creation; and it has been picturesquely filled in with the elaborate details of Talmudic literature, which Louis Ginzberg brought together in his monumental compilation, *The Legends of the Jews* (Philadelphia, 1909–1928). Undeterred by Mosaic warnings against enumeration, the Rabbis seem to have been fascinated by statistics, especially round numbers. They count eight hundred kinds of roses and myrtles, for instance, and sixty myriads of angels singing away in each corner of Eden. They report that the tree of life has fifteen thousand different tastes and perfumes, and that it would take five hundred years to cross an area equidistant to the diameter of the trunk of the tree of knowledge. The highest reward of the just is to sit under canopies and listen to God expounding the Torah.

Such is the nostalgic retrospect of a bookish people, far removed from their promised land or agrarian state. Adam and Eve, they surmised, had spent no more than six or seven hours in that garden. The key to the episode is that it was closed by the Fall; and so it remains the mythical prologue to history, the timeless preserve of an inaccessible perfection. "No one stays in Eden," James Baldwin has written in another connection. Yet everyone goes back to the ancestral sources in his own fashion, reenacting the myth of our common progenitor Seth, retracing the footsteps of our ultimate parents down a green path to their proscribed abode, yearning for the days when man lived in primordial innocence with the beasts and near to God, close to the tree of life and uncontaminated by the tree of knowledge. When the fable was allegorized by Saint Ambrose in his graphic treatise, *De Paradiso*, Eden stood for the soul; Adam symbolized the understanding and Eve the senses, with the serpent as delectation. This interpretation would seem to condemn the very meaning of Eden, which had its derivation from a Hebrew word for pleasure. The early Christian theologians were misogynists, who dated the loss of paradise not from the expulsion or the apple but from the creation of woman. Andrew Marvell would succinctly agree:

> *Such was that happy garden state,*
> *When man walked there without a mate . . .*
> *Two paradises 'twere in one*
> *To live in paradise alone.*

This would accord with Thoreau's cult of solitude at Walden, if not with Melville's "Paradise of Bachelors"—which he situated, not on Tahiti or the Marquesas, but in the convivial masculine society of the Temple at London. His friend Hawthorne, on the other hand, looked upon marriage as a renewal of Eden and highlighted his stories with paradisal imagery. And Omar Khayyám voiced his approval of *solitude à deux* by affirming that the presence of the beloved, along with a book, a jug, and a loaf, could turn a desert into an oasis: "Oh, Wilderness were Paradise enow!"

Eden as the precinct of sensuous delight, *hortus deliciarum*, could be only the most primitive version, the pastoral prefiguration of paradise. The latter word, deriving in Hebrew through the Greek from the Old Persian, is haloed with a distinctly Christian aura. Though it originally signified an orchard, park, or garden, its connotations have been vastly sublimated. The moment of transcendence could be marked by Luke's narrative of the crucifixion, when Jesus promises the good thief: "Today thou shalt be with me in paradise." Where the emphasis was mainly retrospective in the Old Testament, looking toward a lost heritage, it is prospective in the New Testament, looking toward a future dispensation. Meanwhile the location has been shifting skyward, so that Saint Paul can speak of being "caught up into paradise" and hearing "unspeakable words, which it is not lawful for a man to utter." Given the custom of burial, it has been the inherent tendency of many mythologies to set the habitat of the dead underground, in some sort of Sheol. But the tendency to look up to deity, to locate the gods in the skies, engendered a countermovement, leaving the souls of the damned in their underworld while translating those of the blessed to the heavens. The deep concern of the Prophets for redemption, adumbrated when the second Isaiah foretold of new heavens and a new earth, was elaborated into a chiliastic spectacle by the Revelation of St. John, with its background of early Christian persecution and its mystagogic portents of the Millennium and the Last Judgment.

The Biblical story commences in a garden and concludes in a city. The culmination of John's apocalypse, the panorama of New Jerusalem aglitter with precious stones and resounding with harps, arises in sublime compensation for Sodom or Babylon. Saint Augustine will unfold an analogous tale of two cities: *civitas dei*, the holy city of the Catholic Church, and *civitas terrena*, the worldly corruption of the Roman Empire. When heaven is visualized as an extramundane metropolis, it reflects an urban civilization; but it may also be a reaction from an all too fleshly city toward the imaginary garden again. Here the religious nostalgia is reinforced by the literary conventions of pastoralism. Ernst Robert Curtius has shown how the medieval Latin poets repeatedly depicted the same ideal landscape, the *locus amoenus* or pleasance. Tertullian, speaking of paradise as a place of divine pleasantness (*"divinae amoenitatis"*), likened it to the Elysian Fields. Vergil's classic depiction of them, like Ovid's reverberating description of the golden age, furnished the words and images for many poems on Eden. Some of those have been collected by Arturo Graf in the appendix to his monographic study, *La Leggenda del Paradiso Terrestre* (Rome, 1892). "There is a certain place . . . (*Est locus . . .*)," they typically begin, and go on to specify its negative amenities: no chill nor blaze, no crime nor sickness, *et cetera*. Such is the hallowed spot from which the Phoenix takes its flight, in Latin verse and Anglo-Saxon paraphrase, to emerge as a symbol of resurrection.

It is characteristic of Dante, who found a place within his field of vision for everything, that his poem should comprehend both past and future. The past becomes the present through his encounters and recognition scenes, his dialogues with his *dramatis personae*, and the monologues of his mythical, legendary, and historical characters. The present becomes the future through the grandiose scheme of his work, his dramatization of Christian eschatology, the afterworld where justice is unsparing to those popes and emperors who have abused it. We can recognize elements of personal retribution in the attitudes of this spiritual pilgrim who likewise happened to be a political exile. The city from which he was banished reappears, just as it does in Florentine paintings of the Holy Land, where the architecture looks Italian and the cherubim have Tuscan faces. His claims to truth must be reaffirmed at the levels of allegory, since his supernatural journey is literally fictitious, as it were a pseudo-apocalypse; yet his shrewd and poignant insights lend bodily substance to what, at other hands, might have become a sequence of weightless excursions in outer space. In the twenty-eighth canto of the *Purgatorio*, mingling the canonical traditions with bold touches of his own, he reveals the Terrestrial Paradise at the summit of the purgatorial mountain. Matelda, the tutelary spirit who welcomes the poet to this "nest of mankind," explains that it was first given by God to man as "a pledge of eternal peace"—a foretaste of the Celestial Paradise. It is explained in the *De monarchia* that the former typifies earthly happiness, to be attained through moral teaching, while the latter stands for eternal happiness, to be sought through religious teaching.

The peace that Dante will not know on earth, he makes clear in his rendering of the Lord's Prayer, will be assured to us by the coming of God's kingdom. The identity of man's peace with God's will is definitively enunciated by Piccarda Donati, when Dante encounters her not far beyond the threshold of heaven: "*e la sua volontate è nostra pace.*" It is her contentment with her modest station in the moon's sphere that helps him to realize "how everywhere in heaven is paradise (*com' ogni dove / in cielo è Paradiso*)." In equating paradise with the firmament, he has been guided by the astronomical knowledge of his day, and Beatrice delivers an informative lecture explaining the spots on the moon. The Ptolemaic universe, with its nine concentric spheres —the moon, the planets, the sun, the fixed stars, the *primum mobile*, and finally the empyrean provides a cosmological equivalent for the concave circles of hell or the convex stages of purgatory. As the soul moves upward, propelled by light, the setting is less visibly picturesque than the sublunary perspectives; the personages are more and more luminously depersonalized. But "the general form of paradise (*la forma generaldi Paradiso*)," though elusive, is not wholly inexpressible. It is expressed by the very magnitude of the spatial arrangements. Processions and pageants wind their way across Dante's path, singing hymns and celebrating festivals; while the white rose, emblematic, sempiternal, and multifoliate, turns out to be a prodigious kind of grandstand, with seats reserved for the hierarchy of doctors and saints and all who will have been redeemed at the grand finale.

It is this happiest of conceivable endings that justifies the title of *Commedia*. So far as suspense goes, the drama is virtually over by the time we reach the *Paradiso*, and what happens there is predominantly cast in the lyrical mode. The *Inferno* is epical but static, because its issues have been settled for all time. Paolo and Francesca are bound together for a bittersweet eternity, Ugolino can never do more than gnaw upon the skull of his worst enemy, and Satan—no longer walking up and down the earth—is immobilized in a pit of ice. The *Purgatorio* is the dramatic phase where the outcomes are still being decided, where the spectator Dante becomes an actor and threads his way among the other penitents. But if the *Paradiso* resolves the tensions, it vibrates to its planetary gyrations in a perpetual dance; the choreographic movement of the angels is harmonized with the music of the spheres. After Saint Bernard's prayer on behalf of Dante, he completes his pilgrimage with a climactic vision which surpasses our power of speech: "*il mio veder fu maggio / che il parlar nostro.*" The fulgurations are too blinding for us to witness the recognition scene, when he beholds the triune face of God. This reunion with the Unmoved Mover brings the poem, in the extra line completing its last tercet, to an acknowledgment of its motivating force: "the love that moves the sun and the other stars (*l'amor che muove il sole e l'altre stelle*)." The poet's soul, caught up in that cyclic motion, will revolve with it forever.

It would be hard to imagine a consummation more remote from the oriental Nirvana, where the reincarnate souls ascend through a long plurality of successive paradises to that final beatitude which can be nothing but oblivion. Fully to understand Dante's afterworld would be, in his own metaphor, squaring the circle. Milton, perhaps because he was so well aware of Galileo's new astronomy while continuing to make a stage design out of Ptolemy's geocentric cosmology, is even more explicit in putting us off. His Raphael is quite elliptical in describing the hierarchs, as they surround the Almighty's throne with ten thousand ensigns:

> "*in Orbes
> Of circuit inexpressible they stood,
> Orb within orb, the Father infinite.*"

The Great Architect, so the affable archangel cautions Adam, may laugh at man's ambitious calculations and scientific conjectures:

Appendix A

"how gird the Sphear
With Centric and Eccentric scribl'd o're,
Cycle and Epicycle, Orb in Orb."

Milton's direct approach to the court of heaven is introduced by the refulgent invocation to light that prefaces his Third Book. The identification of God Himself with light gathers its special poignance from the realization that the visionary is blind. Small wonder if the phenomena that he contemplates seem to be less visible than Dante's contemplations. Wisely Milton dwells upon their inwardness: Satan carries "within him Hell," and the Archangel Michael leaves Adam and Eve with the comforting prediction of "A Paradise within thee, happier farr." Actually we hear more—indeed we see more—of hell than of the heavens in *Paradise Lost*. The realm of darkness is conceived as a parody of the fields of light, presented at the outset in chiaroscuro and monumentally reconstructed in Pandemonium. The heavenly episodes that we best remember are the battle scenes, "Warring in Heav'n against Heav'n's matchless King," where the Son is armed in "Celestial Panoplie" and the "dev'lish machination" of the Adversary leads to the invention of gunpowder. Without accusing Milton of taking the devil's side, we could agree with Blake that he had more liberty to deal with the rebellious infernal forces. Most of Milton's readers are more at ease with the diabolic, we must admit, than with what Allen Tate has called "the angelic imagination."

To be "lowlie wise," to "Dream not of other Worlds," is Raphael's advice to Adam and Eve. "Heav'n is for thee too high." They have every reason to be content with their "delicious Paradise" on earth. The poet ransacks Greco-Roman fable for comparisons to embellish the topography of their garden and to set the "Silvan Scene" in the "woody theatre" of their tragedy. The charms of nature itself, orchestrating the Fall with a sigh of universal sympathy, have never been set forth with greater artifice. "Properly speaking," Milton declares in a parenthesis of *De doctrina christiana*, "Paradise is not heaven." With some consistency he maintains the distinction throughout his works, reserving the term for the Terrestrial Paradise, which in some ways he seems to favor over the celestial heaven—a preference consistent with his Mortalism, his reluctance to consider the soul apart from the body. "O Earth, how like to Heav'n, if not preferr'd / More justly. . . !" Satan exclaims. He is an untrustworthy spokesman, to be sure, and the Son—inevitably—prefers his Father's kingdom to those of this world in the sequel. Yet if amends are made with *Paradise Regained*, and Christ resists the temptation to which Adam has yielded, the consequence will again be "*Eden* raised in the wast Wilderness." The concluding anthem of the angels can promise: "A fairer Paradise is founded now / For *Adam* and his chosen sons." But that cannot be other than the internal paradise foreseen by Michael, when he predicts a happier day for the couple departing from Eden.

If *Paradise Regained*, by virtue of its happy ending, is a comedy in the Dantesque sense, then *Paradise Lost*, with its double fall, is the tragedy of tragedies. As opposed to the trinitarian symbolism of Dante's progression through the three well-ordered Catholic afterworlds, the absence of Purgatory from the Protestant outlook intensifies the polar opposition between heaven and hell, which are in dynamic conflict through both of Milton's epics. If he individualizes where Dante systematized, it is because iconoclasm has meanwhile been challenging dogma. The *Divina Commedia* could be read as a guidebook which would help believers to advance from wretchedness to a state of blessedness, as it is suggested in the epistle dedicating the *Paradiso* to Can Grande della Scala. The Miltonic goal is theodicy, a justification of God's ways to man, but its moralistic purpose is tempered by the esthetic canons of classical art. John Bunyan could offer guidance to striving Christians on the evangelical plane of a popular handbook telling them what they should, or should not, do to be saved: *The Pilgrim's Progress from This World to That Which Is to Come*. The practical and plainspoken manner of Bunyan's allegory seems to be more effective along the road and across an English-looking countryside, where pitfalls are pointed out, than at the terminus, a conventionally gilded evocation of the Celestial City. In his satirical tale, "The Celestial Railroad," modernizing the theology as well as the technology, Hawthorne could reverse the direction and send his pilgrims on a grand tour to hell.

The allegorical purport of *The Faerie Queene* is ethical rather than theological. As an idealized picture of Elizabethan England, blending various myths and supernatural motifs into its idealization of nature, Spenser's Fairyland lies well out of this world yet not quite in the next. Its fabulous terrain is fertile soil for earthly paradises, such as the Garden of Adonis glimpsed in Book III, where the fair Amoret has been "trained up in true feminitee," tenderly nurtured amid the haunts of pagan voluptuousness. In Book II it is the Bower of Bliss, where Sir Guyon, the champion of temperance, climaxes his adventures by dauntlessly resisting and putting down the blandishments of the temptress Acrasia. The sensuous beauty of this "daintie Paradise" is invidiously compared with many a Greek prototype—to which Spenser adds, with a touch of puritanic compunction, "Or *Eden* selfe, if ought with Eden mote compare." Elsewhere, in one of his *Amoretti*, the not quite attainable bosom of the poet's beloved is termed "the bower of blisse, the paradice of pleasure." Paradise, traditionally associated with carnal temptation, thus presents a demoralizing ambush of forbidden delights to the virtuous knights of Spenser and his predecessors in Christian heroic romance, Ariosto and Tasso. Those notorious gardens of their respective enchantresses—where Ruggiero is seduced by Alcina in the *Orlando furioso*, or where Rinaldo dallies with Armida in the *Gerusalemme liberata*—are decadent and illusory versions of Eden, Ariosto's "birthplace of love."

Such enchantments, though malign, are accepted as truly magical. We hear reports of other snares and delusions which, while pretending to the miraculous, were contrived by perverse human ingenuity. Mandeville has an anecdote about a certain rich man, living on the eastern Isle of Mistorak, who redecorated his castle and grounds in that paradisal style to which we have by now become accustomed: precious stones, plashing wines, musical accompaniments, delicacies served by damsels and striplings dressed in cloth of gold to simulate angels. The subtle deceit, as Mandeville phrases it, was to befuddle the knightly visitors into laying down their lives for their host, in the belief that they would be thereby entitled to spend an eternal life on his premises. This might serve as a cautionary example of a fool's paradise. Those who were disinclined to be taken in might become wary, not merely of their over-enterprising fellow men, but of institutions and doctrines which put off the fulfillment of their glittering promises until after death or else protracted it into an endless future. Was immortality to be taken for granted, or was it an illusion? What did men know about heaven, after all, they asked themselves in their Enlightenment? An article in the *Encyclopédie* pointed out that the notion of a paradise in the sky had been rendered obsolete by modern astronomers; if *le paradis* existed, it was "not a place but a change of state." As for the Millennium, it supplied an occasion for some of Gibbon's most withering ironies:

> So pleasing was this hope to the mind of believers, that the *New Jerusalem*, the seat of this blissful kingdom, was quickly adorned with all the gayest colours of the imagination. A felicity consisting only of pure and spiritual pleasure would have appeared too refined for its inhabitants, who were still supposed to possess their human nature and senses. A garden of Eden, with the amusements of the pastoral life, was not suited to the advanced state of society which prevailed under the Roman empire. A city was therefore erected of gold and precious stones, and a supernatural plenty

of corn and wine was bestowed on the adjacent territory; in the free enjoyment of whose spontaneous productions, the happy and benevolent
people was never to be restrained by any jealous laws of exclusive
property.

Gibbon's periods are far more elegant than the revivalistic strains of
"The Sweet Bye and Bye," but the same note of skeptical reservation
can be heard in Joe Hill's burlesque: "You'll get pie in the sky when
you die." Stated more positively, the implication was a socialistic demand
for more pie on earth—or, as Heinrich Heine sang, for roses and myrtles,
beauty and happiness, yes, and green peas for everybody, leaving the
heavens to the angels and sparrows.

> *Ja, Zuckererbsen für jedermann,*
> *Sobald die Schoten platzen!*
> *Den Himmel überlassen wir*
> *Den Engeln und den Spatzen.*

We deflect our gaze from the welkin, then, to the garden once more.
Some of the learned authorities speculated that the Terrestrial Paradise
had been washed away by the Flood; others argued that it had survived
because of its position on a mountain-top. Enoch and Elijah still lived
there, it was believed, having been translated bodily; and Alexander
the Great had vainly tried to storm the verdant summit. Travelers' tales
connected the territory with the mysterious land of Prester John. One of
Columbus' favorite books, the *Ymago mundi* of Pierre d'Ailly, gave
it a standing in fifteenth-century geography and summed it up in a
reminiscent phrase as "*locus amoenissimus.*" Hence Columbus came to
feel that he had all but rediscovered it during his third expedition in
1498. He assumed that it was in the Orient, of course, as he assumed
that he was: "in the ocean sea at the end of the East." The actual spot
that he seems to have had in mind was somewhere near the peninsula
of Paria, at the mouth of the Orinoco River, in what would soon be
named the Spanish Main. Believing that fateful tract could not be entered without God's permission, he did not investigate further; but in an
eloquent letter to his royal patrons, Ferdinand and Isabella, he marshaled
the observations and precedents in favor of this conclusion. He was now
of the opinion that the earth was pear-shaped rather than round, that
the newly discovered hemisphere was shaped like a woman's breast, and
that the Earthly Paradise was located at a high point corresponding to
the nipple.

Samuel Eliot Morison, in his compelling biography, *Admiral of the
Ocean Sea* (Boston, 1942), explains how Columbus might have arrived

at such a theory by miscalculating his altitudes. Yet there may have been a deeper impulsion at work—not unrelated to that primal urge which prompted Edmund Spenser to describe his lady's breasts as a bower of bliss—so that Columbus, seeking the aboriginal site of human generation, would nostalgically envisage it as a maternal archetype. At all events, it inspired Bishop Las Casas, the sixteenth-century chronicler of the Indies, to an erudite digression authenticating the Earthly Paradise and distinguishing it from pagan superstitions about the Elysian Fields. Later voyagers, notably Amerigo Vespucci, would localize it southward; Richard Hakluyt, in his chronicles of the English navigations, would place it south of the equinoctial line (Drayton, in his ode addressed to Hakluyt, hailed Virginia as "Earth's onely paradise"). Its role in the discovery and colonization of Brazil has been canvassed by Sérgio Buarque de Holanda in *Visão do Paraíso* (Rio de Janeiro, 1959), while its influence upon the relations between Europe and the United States has been studied by Charles L. Sanford in *Quest for Paradise* (Urbana, 1961). With the economic development of the Americas, Eldorado must have seemed a more pertinent image than Eden, and the search for the noble savage had to be pushed ever westward to the South Sea isles. With the decolonization of postwar years and the emergence of underdeveloped nations, the horizons of primitivistic escape have been closing in upon us. The impact of these changes on the Western conscience and consciousness has been registered lately by Henri Baudet in a far-seeing little treatise (New York, 1965), entitled—what else but *Paradise on Earth?*

Eden is always set far apart from civilization in space or time. There was a time—already past for Shakespeare's John of Gaunt—when England could be hailed as "This other Eden, demi-paradise." But that green world had totally receded by the epoch of the Industrial Revolution, and Blake's prophetic writings form a program for messianic revival: to abolish "the dark Satanic mills" and to build a New Jerusalem "In England's green and pleasant land." Englishmen impatient for that advent might cross the Atlantic. Among the colonists, William Byrd of Westover sought "the Land of Eden" in the Virginian backwoods, just as Thomas Morton of Merrymount sought a "New Canaan" on Massachusetts Bay. Among the emigrants, Martin Chuzzlewit is lured by a prospectus for the Eden Land Corporation on the banks of the Missouri River; but the "flourishing city" advertised by promoters is as yet no more than a "hideous swamp"; and Dickens' young surveyor, after having nearly succumbed to its fevers, returns to the Old World a poorer and wiser man. The American record is full of other Edens raised in the wilderness with greater success, demi-paradises brought up to date with all the latest conveniences of Utopia. The Edenic impulse, however, has been at odds with the Utopian impetus. Reviewing a book by a German technocrat, J. A. Etzler, *The Paradise within Reach of All Men*, Thoreau sharply recoiled from its campaign for salvation by labor-saving devices:

> Thus is Paradise to be Regained, and that old and stern decree at length reversed. Man shall no more earn his living by the sweat of his brow. All labor shall be reduced to "a short turn of some crank," and "taking the finished articles away." But there is a crank,—oh, how hard to be turned! Could there not be a crank upon a crank—an infinitely small crank?—we would fain inquire. No, alas! not. But there is a certain dim energy in every man, but sparingly employed as yet, which may be called the crank within, quite indispensable to all work. Would that we might get our hands on its handle! In fact, no work can be shirked. It may be postponed indefinitely, but not infinitely. Nor can any really important work be made easier by coöperation or machinery.

This would seem to be one of those situations where Thoreau stands alone, where the railroad has rushed by Walden Pond, where the crank within has unfortunately been superseded by the push-button without. "Of course," Thoreau was to jot in his journal, "we do not expect that our paradise will be a garden." His daily life in the woods or on the pond or at the bean-field was more like the hard-working routine of Adam after the Fall. Nor would he have wanted to be exempt from the after-effect of Original Sin upon nature: "the penalty of Adam," as Shakespeare put it, "The seasons' difference." Spring had been eternal before the Fall. Now, after the summer birds, the autumn colors, the winter snows, Thoreau noted in *Walden*: "As every season seems best to us in its turn, so the coming in of spring is like the creation of Cosmos out of Chaos and the realization of the Golden Age."

It may be that so exceptional a personality could succeed in internalizing his individual paradise. Wordsworth, in a fragment of *The Recluse*, held that anyone could do so under the proper conditions and that such perceptions could be externalized:

> Paradise, and groves
> *Elysian, Fortunate Fields—like those of old*
> *Sought in the Atlantic Main—why should they be*
> *A history only of departed things,*
> *Or a mere fiction of what never was?*
> *For the discerning intellect of Man,*

When wedded to this goodly universe
In love and holy passion, shall find these
A simple produce of the common day.

But this is too abrupt a come-down from the unattainable to the commonplace. Paradise would soon lose its luster, for most of us, if it were so accessibly near at hand. It is the impossibility of their quest that makes heroes out of William Morris' wayfarers in *The Earthly Paradise*. The realization of the unrealizable ideal must forever be projected into the future, just as the sense of retrospective felicity is all the more felicitous because it resides in the past. The truest paradises, lamented Marcel Proust, are those that we have lost (*"car les vrais paradis sont les paradis qu'on a perdus"*). His innocent childhood hours in those Parisian gardens so incongruously known as the Champs Elysées, like the special heaven that lay about Wordsworth in his infancy, were perfect because they were irretrievable except through the nostalgic illuminations of art—the only other world with which Proust ultimately reckoned. Only the artist has the privilege of seeing his personal vision of perfection take tangible form. Hence Poe remarked of Claude Lorrain: "No such paradises are to be found in reality as have glowed on the canvas of Claude."

André Malraux recalls an exchange with Yehudi Menuhin over the question: "What does music most constantly convey to you?" M. Malraux's reply was the single word, "Nostalgia," which he has recently glossed for us with the comment: "The great music of Europe is the song of Paradise Lost." As an esthetician who is both a modernist and—so it turns out—a traditionalist, M. Malraux would discern the most potent meaning in the evocation of cultural inheritance at a wordless and idealized remove. The moralists, regarding the loss of Eden as a fortunate lapse, *felix culpa*, could look ahead to man's destiny rather than back toward his origins, in the pious hope that paradise could be regained by his moral exertions, together with divine grace. His unwillingness to accept his mortality, along with his desire to participate more actively in the mysteries of existence, to know the unknown, not to say the unknowable, found encouragement among the theologians. Happiness is always in the past or in the future, Schopenhauer has observed, while the present is always cloudy. To which we might subjoin a remark of the Rumanian essayist, E. M. Cioran, that all paradisical visions take place in a static world, in a time that is out of time, an everlasting spring or unending youth. Nonetheless they have animated the history of the only world we know with any certainty, luring Columbus on toward a mirage of repose on the very bosom of Mother Earth and mitigating Dante's troubled dreams with intimations of continual love and eternal peace.

[B]

SOME PARADOXES OF UTOPIA

YOU REMEMBER Shakespeare's Gonzalo, the merry old councillor in *The Tempest*, who wanted to be king of the island so that he could abolish monarchy. Cynical companions pointed out his political inconsistency: "The latter end of his commonwealth forgets the beginning." This is the dilemma of authority, which either keeps ideal commonwealths from coming into existence or else keeps existing commonwealths from ever becoming ideal. The best regimes have traced their institutions back, through the convenient obscurity of the legendary past, to some wise lawgiver: Sparta to Lycurgus, Athens to Solon, and Thomas More's Utopia to a certain King Utopus. The scientific program of the New Atlantis is credited by Bacon to the foresight of another ancient king, Salomona. The hypothetical constitution of James Harrington's *Oceana*, which influenced our American founding fathers, is said to have been framed by a single man. History is more complicated in this respect, as in others. The faltering statesmanship of Plato at Syracuse stands in unhappy contrast to *The Republic*. The hesitations posed by More, upon entering the royal service, found their grimly ironic confirmation in the martyrdom that crowned his public career. The world of his travails is better described by his contemporary, Machiavelli, in *The Prince*.

Yet the critique of actual conditions, in the first book of the *Utopia*, counterweights the meliorating vision of the second. Ideology as Karl Mannheim defined it, an implicit belief in the *status quo*, has continually been challenged by utopianism, which in turn has generated mythical beliefs. These have been portents, if not guides to action—"premature truths," in the phrase of Lamartine. "Progress," according to Oscar Wilde in one of his serious moods, "is the realization of utopias." Nonetheless those myths became such bywords for impossibility that Marx and Engels drew a sharp line between Utopian Socialism, which they dismissed as impractical, and their own kind of socialism, which they termed Scientific. They were utopians, in spite of themselves; for, in the progress of the socialist movement, the elements of idealism and pragmatism have been too intermixed to justify so clear-cut a distinction. The central problem has been Gonzalo's paradox: in order to redistribute power, one must first possess it; and those who have possessed and tasted it, whether by more traditional means or by revolution, have proved notoriously reluctant to give it up. The present is always imperfect, while the future may be envisioned as perfect since it is unattainable by definition.

We can never attain the future because of the fact that it turns into the present just as soon as we reach it. However, we can influence the shape of things to come by our attitudes and expectations. More showed his acute awareness of the contradictions inherent in his theme when he coined the name "Utopia," punning on "Eutopia" and implying that the good place was nowhere. This and the innumerable other model societies, to which he had thereby given a label, have all been small in scale and isolated from the rest of the world. Our limited access to them has been through the fictive adventures of an eager traveller not unlike ourselves, who is generally taken in hand by a sage and persuasive native. Dialogue can be a tricky genre, as Plato demonstrated when he rigged his arguments for Socrates, and our visitor is apt to be converted at the outcome of his conducted tour. All of his objections will have been conclusively answered; all of the exhibits and experiences will have worked *ex hypothesi*. Since we are dealing with fiction, we cannot submit its hypotheses to any empirical test. The author has it his way for the obvious reason that he is the author. With Edward Bellamy, he pronounces his own magic: "Abracadabra, the conquering word."

Every man is entitled to conceive, as so many have done, as Robert Burton did, "a utopia of mine own." Such a speculation could not but mirror the concerns of each particular utopist. Witness the heretical priest, Tommaso Campanella, and the rationalistic innovations embodied in his City of the Sun. Often the utopian reflection is the opposite of a burdensome actuality: for example, More, the dedicated lawyer, allowed no lawyers in his personal realm. Some of its other aspects seem to express his character more directly—the ascetic character of a man who spent four years in a Carthusian monastery and wore a hair-shirt under his Tudor garments. The garments of his Utopians are monastic, uniform and colorless. Their meals are served in refectories, and their daily lives are regulated by an exacting self-discipline. The same geometrical spirit seems to pervade the domestic arrangements and the ground rules of the other utopias. They also tend to be located on rectangular islands or perhaps surrrounded by cone-shaped mountains; their cities are laid out in parallelograms; and the net esthetic effect is that of symmetrical monotony. Individuals are regimented and human reactions standardized, while the social structure is bureaucratized to a military extent.

Or so it well might seem to the disengaged bystander. That the non-conformist, a potential Thoreau, could extend his experiment in living to the point where it presses conformity upon others—this is the situation confronted by B. F. Skinner in *Walden II*. The paradoxical aim of most utopists is the organization of anarchy. But any scheme is bound to look schematic, however humane its intention; every plan for collective activity must begin on the two-dimensional plane of a blueprint. Reformers, most of them peacefully inclined, have a habit of thinking in militaristic analogies. Fourier chose the phalanx for his communal unit, and Bellamy proposed to recognize society by recruiting it into an industrial army. We need not be alarmed at such well-meaning efforts to beat swords into plowshares. Yet, given the opportunity to play the demiurge and dream up brave new worlds, we may be somewhat disappointed by the lack of variety or imagination in these self-repeating designs. On the other hand, we should be impressed by the very sameness of their professed objectives, the consistency with which they address themselves to recurrent problems. If their untried programs seem unduly abstract, the ills they seek to cure remain all too concrete.

A comparative study of these unrealized projects, which we may call utopiology, would tell us much about the cultures and periods that engendered them. It would form a critical commentary upon the administration of justice, the ownership of land, production and exchange, employment and leisure, the relationship of the sexes, the education of children, religion and science and art. It would have little to relate about foreign policy or international traffic, since utopias lie outside the bounds of diplomatic recognition. The most persistent issue would involve the holding of property. One of Robert Owen's followers from his colony at Yellow Springs, Ohio, testifies that the British industrialist discerned the root of all evil "in the laws of *meum* and *tuum*," believing "that a state of society where there is nothing *mine* or *thine* would be a paradise begun." The utopian line of thought that runs unbroken, from primitive Christianity to Soviet Communism, is the principle that men should own all things in common. Of almost equal persistence is the patriarchal image of the utopians as one happy family: "the enlargement of home—the extension of family union beyond the little man-and-wife circle to large corporations," in the words of John Humphrey

Noyes, the founder and virtually the only begetter of the Oneida Community.

As a way of living, this has both the advantages and the limitations of tribalism or parochialism. If it coexisted among the nations, it would be rather less of a pilot project than a nostalgic retreat. Today it could be no larger or more self-sufficient than, let us say, Andorra or Luxembourg. Utopia, as a historical manifestation, has been the expression of certain times rather than others. To the Middle Ages, with their feudal hierarchies and their ultimate trust in an otherworldly City of God, it would have been inconceivable. In its secular quest for the good life, it is the product of Renaissance humanism, abetted by a few classical recollections, and responsive to the aspirations of the succeeding centuries toward democracy, enlightenment, and humanitarianism. More than a response, it has been a herald for such modern issues as the status of women. It has been experimental, as well as libertarian, in its approach to the question of sex and marriage. Already Campanella, in the seventeenth century, had pioneering notions about eugenics. Noyes, in the nineteenth, evolved a drastic system of controls over procreation. The Shakers, pledged to a semi-monastic cult of celibacy, eliminated their chances of survival by sublimating their sexual impulses in ecstatic dances.

America, the land of Europe's futurity, provided a fertile soil for the largest number of earnest endeavors to put utopian theory into practice. Some of the original colonies, insofar as they deliberately broke with old-world traditions, could be viewed in that light. Coleridge and Southey, in their youthful radicalism, hoped to establish a Pantisocracy —or rule of all—with a settlement on the banks of the Susquehanna, combining "the innocence of the Patriarchal Age with the refinements of European culture." Though they did not get across the Atlantic, others did who were scarcely less visionary. Etienne Cabet, after having written his popular romance about an imaginary journey to Icaria, sponsored a series of little Icarias in various parts of the country. Fanny Wright, the freethinking Scottish feminist, sought to incorporate a haven for Negro emancipation into her progressive community at Nashoba, Tennessee. Fourierism, a major influence on American intellectuals of the Golden Day, set up its main phalanstery at Red Bank, New Jersey, and took over the Transcendentalist enclave at Brook Farm. The early days of the latter were etched in acid by *The Blithedale Romance*. Hawthorne, who had briefly participated, exposed that demon of individualism which sooner or later ensnared the hopes for socialism.

Sooner, in most cases, rather than later. Few of these communities managed to survive for much more than a decade, while remaining true to the tenets of their initial compact. Those that lasted longer, and continued to flourish, were held together by a religious commitment—"the earnest kind," Noyes added in his *History of American Socialisms* (Philadelphia, 1870), "which comes by recognized afflatus, and controls all external arrangements." Thus the Rappites, the pious Lutheran wine-growers who founded New Harmony on the banks of the Wabash, stayed there for twelve years and then moved on to further prosperity elsewhere. Their Indiana village was bought out by Robert Owen, whose philanthropic undertaking was science-oriented. The Owenites banished religion along with alcohol, but within two years they had abandoned the principles of their patron. Capitalism re-emerged in the shape of a distillery, and gradually the churches were reactivated. Similarly at Nauvoo, Illinois, the Mormons were succeeded by the Icarians, who splintered into increasingly fractious sub-groups, while the Latter-day Saints proceeded westward to consolidate the zeal of their sect. It is not the least of the paradoxes before us that the quest for a more rational *modus vivendi* should have gone astray or been given up, except when it has been animated and accompanied by the special devotion of a *mystique*.

This would lend its force to the revival of an ancient creed, as with Zionism, or to what Bellamy called "the religion of solidarity," as it is currently practised in the Soviet Union. The element of utopianism in both instances, though it finds a last resort in the *kibbutz* or the *kolkhoz*, is hard pressed by the encroachments of nationalism. Meanwhile the development of machinery has been propelling utopian thought toward the sphere of science-fiction. Bellamy's contribution lay not so much in his fictitious inventions—which adumbrated the radio, the credit-card, and other mixed blessings—as in his nationalization of them to solve the crises of his time: strikes, trusts, and panics of the Eighteen-Eighties. His complete acceptance of urbanization, which has been so explicit a feature of most utopias, prompted the criticism of William Morris, whose *News from Nowhere* harks back to the medieval past and toward a reforestation of the pastoral. Samuel Butler, too, had been an intellectual Luddite; the key to the happiness of his Erewhonians was their decision to sabotage their machines, rejecting industrialism and returning to nature. But *Erewhon*, as its inverted title indicates, not to mention its setting in the Antipodes, is basically a utopia upside down, a dystopia.

Utopia has always mingled satire against things as they are with its fantasy about things as they might be. Its transformation into dystopia happened almost imperceptibly on its progression from the nineteenth into the twentieth century. The precipitating factor was technology, which appeared so opportune in prospect, but which seems more ominous once it has taken command. During the last two or three generations, as the literary models have been brought up to date, they have seemed decreasingly attractive. This reversal can be dated somewhere between the pseudo-scientific ebullience of H. G. Wells and the penitent modernism of Aldous Huxley. Those highly organized and mechanized vistas which Evgeni Zamyatin opened up in his sardonic novel, *We*, actually foreshadowed some of the grimmest regimentations of totalitarianism. When we consider the trends toward the fulfilment of George Orwell's prophecies, we may feel that the year 1984 has come too close for comfort. The by-products of utopianism surround us with municipal improvements: cooperatives, garden suburbs, city-planning, low-cost housing, all the ameliorations of social welfare. Politicians assure us that the Great Society is just around the corner. Behavioral scientists promise to make our offspring worthy of it by unprecedented achievements of human engineering. It seems retrograde to share Max Beerbohm's doubts:

> *So this is Utopia,*
> *Is it? Well—*
> *I beg your pardon;*
> *I thought it was Hell.*

Yet there is a doubleness in the utopian perspective, which is reflected by the title and time-scheme of *Looking Backward: 2000–1887*. Bellamy's book, composed in 1887, looks ahead to 2000 A.D., the year he has undertaken to survey. Originally he had taken the year 3000 as his vantage-point, but optimism accelerated his timing. Consequently we are now standing much nearer to his anticipated bimillennium than to his period of composition. The changes registered in the eighty years since publication—our fashions, pastimes, buildings, communications, and transportation—would to him have seemed indeed futuristic. The closing year of the twentieth century is not simply his idealistic projection of the late nineteenth; it is a foothold for his retrospective stance. His most penetrating scrutiny was directed toward the realities of his era: the contemporary unrest, turmoil, and uncertainty. It is a nightmare from which the hero escapes to the happier dream of an earthly afterworld. He ends by feeling guilty for having missed the difficult interval between the two ages, for not having played a part in the delivering struggle that led his brethren from the one to the other. The point is made explicit by a sermon: "I would fain exchange my share in this serene and golden day for a place in that stormy epoch of transition."

[C]

A NOTE ON ICONOGRAPHY

THE MYTH OF THE GOLDEN AGE, as we have had some occasion to note in passing, has brought out responses and interactions within the sphere of the visual arts. Yet though the phrase is frequently—and sometimes rather imprecisely—mentioned by the art historians, they have uncovered no central pattern grandly sustained, as they have successfully done with so many other Greco-Roman myths. They have cast incidental light on a number of interesting points of contact, as the notes to this book will acknowledge. In his notable essay, "*Et in Arcadia Ego*: Poussin and the Elegiac Tradition," Erwin Panofsky corrected a longstanding misconception by reversing the iconological method: by using the pictorial evidence to interpret the historical documentation. He demonstrated that the intended effect of Poussin's famous painting, and of its predecessor by Guercino, and of the Latin motto that both took for their title, was to undermine the notion of Arcadianism as a life of untroubled bliss, since the Arcadians too must be visited by death. Artists may prefer to dwell upon the more euphoric episodes, to be sure, but even the bucolic poets seem to reach their heights in the elegy. The special pathos of the pastoral vision is that the beholder can never expect to attain it; like the golden age, it has gone by. As Kenneth Clark suggests in a comment on Claude Lorrain:

> . . . The Virgilian element in Claude is, above all, his sense of a Golden Age, of grazing flocks, unruffled waters and a calm, luminous sky, images of perfect harmony between man and nature, but touched, as he combines them, with a Mozartian wistfulness, as if he knew that this perfection could last no longer than the moment in which it takes possession of our minds.

Here the commentator, grasping perhaps too eagerly at the seductive postulate of *ut pictura poesis*, may be indulging in something of a pathetic fallacy. Vergil's conscious sense of the golden age was articulated, after all, not in his evocations of rural nostalgia but in the triumphal panoply of the *Fourth Eclogue* and the imperial prophecies of the *Aeneid*. The synesthetic cross-reference to Mozart betrays the cultural sentimentalism of the modern observer. Sir Kenneth's point is more securely taken when he compares Poussin's *Seasons* with *Paradise Lost*, since the subject-matter of the one is an explicit consequence of the story told by the other—of the fall, or, in classical terms, the demise of the golden age. But this means that Poussin is post-Saturnian, just as Milton is postlapsarian. Moreover, since the four seasons must be rendered by four successive paintings, the painter has a comparatively rare opportunity for presenting a sequence in time. Dostoevsky's interpretation of Claude would seem to agree with Sir Kenneth's: we are witnessing the sunset of an idyll. Dostoevsky was imposing his own guilt-ridden and messianic sense of the golden age upon a picture of Acis and Galatea, which he arbitrarily retitled. Yet he saw clearly that the essence of such painting is to recapture the moment of happiness in an eternal stasis.

The museums are full of idealized landscapes, sparsely and pleasantly populated with swains and shepherdesses, as well as fauns and nymphs and other mythical beings, into which we all are free to read our private fantasies of the great good place. But, since Arcadia is a spatial concept, it lends itself more readily to graphic representation; whereas the golden age, being temporal, is best suited to narration, and cannot be made visible except under certain limiting conditions. The beauty of youth and the exfoliation of spring, under any circumstances, are always paintable. It has been suggested, and we have noted, that the symbolism of primal verdure in Botticelli's *Primavera* is not unconnected with our theme. From the rococo pastoralism of Watteau to the naive primitivism of *le douanier* Rousseau or Edward Hicks, art has fed man's yearning to be reconciled with his natural environment. To the extent that mythology deals with prehistory and that the foreworld is envisaged as a happier state, there must be innumerable mythological paintings which could be loosely identified with a golden age. Yet the Renaissance painter who seems to have come closest to nature in bringing out the relation of men and beasts, Piero di Cosimo, was what we should term a hard primitivist, without a trace of idealization in his treatment of either.

The fascinating study by Richard Bernheimer, *Wild Men in the Middle Ages* (Cambridge, Mass., 1952), argues that this vein of savage energy was humanized by Luca Signorelli. But the argument is pressed too far by pointing to Signorelli's *Rule of Pan*, with its attendant flute-players, as a focus for Hesiod's myth of the ages. Arcadia is one myth; the golden age is another; and, though they have significant linkages, art history does not help by confounding the two. If the latter is more easily narrated than depicted, one reason lies in its generality. It collectively sketches the earlier stages of mankind, rather than emphasizing specific acts or individual protagonists. As we have likewise seen repeatedly, it takes a critical—and therefore a negative—viewpoint. Its awareness of later evils is keen, while positive ideals are vaguely stated: no wars, no property, *et cetera*. These are sentiments rather than characteristics, and can most effectively be conveyed by a verbal means of expression, the rhetorical *topos*. In lieu of a hero or heroine, two superhuman figures preside over the anonymous races of men, hovering somewhat obscurely in the background. Dike-Astraea does not become conspicuous until she decides to absent herself. Kronos-Saturnus, whose career has involved some ungolden deeds, stamps his image on the scene by leaving it. He, too, is lamented after his departure.

His identity as god of time gave him his predominant role in our myth. But the different roles he played in other myths—his Saturnalian reappearance as a Roman progenitor, the saturnine aspect of his planetary embodiment—ended by blurring the outlines of his figure. The influential compilation of Colard Mansion, *La Bible des poetes de Ovide Methamorphose* (Bruges, 1484), opens with a full-page woodcut of Saturn, enshrined amid an almost surrealistic assortment of self-contradictory attributes, munching an infant while being emasculated. A fourfold allegorical exegesis, inherited from Ovidian moralizations by the fourteenth-century Benedictine scholar, Petrus Berchorius, vainly attempts to resolve those contradictions. Though they can be verbally rationalized, it is more difficult for them to be visually projected. In general the illustration of books, inasmuch as it is designed to follow a narrative continuity, has proved more responsive to the myth of four ages than the larger representational media. Ovid's *Metamorphoses* is the controlling influence here as elsewhere, and the rich collection of French sixteenth-century illustrated editions in the Harvard College Library Department of Printing and Graphic Arts has been amply and handsomely catalogued (Cambridge, Mass., 1964). For example, the free prose translation known as *Le grand Olympe des hystoires poetiques* (Paris, 1539) is thickly interspersed with small and sketchy woodcuts.

Among these only three ages are represented, though the text retains all four: in the first the people are dancing, in the second they are plowing, and in the third they are engaged in what looks like heavy industry. A similar condensation, reducing a tetralogy to a trilogy, appears in *La Metamorphose d'Ovide figuree* (Lyons, 1557), where three elegant illustrations, attributed to Bernard Salomon, leap over the brazen age and lead directly from the agricultural silver age to the military iron age. Their delineation of the golden age (bordered by theatrical grotesques and quasi-Pompeian ornaments, and reproduced as the frontispiece to this book), shows five pairs of lovers in appropriate poses against a campestral setting. The second of the two summarizing quatrains, departing from Ovid and foreshadowing Tasso, sounds the praise of free love. Even in the fairly close verse translation of Ovid's *Trois premiers livres* (Lyons, 1556), where the first and second books have been translated by Clément Marot, the corresponding picture stresses the amatory side of the pastoral outlook. The silver age is symbolized by a circle, horizontally and vertically divided into four sectors, each of them depicting one of the seasons. The brazen age is given warlike depiction, and the iron age is delineated on the same page allegorically. There we see the personified virtues (Faith, Truth, Shame) winging their way to the heavens, while the demonic vices (Fraud, Treason, Violence) remain in possession below.

The book-illustrator has more scope for pursuing his subject serially than the painter in oils who works with a single canvas—and, of course, the letterpress can fill in what is left out on the block or the plate. A simultaneous presentation, like that of Lucas Cranach the Elder, projected the whole story of the fall within one picture-frame by redepicting Adam and Eve at every stage of their sojourn in Eden. Cranach's *Golden Age* need not stand alone, since he has also treated *The Silver Age*. His conception of that ensuing epoch, his ungainly nudes clubbing one another in universal strife, can but accelerate the cycle to an untimely termination. His *Golden Age*, which he painted at least three times, stands in contrast not merely to this dismal affray; it is pagan comedy, as contrasted with the Christian tragedy of the *Paradise*. The garden, with its tame animals, is highly domesticated; and, beyond its enclosure, we discern anachronistic glimpses of distant architecture. Three men and three women dance around a tree, while other nude couples embrace in semi-recumbent posture or else disport themselves in an artificial pool. This last feature links the painting with Cranach's *Fountain of Youth*, where the gaiety of the bathers is offset by the senility of the unrejuvenated. Rejuvenation, that major theme of the Renaissance handled so lyrically by the Italians, turns grotesque in the cold northern light.

In any case, the Florentine fresco-painters had full scope for treating continuous themes through related sequences—none more than Giorgio Vasari, when he served as architect and principal decorator of the Palazzo Vecchio. In fulfilling his Medicean assignment, it is no surprise that he reverted to the Saturnian reign for his inspiration. The striking fact is that he stayed there as long as possible, ignoring the ages of subsequent decline, while elaborating symbolic allusions from his Titanic subjects to his ducal employers. A prolific and derivative artist, Vasari was better as a first-hand *Kunstforscher*, and he has left us his own iconology, following the *Genealogiae deorum* of Boccaccio. In a set of affable dialogues, *Ragionamenti* (Florence, 1588), he himself takes a princely visitor on a guided tour. The Terrazzo di Saturno is dominated by the grand old Titan, receiving the fruits of Tuscany in homage and assuming various other guises; for, as we hear in the next dialogue, Saturn has ten varying qualities; he can be melancholy, proud, eternal, jocund, crafty, bold, niggardly, seductive, sagacious, and deceptive. All the germane motifs are eclectically introduced: Astraea holds an uncharacteristic pair of scales. Saturn's adventures continue through the chamber of Ops, his consort, where he and Janus are portrayed asleep, watched over by feminine personifications of Liberty and Tranquility, "who made sweet the slumber of the golden age."

Those golden slumbers were all too indicative of a basically uneventful scenario. Three small allegories by Jacopo Zucchi, one of Vasari's manneristic disciples, hang in the Uffizzi galleries. Here again the age of brass, too transitional to have made a distinctive impression on artists, has dropped out altogether. The motto, "*O belli anni del' oro,*" on a banner borne aloft by flying figures, reminds us that this particular rendering was contemporaneous with Tasso's *Aminta*. The vista extends from a horticultural foreground toward a craggy hill which rises steeply in the distance. At every level the garlanded nudes are enjoying their idleness: dancing, bathing, playing, fondling one another, plucking flowers, gathering their spontaneous nutriment. Two *putti*, male and female, are urinating downstream. Any deviation from the established routine, homely though it be, rearouses a flagging interest. An ingenious easel-painter could contribute an episode to the legend, adapting it to his own style and mood, as Salvator Rosa did in his *Descent of Astraea*. There the goddess is pictured not departing but arriving, seated upon a cloud, attended by winged *putti*, and bearing both sheaf and scales. This majestic apparition is making a humble retreat to a picturesque hamlet, where she is being greeted by the surprised *contadini*, dressed in rustic garments of the painter's day, with their children and sheep.

As a semi-official emblem, a veritable trophy of the Medici, a constant source of decoration for their pageants and theatricals, the myth grew wearier with each variation. Four seventeenth-century murals by

Pietro da Cortona tell the whole tale again, in baroque *tableaux*, on the festooned walls of the Pitti Palace. Their golden age is shaded by the traditional oak-tree, whose branches are being shaken for acorns—the classic pose. The silver age seems to welcome the prospect of tilling and hunting. The brazen age, increasingly urban and bellicose, yields to an iron age of rapine, arson, and ruin. The latent pacifism behind such treatments of war, though it might find corrosive manifestation through a Callot or a Goya, was unlikely to thrive on courtly patronage. Princes and generals stood in greater need of glorification and the heroic mode. The modern era, being so much more literally an age of iron than the preceding periods, may have come to regard their self-denunciations as obsolete. So far as it recoiled from the constrictions of property or hoped to realize some communal ideal, it adopted the stance of militant revolution. Sir Kenneth Clark attributes the loss of belief in a golden age to the scientific approach of Malthus and Darwin. Yet if hard primitivism destroyed the old dream of the past, it opened the way for a soft millennialism, a golden age in the foreseeable future.

This, however devoutly to be wished, would offer little to illustrate with concreteness. The original myth survived into the nineteenth century as an academic exercise. After having been taken up and abandoned by so belated a classicist as Ingres, it might well be said to have had its day. Ingres was commissioned by the Duc de Luynes to paint four lunettes of the respective ages for the Château de Dampierre. When he gave up the commission after a decade of preparation and perplexity, of studying Ovid and making some five hundred drawings from life, Ingres had not quite completed his *Golden Age* and—skipping the two others—had barely started his *Iron Age*. In short, he confirmed that tendency which we have been observing to reduce a tetraptych to a diptych, a gradation of ages to a polarization of past and present. Even so, the present eluded him, while the past attracted his serious efforts. These were extensive, if one may judge from his small-scale replica now in the Fogg Museum. Therein, in a fruitful grove interspersed with wildflowers and domestic animals, by a plashing waterfall and before a rocky mountain, he assembled about seventy figures, mostly nude, around his presiding Saturn. Several of them are mythologically recognizable: Astraea, Venus, Flora, Hebe, the Graces, Pan and his satyrs. Children play among them; the grouping seems to concentrate on families rather than lovers.

It is a triumph for artful composition that, in so large a crowd of naked people, nothing is exposed that could offend the prudish taste of the bourgeois spectator. And that, in turn, is a far cry from the days when the myth held meaning—so far that Ingres, in his correspondence, wondered what to do with these personages whom he had taken such pains to convoke. Rodin could recall an evocative phrase, *Eternal Springtime*, when he sculptured an embracing couple, and—probably because of his medium—could call a powerful nude *The Age of Bronze*. But these were literary reminiscences, marginally and sporadically attached to the plastic arts. Classical mythology was among the casualties of the artists' battles against academism, and pastoralism has been replaced today by other modes of wish-fulfilment and oversimplification. It would seem, in retrospect, that artists profited much less than men of letters from our myth. In the iconography of the golden age, we look in vain for the artistic peers of Tasso, Montaigne, Shakespeare, Cervantes, or Dostoevsky, to name no lesser masters. One of the explanations may be inherent in the nature of the material, the need for an extra dimension expressive of time. Another may reside in this paradox: that an attitude grounded upon a critique of the *status quo* should, because of art's dependence on its high-placed patrons, be transposed to a panegyric.

[❀]

Notes

The numbers at the left refer to the foregoing pages. These are linked to the references that follow here by the cited names or titles or catch-phrases. In certain cases, where there are successive allusions to the same text, a single reference may carry over. Where the texts have been frequently reprinted and are variously available, and where the specific edition has no special bearing, chapter or section will be indicated rather than place, date, and page.

I. PREHISTORY

3 Homer / *Odyssey*, iv, 565, as translated by Robert Fitzgerald (New York, 1961), p. 81.

Mircea Eliade / *The Myth of the Eternal Return*, tr. W. R. Trask (New York, 1954).

4 Kenneth Clark / *Landscape into Art* (Boston, 1961), p. 54.

Petrarch / *Le Rime di Francesco Petrarca, Canzone* xxiii, 1.

5 Novalis / *Gesammelte Werke*, ed. Carl Seelig (Herrliberg-Zurich, 1945), II, 35 (*Fragmente*, 97). See also George Boas, *The Cult of Childhood* (London, 1966).

Arthur Lovejoy and George Boas / *A Documentary History of Primitivism and Related Ideas in Classical Antiquity* (Baltimore, 1935), p. 7.

Horace / *Epodes*, ii, 1, 2. See M. S. Røstvig, *The Happy Man: Studies in the Metamorphosis of a Classical Idea* (Oslo, 1954).

6 "The Former Age" / *The Complete Works of Geoffrey Chaucer*, ed. F. N. Robinson (Boston, 1933), p. 629 (l. 50).

Arcadia / See Bruno Snell, "Discovery of Arcadia," *The Discovery of Mind: The Greek Origins of European Thought* (Cambridge, Mass., 1955), and Erwin Panofsky, "*Et in Arcadia Ego:* Poussin and the Elegiac Tradition," *Meaning in the Visual Arts* (New York, 1955).

hymn to Pan / *Homeric Hymns*, xix, 30.

"O happy *Hobbinoll.* . ." / Edmund Spenser, *The Shepheardes Calender*, vi, 9–10.

7 "*utinam ex vobis unus.* . ." / Vergil, *Eclogues*, x, 35.

Alexander Pope / "A Discourse on Pastoral Poetry."

Charles Renouvier / *Uchronie: L'Utopie dans l'histoire* (Paris, 1901).

8 "*O tempora!* . . ." Cicero, *In Catilinam*, I, i, 2.

Boethius / *Philosophiae consolatio*, II, *Metrum* v, 23, 24.

"Anywhere out of the world" / Charles Baudelaire, *Le Spleen de Paris*, xlviii; Thomas Hood, "The Bridge of Sighs."

a German scholar / Alfred Doren, "*Wunschräume und Wunschzeiten*," *Vorträge der Bibliothek Warburg* (1924–5), pp. 158–205.

10 Stith Thompson / *Motif-Index of Folk-Literature* (Bloomington, Ind., 1955), I, 194 and *passim*.

the prophecy in the Norse Eddas / See A. C. Bang, *Voluspá und die Sibyllinischen Orakel* (Vienna, 1880).

S. N. Kramer / *History Begins at Sumer* (New York, 1959), p. 222.

11 "the negative formula" / H. R. Patch, *The Other World according to Descriptions in Mediaeval Literature* (Cambridge, Mass., 1950), p. 12 and *passim*.

poem about the phoenix / C. W. Kennedy (tr.), *Early English Christian Poetry* (London, 1952), p. 231.

Karl Marx / *Zur Kritik der Politischen Ökonomie* (Stuttgart, 1919), pp. 47, 156ff.

12 Homer / *Iliad*, iii, 64; *Odyssey*, iv, 14.

Lucian / *Saturnian Letters*, i, 20.

Plato / *Cratylus*, 398.

Genesis / ii, 11, 12.

Pindar / *Isthmian Odes*, v, 1–3.

Robert Burton / *The Anatomy of Melancholy*, III, l, ii, 1.

Petrarch / *Le Familiari*, xx, 1.

"*auri sacra fames*" / Vergil, *Aeneid*, iii, 57.

13 Marx / Op. cit., p. 160.

Viktor Rydberg / Translated from Paulus Svendsen, *Gullalderdrøm og Utviklingstro: en idéhistorisk Undersokelse* (Oslo, 1940), p. 282.

Lewis Mumford / "Utopia, The City and the Machine," *Daedalus: Proceedings of the American Academy of Arts and Sciences* (Spring, 1965), XCIV, 2, 272ff.

Plato's *Republic* / III, xxi, 415.

Isaiah / lx, 17.

Daniel / ii, 31–5.

14 Hesiod / See J. G. Griffiths, "Archaeology and Hesiod's Five Ages," *Journal of the History of Ideas* (January, 1956), XVII, 1, 108–19; H. C. Baldry, "Hesiod's Five Ages," loc. cit. (October, 1956), XVI, 4, 553–4; and J. G. Griffiths, "Did Hesiod Invent the Golden Age?," loc. cit. (January, 1958), XIX, 1, 91–3.

George Grote / *A History of Greece* (London, 1862), I, 62.

15 Aratus / *Phaenomena*, 96–136.

16 J. G. Frazer / *The Golden Bough* (London, 1913), IX, 344.

Vergil / *Aeneid*, viii, 323–5.

Some of the interpreters / W. W. Tarn, "Alexander Helios and the Golden Age," *Journal of Roman Studies* (1932), XXII, 2, 135–159; Harold Mattingly, "Virgil's Fourth Eclogue," *Journal of the Warburg and Courtauld Institutes* (1947), X, 14–9; Jérôme Carcopino, *Virgile et le mystère de la IVe églogue* (Paris, 1930).

17 Augustus Caesar / *Aeneid*, vi, 791–4.

18 Calpurnius Siculus / *Eclogues*, i, 41–4.

Petrarch / See Konard Burdach, *Rienzo und die geistige Wandlung seiner Zeit* (Berlin, 1928), pp. 81–90.

Pope / "Messiah: A Sacred Eclogue in Imitation of Vergil's Pollio," ll. 7, 8. See also R. A. Brower, *Alexander Pope: The Poetry of Allusion* (Oxford, 1959), pp. 35–62.

Dante / *Purgatorio*, xxii, 70, 71.

19 Milton's hymn "On the Morning of Christ's Nativity" / ll. 133–5.

Ovid / *Metamorphoses*, i, 73–150.

George Sandys / *Ovid's Metamorphosis* (Oxford, 1632), p. 3.

20 James Joyce / *Finnegans Wake* (New York, 1939), p. 3.

Ernst Bloch / *Das Prinzip Hoffnung* (Frankfurt, 1959), I, 129.

Pythagoras / Ovid, *Metamorphoses*, xv, 96–103.

21 Vergil / *Georgics*, ii, 149.

Shakespeare / *As You Like It*, II, i, 5, 6.

Bacon / "The speeches drawn up for the Earl of Essex in a device before Queen Elizabeth, on the anniversary of her accession to the throne, November 17, 1595," *Works*, ed. James Spedding, R. L. Ellis, and D. D. Heath (London, 1859–1869), VII (I, 1862), 379.

22 Vergil / *Georgics*, i, 125–54.

less poetic accounts / See W. K. C. Guthrie, *In the Beginning: Some Greek Views on the Origins of Life and the Early State of Man* (Ithaca, N. Y., 1957), especially pp. 95ff.

23 Ovid / *Amores*, III, viii, 35–49.

Chaucer / Op. cit., ll. 27–30.

Boethius / Op. cit., II, *Metrum* v, 30.

"precious periles" / Chaucer, *Works*, ed. Robinson, p. 393.

"precious bane" / Milton, *Paradise Lost*, i, 692.

Georgius Agricola / *De re metallica*, tr. H. C. and L. H. Hoover (London, 1912), p. 7.

"Curst Steele. . ." / Sandys, op. cit., p. 4.

24 "*Aurea sunt vere nunc saecula. . .*" / Ovid, *Ars amatoria*, ii, 277.

Tibullus / *Elegies*, II, iii.

Theocritus / *Idylls*, xii, 15, 16.

Empedocles / Lovejoy and Boas, op. cit., p. 33.

"*Liber amor. . .*" / *Anthologia Latina*, no. 914, 69–70 (quoted from Lovejoy and Boas, op. cit., p. 69).

John Donne / *Elegies*, xvii, 39.

Juvenal / *Satires*, vi, 10.

25 Lucretius / *De rerum natura*, V, 965.

Seneca / *Hippolytus*, 525–39; *Octavia*, 397–406; *Epistulae morales*, xc, 14.

26 Cicero / *Epistulae ad Atticum*, ii, 19. Cf. Lovejoy and Boas, op. cit., 95n.

Petrarch / *Rime, Canzone* 1, 23, 24.

"*pabellón al siglo. . . dorado*" / Luis de Góngora y Argote, *Obras Completas*, ed. Juan Mille y Gimenez (Madrid, 1943), p. 547 (*Fabula de Polifemo*, xi).

Ezra Pound / "Hugh Selwyn Mauberley," in *Selected Poems* (New York, 1949), p. 61.

Cesare Ripa / *Iconologia* (Rome, 1603), p. 138.

27 Plutarch / *Morals*, tr. Philemon Holland (London, 1603), p. 42.

Vincenzo Cartari / *The Fountain of Ancient Fiction*, tr. Richard Lincoln (London, 1599), D iii—a free English adaptation of *Le Imagini de i dei de gli antichi* (Venice, 1571), pp. 36ff.

28 Marsilio Ficino / See Raymond Klibansky, Erwin Panofsky, and Fritz Saxl, *Saturn and Melancholy: Studies in the History of Natural Philosophy, Religion, and Art* (London, 1964), pp. 254ff; cf. Rudolf and Margaret Wittkower, *Born under Saturn* (New York, 1963), pp. 102ff.

"*cunctis universa communia*" / Giovanni Boccaccio, *Genealogie deorum gentilium libri*, ed. Vincenzo Romero (Bari, 1951), II, 391.

"*omnia . . . omnibus . . . communia*" / *Natalis Comitis Mythologiae sive explicationum fabularum libri x* (Venice, 1581), p. 77.

Seneca / *Epistulae morales*, xc, 38.

Cicero / *De officiis*, I, vii, 21; xvii, 54; xvi, 51.

Acts of the Apostles / ii, 44; iv, 32–5.

Saint John / xvii, 10.

29 Plautus / *Trinummus*, (II, ii) 329.

collection of adages / See M. M. Phillips, *The "Adages" of Erasmus* (Cambridge, 1964), pp. 11, 111, 112.

mine and *not mine* / Plato, *Republic*, V, ix, 462c.

"*wer myn das din*" / *Sebastian Brants Narrenschiff*, ed. Friedrich Zarncke (Leipzig, 1854), p. 80.

Alexander Barclay / *The Ship of Fools* (Edinburgh, 1874), II, 103.

Antonio de Guevara / *The Dial of Princes*, tr. Sir Thomas North (London, 1557), f. 43 (I, xxxi).

30 John Locke's apologia / *Two Treatises of Government*, ed. Peter Laslett (Cambridge, 1960), p. 304 (II, v).

Erasmus / *Stultitiae laus*, ed. I. B. Kan (Hague, 1898), p. 58.

Thomas Hobbes / *Leviathan*, I, xiiii.

II. ETHICS

32 Lactantius / *Divinarum institutionum libri septem*, in J. P. Migne (ed.), *Patrologia Latina* (Paris, 1844), VI, 566, 567.

rapid historical summary / E.g., H. J. Massingham, *The Golden Age: The Story of Human Nature* (London, 1927), p. 43.

33 Alanus de Insulis / *Anticlaudianus*, in Thomas Wright (ed.), *The Anglo-Latin Satirical Poets and Epigrammatists of the Twelfth Century* (London, 1872), II, 483. Cf. C. S. Lewis, *The Allegory of Love* (Oxford, 1936), pp. 99, 102.

Saint Thomas Aquinas / *Boetius de philosophica consolatu* (Strassburg, 1501), xl.

Bernard of Cluny / *De contemptu mundi*, in Wright, op. cit., ii, 43.

Modoin / See F. J. E. Raby, *A History of Secular Latin Poetry in the Middle Ages* (Oxford, 1934), I, 205.

Hilarius / *Versus et ludi*, ed. J. B. Fuller (New York, 1927), p. 71.

Ernst Robert Curtius / *European Literature and the Latin Middle Ages*, tr. W. R. Trask (New York, 1953), especially pp. 195–200.

Alfred Jeanroy / *La Poésie des Troubadours* (Paris, 1934), II, 128.

34 Theodulus / Joannes Osternacher (ed.), *Theoduli ecloga* (Linz, 1902), p. 32.

Dante / *Inferno*, xiv, 96, 103, 114.

35 Dante/ *Purgatorio*, xxii, 148; xxviii, 139–41.

"*En ce deliteuz paradis. . .*" / Cornelis de Boer (ed.), "*Ovide moralisé*": *Poème du commencement du XIVme siècle* (Amsterdam, 1915), I, 809–12.

36 "*Sans labourer*" / Cornelis de Boer (ed.), *Ovide moralisé en prose* (Amsterdam, 1954), I, xiii, p. 47.

Arthur Golding / *The xv. Bookes of P. Ovidius Naso, entytuled Metamorphosis* (London, 1567), A7.

Jean de Meun / *Le Roman de la rose*, ed. Ernest Langlois (Paris, 1924), V, 29, 26, 33.

37 "*Qu'onques amour e seignourie. . .*" / Ibid. (1921), III, 82; cf. Ovid, *Metamorphoses*, ii, 846, 847.

Curtius / Op. cit., p. 125.

sixteenth-century illustrations / See Frontispiece and Appendix C.

Fanny Hill / John Cleland, *Memoirs of a Woman of Pleasure* (New York, 1963), pp. 163, 164.

38 E. H. Gombrich / "Renaissance and Golden Age," in *Norm and Form: Studies in the Art of the Renaissance* (London, 1966), pp. 29–34.

Baldassare Castiglione / *The Book of the Courtier*, tr. Thomas Hoby (London, 1577), Ti^v.

Marsilio Ficino / *Opera* (Basel, 1576), p. 944.

39 Giorgio Vasari / *Le Vite de' piu eccellenti pittori, sculptori e architectori* (Milan, 1964), III, 193.

Aby Warburg / "Sandro Botticellis 'Geburt der Venus' und 'Frühling'," *Gesammelte Schriften* (Leipzig, 1932), I, 1–45.

Pontormo / Vasari, op. cit., VI, 153.

40 Nardi's verses / *Canti carnascialeschi del Rinascimento*, ed. C. S. Singleton (Bari, 1936), p. 250.

masques and festivals / See A. M. Nagler, *Theatre Festivals of the Medici* (New Haven, 1964), pp. 11, 61, 154.

41 Politian / *Stanze per la Giostra*, I, xx, xxi

42 Lorenzo / *Selve d'amore*, II, xxxv, cxix, lxxxv, lxxxiv, cv, lxxxiii.

43 Jacopo Sannazaro / *Arcadia*, Eclogues iii, vi, ix, and especially x.

44 an Arcadian academy / See Giuseppe Toffanin, *L'Eredità del Rinascimento in Arcadia* (Bologna, 1923).

Tasso / *Aminta*, V, i, 8.

45 "*Pastor, non mi toccar...*" / Ibid., III, i, 105.

crudeltate / Ibid., IV, i, 116, 117.

la gente prima / Ibid., I, i, 20.

"*...regna l'oro.*" / Ibid., II, i, 57, 58.

46 "*Il mondo invecchia...*" / Ibid., II, ii, 71, 72.

Samuel Daniel's translation / *Complete Works*, ed. A. B. Grosart (London, 1885), I, 260.

47 Catullus / *Carmina*, v, 1, 3–5.

48 Sperone Speroni / *Opere* (Venice, 1740), IV, 49.

Dante / *Inferno*, v, 56.

Plautus / *Menaechmi* (IV, ii), 589.

Ben Jonson / *Cynthia's Revels*, V, iii, 630.

John Marston / *Sophonisba: The Wonder of Women*, IV, i, 191.

Rosemond Tuve / *Allegorical Imagery: Some Mediaeval Poets and Their Posterity* (Princeton, 1966), p. 254n.

John Donne / *Elegies*, xvii, 48, 49.

49 Henry Reynolds / *Torquato Tasso's Aminta Englisht* (London, 1628), D2.

Richard Lovelace / *Poems*, ed. C. H. Wilkinson (Oxford, 1925), p. 146.

Mrs. Aphra Behn / *Works*, ed. Montague Summers (London, 1915), VI, 141.

Il disonóre dell' onore / See G. A. Borgese, "The Dishonor of Honor," *Romanic Review* (February, 1941), XXXII, 1, 44/55.

50 "This is the place. . ." / Edward Fairfax (tr.), *Godfrey of Boulogne, or the Recoverie of Jerusalem* (London, 1624), p. 279.

Del piacere onesto / Torquato Tasso, *Dialoghi*, ed. Ezio Raimondi (Florence, 1958), III, 285–96.

A masque for the Medici / Nagler, op. cit., p. 28.

Giordano Bruno / *Lo Spaccio della bestia trionfante*, III, i.

51 Dryden / Preface to *Sylvae*.

Jonson / *Volpone*, III, iv, 91, 92.

Sir John Fanshawe / Guarini's *Il Pastor Fido*, ed. W. F. Staton, Jr., and W. E. Simeone (Oxford, 1964), p. 10.

52 critical treatises / See Bernard Weinberg, *A History of Literary Criticism in the Italian Renaissance* (Chicago, 1961), II, 656, 683, 1074, 1079.

Cardinal Bellarmino / See W. W. Greg, *Pastoral Poetry and Pastoral Drama* (London, 1906), p. 203.

John Fletcher's pastoral tragicomedy / *The Faithful Shepherdess*, III, i, 135, 211.

53 "Not Natures law perchance . . ." / Fanshawe, op. cit., p. 109; G. B. Guarini, *Il Pastor fido*, IV, v.

"Husband and lover. . ." / Fanshawe, op. cit., p. 126; cf. *Il Pastor fido*, IV, ix.

"*S'ei piace, ei lice*" / Tasso, *Aminta*, I, ii, 343.

"*Piaccia se lice*" / *Il Pastor fido*, IV, ix.

54 Goethe / *Torquato Tasso* (II), 994, 1006.

Edmund Spenser / *The Faerie Queene*, VI, xi, 6; IV, viii, 30.

56 "*leur voiloir et franc arbitre*" / François Rabelais, *Gargantua*, lvii.

Thelemia / Francesco Colonna, *Les Songes de Poliphile*, ed. A. M. Schmidt (Paris, 1963). Cf. V. L. Saulnier, "*L'Utopie en France: Morus et Rabelais*," in *Les Utopies à la Renaissance* (Brussels, 1963), p. 160.

"Doing as One Likes" / Matthew Arnold, *Culture and Anarchy*, ii.

57 encomium on borrowing and lending / Rabelais, *Le Tiers Livre*, iv.

harangue on codpieces / Ibid., viii.

III. GEOGRAPHY

58 "The people of the golden age. . ." / R. W. Emerson, *The Journals and Miscellaneous Notebooks*, ed. W. H. Gilman, G. P. Clark, A. R. Ferguson, and M. R. Davis (Cambridge, Mass., 1960), I, 293, 294.

Seneca / *Medea*, 379.

59 Columbus / *Select Letters*, tr. and ed. R. H. Major (London, 1847), p. 145.

"Tomorrow to fresh Woods. . ." / Milton, *Lycidas*, 193.

Columbus / Op. cit., p. 5.

60 Leonardo Olschki / *Storia letteraria delle scoperte geografiche* (Florence, 1937), pp. 11–21.

H. N. Fairchild / *The Noble Savage: A Study in Romantic Naturalism* (New York, 1928), p. 4.

Peter Martyr / *De novo Orbe, or The Historie of the west Indies*, tr. Richard Eden and Michael Lok (London, 1612), p. 140^v.

"These natives. . ." / Quoted by R. R. Cawley, *The Voyagers and Elizabethan Drama* (Boston, 1938), p. 290; cf. Peter Martyr, op. cit., p. 249^r.

61 "The inhabitants of these Ilandes. . ." / Ibid., p. 15^r.

Richard Eden / Ibid., 51^r, 69^r, 133^v, 75^r, 99^v, 24^v.

62 Bartolomé de Las Casas / See *Hakluytus Posthumus or Purchas His Pilgrimes* (Glasgow, 1906), XVIII, 87.

Columbus / Op. cit., p. 196.

Book of Metals / Edward Arber (ed.), *The First Three English Books on America* (Birmingham, 1885), p. 355.

Michael Lok / Peter Martyr, op. cit., p. 249ʳ.

63 Sir William Davenant / *Dramatic Works,* ed. W. H. Logan and James Maidment (Edinburgh, 1873), IV, 19, 88.

64 Ralegh / *The Discovery of Guiana,* ed. V. T. Harlow (London, 1928), p. 17; cf. Milton, *Paradise Lost,* xi, 414–6. See also Constantine Bayle, *El Dorado fantasmo* (Madrid, 1930).

Amerigo Vespucci / *Letters,* ed. C. R. Markham (London, 1894), pp. 9, 46, 47.

65 André Thevet / See Gilbert Chinard, *L'Exotisme américain dans la littérature française au XVIe siècle* (Paris, 1911), pp. 99–102.

Geoffroy Atkinson / *Les Nouveaux Horizons de la Renaissance Française* (Paris, 1935), pp. 137–68.

Jodocus Hondius / Translated from Atkinson, op. cit., p. 142.

Marc Lescarbot / Translated and paraphrased from Atkinson, op. cit., p. 145.

66 The Portuguese / See Sérgio Buarque de Holanda, *Visão do Paraíso: os motivos edênicos no descrobimento e colonização do Brasil* (Rio de Janeiro, 1959).

Philip Amadas and Arthur Barlow / Richard Hakluyt, *The Principal Navigations Voyages Traffiques and Discoveries of the English Nation* (Glasgow, 1904), VIII, 305.

A poem . . . reprinted by Hakluyt / Ibid., X, 446.

Michael Drayton / *The Muses Elizium,* "The Description of Elizium," 37.

Byron / *Don Juan,* xiii, 43.

William Camden / *Britannia* (London, 1607), p. 3.

67 Captain John Smith / *Travels and Works,* ed. Edward Arber (Edinburgh, 1895), p. 627.

Peter Martyr / Op. cit., pp. 16ᵛ, 133ʳ.

Drayton's ode "To the Virginian Voyage" / 24, 37f.

Cotton Mather / *Magnalia Christi Americana* (Hartford, 1852), I, 27.

California / See A. F. Rolle, *California: A History* (New York, 1963), pp. 31f.

H. H. Bancroft / Quoted by J. D. Hart, *American Images of Spanish California* (Berkeley, 1960), p. 32.

68 François Barbé-Marbois / Cited by René Rémond, *Les Etats-unis devant l'opinion française: 1815-1852* (Paris, 1962), p. 489.

Henry James / *The Europeans*, iii.

"a larger . . . house" / H. D. Thoreau, *Walden*, "The House-Warming."

Emerson / "Resources," *Letters and Social Aims.*

Herman Melville / *Typee*, xvii.

69 *La Bible des poètes* / Colard Mansion, *La Bible des poetes de Ouide Methamorphose. Translate de Latin en Frãcoys. . .* [Paris, ca. 1520].

Lemaire de Belges / *Oeuvres*, ed. J. Stecher (Louvain, 1882), I, 39.

70 *Contrefait de Renard* / See C. V. Langlois, *La Vie en France au Moyen Age* (Paris, 1925), II, 297.

Clément Marot / *Oeuvres lyriques*, ed. C. A. Mayer (London, 1964), p. 354; *Oeuvres diverses*, ed. C. A. Mayer (London, 1966), p. 129.

Béranger de la Tour d'Albénas / *Le Siècle d'or et autres vers divers* (Lyons, 1551).

Honoré d'Urfé / *L'Astrée*, ed. Hugues Vaguenay (Lyons, 1925), I, 3.

pastoral masque / Pierre de Ronsard, *Oeuvres complètes*, ed. Gustave Cohen (Paris, 1966), I, 918, 920, 930.

71 *Les Sereines* / Ibid., I, 1011.

A fifth eclogue / Ibid., I, 986.

le grand pasteur Carlin / Ibid., I, 933.

Hynne de l'or / Ibid., II, 264.

Les Armes / Ibid., II, 311.

72 "*le mari de Rhée*" / Ibid., II, 111.

Guy de Brués / *Dialogues*, ed. P. P. Morphos (Baltimore, 1953), pp. 97f.; see also pp. 187f, 260f.

Jean-Antoine de Baïf / See F. A. Yates, *The French Academies of the Sixteenth Century* (London, 1947), pp. 43–5.

"*le siecle . . . de celle gent doree*" / Jean-Antoine de Baïf, *Euvres en rime*, ed. Charles Marty-Laveaux (Paris, 1881), I, 107.

Joachim Du Bellay / *Oeuvres françoises*, ed. Charles Marty-Laveaux (Paris, 1866), I, 226, 227.

73 *Les Isles fortunées* / Ronsard, op. cit., II, 414.

74 *Discours contre Fortune* / Ibid., II, 407.

multitudinous quotations / Michel de Montaigne, *Essais*, ed. Pierre Villey and V. L. Saulnier (Paris, 1965), p. lv.

earliest taste for books / "*De l'institution des enfants.*"

a naturalist / "*De la phisionomie.*"

75 on the cannibals / "*Des Cannibales.*"

"there is nothing in that nation. . ." / John Florio, *The Essays of Montaigne*, ed. George Saintsbury (London, 1892), I, 221.

76 "for me seemeth. . ." / Ibid., I, 222.

"It is a nation. . ." / Ibid., I, 222.

"First, valour. . ." / Ibid., I, 224.

77 "I am not sorie. . ." / Ibid., I, 226.

Voltaire / *Candide*, xvi; cf. *Essai sur les moeurs*, cxlvi.

"We may . . . call them barbarous. . ." / Florio, op. cit., I, 226.

"Cannibals? . . ." / Herman Melville, *Moby Dick*, lxv.

78 his prefatory note / Florio, op. cit., I, 12.

Des coches / Ibid., III, 142.

79 on fathers and children / Ibid., II, 514.

Chateaubriand / See Montaigne, *Essais*, ed. Villey and Saulnier, p. 1140.

Claude Lévi-Strauss / *Tristes tropiques* (Paris, 1956), p. 276.

80 "For may not a Goose. . ." / Florio, op. cit., II, 244.

81 "When I am playing. . ." / Ibid., II, 144.

animalitarianism / See George Boas, *The Happy Beast in French Thought of the Seventeenth Century* (Baltimore, 1933).

82 Giovanni Battista Gelli / *Circe*, tr. Thomas Brown and ed. Robert Adams (Ithaca, N. Y., 1963).

"Saide Guyon. . ." / Spenser, *Faerie Queene*, II, xii, 87.

"*Salvagesse sans finesse.*" / Ibid., IV, iv, 39.

83 Hans Sachs / See Richard Bernheimer, *Wild Men in the Middle Ages* (Cambridge, Mass., 1952), pp. 113–5.

IV. FICTIONS

84 William Hazlitt / "On Thomson and Cowper," *Lectures on the English Poets.*

Stephen Hawes / *The Pastime of Pleasure* (London, 1845), p. 9.

85 George Cavendish / *The Life and Death of Cardinal Wolsey*, ed. R. S. Sylvester (Oxford, 1959), p. 11.

"golden lads and girls" / Shakespeare, *Cymbeline*, IV, ii, 262.

"golden slumbers" / Thomas Dekker, *Patient Grissell*, I, i, 200.

"I had approached . . ." / William Wordsworth, *The Prelude*, xi, 79.

"the green world" / John Keats, *Endymion*, i, 16.

86 The may-games / See William Hone (ed.), *The Every-Day Book and Table Book, or Everlasting Calendar of Popular Amusements, Sports, Pastimes, Ceremonies, Manners, Customs, and Events* (London, 1835), I, 558, 551.

Richard Edwards / In *The Paradise of Dainty Devices*, ed. H. E. Rollins (Cambridge, Mass., (1927), p. 10.

". . . the hobby-horse is forgot." / Shakespeare, *Hamlet*, III, ii, 144; cf. *Love's Labour's Lost*, III, i, 30.

87 Thomas Starkey / *A Dialogue between Cardinal Pole and Thomas Lupset*, ed. J. M. Comper (London, 1871), p. 9.

Saint Ambrose / See A. O. Lovejoy, "The Communism of St. Ambrose," *Essays in the History of Ideas* (Baltimore, 1948), pp. 296–307.

Gratian / See Norman Cohn, *The Pursuit of the Millennium* (New York, 1957), pp. 201–17.

Gregory the Great / Quoted in the introduction to St. Thomas More, *Utopia*, ed. Edward Surtz and J. H. Hexter (New Haven, 1965), p. cxi.

John Wycliffe / *Tractatus de civili dominio*, ed. and tr. R. L. Poole (London, 1875), I, 96.

88 John Ball / *The Chronicle of Froissart translated by Lord Berners*, ed. W. P. Ker (London, 1901), III, 224.

dialogue of *Dives and Pauper* / (London, 1534), p. 241.

William Langland / *Piers the Plowman*, ed. W. W. Skeat (Oxford, 1886), I, 595 (C, *Passus* xxiii, 273–6).

Thomas Tusser / *Five Hundred Pointes of Good Husbandrie*, ed. W. Payne and S. J. Herrtage (London, 1878), p. 141.

Shakespeare / 2 Henry VI, IV, ii, 270–5. Cf. Alfred Hart, *Shakespeare and the Homilies* (Melbourne, 1934), pp. 64f., 34.

89 Sir Thomas Elyot / *The Boke Named the Governour*, ed. H. H. S. Croft (London, 1883), I, 2.

homilies / *Certain Sermons or Homilies appointed to be read in Churches* (London, 1640), pp. 69–70.

Nusquama / *Opus Epistolarum Desiderii Erasmi Roterodami*, ed. P. S. Allen (Oxford, 1910), II, 339.

90 J. W. Allen / *A History of Political Thought in the Sixteenth Century* (London, 1928), p. 154.

"that no equal and just distribution. . ." / More, *Utopia*, ed. Surtz and Hexter, p. 104; tr. Ralph Robynson, ed. J. H. Lupton (Oxford, 1895), pp. 107, 108.

"But I am of a contrary opinion. . ." / Ibid., ed. Surtz and Hexter, p. 106; tr. Robynson, p. 109.

"that Christ instytuted. . ." / Ibid., ed. Surtz and Hexter, p. 218; tr. Robynson, p. 269.

"*O sanctam rempublicam.* . ." / Ibid., ed. Surtz and Hexter, p. 146.

91 probably written somewhat later / See J. H. Hexter, *More's Utopia: The Biography of an Idea* (New York, 1965), pp. 21–30.

the conspiracy of the rich / Ibid., ed. Surtz and Hexter, p. 238–42.

The peroration of Hythlodaeus / *Utopia*, tr. Robynson, pp. 300, 302.

Erasmus / *Opus Epistolarum*, ed. Allen, IV, 3–23.

The Four Last Things / More, *English Works*, ed. W. E. Campbell and A. W. Reed (London, 1931), I, 492.

92 Vespucci / More, *Utopia*, ed. Surtz and Hexter, p. 50.

their definition of virtue / Ibid., pp. 162– 64; tr. Robynson, p. 192.

an enlightened hedonism / See Edward Surtz, *The Praise of Pleasure* (Cambridge, Mass., 1957).

Seneca's *Ninetieth Epistle* / xvi.

liberty of mind / More, *Utopia*, ed. Surtz and Hexter, p. 134; tr. Robynson, p. 152.

93 Guillaume Budé / More, *Utopia*, ed. Surtz and Hexter, pp. 10–2.

rules and regulations / See S. A. Zavala, *La Utopia de Thomas More en la Nueva España* (Mexico, 1937), pp. 7–15, 4. Cf. F. B. Warren, *Vasco de Quiroga and His Pueblo-Hospitals of Santa Fe* (Washington, 1963).

"For not in vain. . ." / Silvio Zavala, "The American Utopia of the Sixteenth Century," *Huntington Library Quarterly* (August, 1947), X, 4, 339.

an absolute heroical poem / Sir Philip Sidney, *The Complete Works*, ed. Albert Feuillerat (Cambridge, 1923), III, 10.

94 "a trifle. . ." / Loc. cit., I, 3.

"A speaking Picture. . ." / Loc. cit., III, 9, 29.

95 *Wunschlandschaft* / See Ernst Bloch, *Das Prinzip Hoffnung* (Berlin, 1955), II, 372–92.

"singuler reputation. . ." / Sidney, loc. cit., IV, 1.

"wanting little. . ." / Loc. cit., I, 14.

"the pleasauntnes of this place" / Ibid., I, 57; cf. IV, 12.

"as though he should never be old" / Ibid., I, 13.

Hazlitt / "On Miscellaneous Poems, etc.," *Lectures on the Dramatic Literature of the Age of Elizabeth*.

"the shepherdish pastimes" / Sidney, loc. cit., I, 118, 119; cf. IV, 42.

96 "a pleasant picture of nature. . ." / Ibid., I, 91.

"a civil wildnes" / Ibid., I, 14.

"the conceites of the Poets" / Ibid., I, 58; cf. IV, 14.

97 "O sweete woods. . ." / Loc. cit., IV, 158; cf. *The Poems of Sir Philip Sidney*, ed. William Ringler (Oxford, 1962), p. 68.

"stage play of Love" / Sidney, loc. cit., IV, 50.

"Arcadia, Arcadia. . ." / Ibid., IV, 100.

98 "Why shulde wee. . .?" / Ibid., IV, 265.

"intermitted historiologie" / Loc. cit., I, 256.

"The daungerous division. . ." / Loc. cit., II, 145; cf. I, 329.

Erwin Panofsky / *Meaning in the Visual Arts*, pp. 295–320.

"*Arkadisch frei*. . ." / J. W. von Goethe, *Faust*, II, 9573.

W. H. Auden / *The Age of Anxiety* (New York, 1947), p. 85.

a Washington conference / Maurice Matloff and E. M. Snell, *United States Army in World War II: Strategic Planning for Coalition Warfare, 1941–1942* (Washington, 1953), pp. 97–126.

99 Queen Elizabeth I / See F. A. Yates, "Queen Elizabeth as Astraea," *Journal of the Warburg and Courtauld Institutes* (1947), X, 27–82.

100 "the righteous Maide" / Edmund Spenser, *Mother Hubberds Tale*, 1, 143–53. See *passim* H. G. Lotspeich, *Classical Mythology in the Poetry of Edmund Spenser* (Princeton, 1932).

"all things to an equall" / Spenser, *Faerie Queene*, V, ii, 34, 30; Proem, 1, 2, 11.

101 "All change is perillous. . ." / Ibid., V, ii, 36.

"later times" / Ibid., II, vii, 18.

"*O gran bontà. . .*" / Ariosto, *Orlando furioso*, I, xxii.

"O goodly usage. . ." / Spenser, *Faerie Queene*, III, i, 13.

Edwin Greenlaw / in *The Works of Edmund Spenser: A Variorum Edition* (Baltimore, 1936), V, 156.

102 the house of Alma / Spenser, *Faerie Queene*, II, viii, 59, 60.

"Where is that happy land. . ." / Ibid., II, Proem, 2.

103 "blisse . . . balefulnesse" / Ibid., II, xii, 83.

"Of Court it seemes. . ." / Ibid., VI, i, 1; xi, 27, 33.

104 the Garden of Adonis / Ibid., III, vi, 34, 42, 44.

the Bower of Bliss / Ibid., II, v, 29; xii, 50.

105 "a vile phrase" / Shakespeare, *Hamlet*, II, ii, 112.

". . . This Gardin. . ." / Spenser, *Faerie Queene*, II, xii, 59, I, 75; i, Argument.

"the baite of bestiall delight" / Ibid., IV, viii, 32.

The dichotomy of art versus nature / See E. W. Tayler, *Nature and Art in Renaissance Literature* (New York, 1964).

106 Francis Bacon / *The Advancement of Learning*, II, xiii, in *Works*, ed. R. L. Ellis, James Spedding, and D. D. Heath (London, 1860), IV, 315.

107 *Aphorisms* / Loc. cit., IV, 102 (*Novum Organum*, I, cxiii).

Sidney / *Works*, ed. Feuillerat, III, 30, 29, 22, 8.

108 Scaliger / See J. P. McIntyre, "Sidney's 'Golden World,'" *Comparative Literature* (Fall, 1962), XIV, 4, 356.

109 "Iron commands gold" / Bacon, "To the Speaker's Excuse," in *Works*, ed. Basil Montagu (London, 1826), VI, 68. Cf. More, *Utopia*, ed. Surtz and Hexter, p. 150.

"the best iron in the world" / "A Speech concerning the article of the general naturalization of the Scotish nation," *Works*, ed. Montagu, V, 73.

"lanthorn of this kingdom" / Bacon, *Works*, ed. Spedding, Ellis and Heath (London, 1859), III, 145.

Lord Macaulay / "Milton," *Complete Works*, ed. Lady Trevelyan (New York, 1866), V, 4.

110 Thomas Love Peacock / *Headlong Hall*, x.

"A poet in our times. . ." / H. F. B. Brett-Smith (ed.), *Peacock's Four Ages of Poetry; Shelley's Defence of Poetry* (Oxford, 1921), pp. 16f.

Shelley's defense / Ibid., pp. 25, 48, 34.

"my golden age. . ." / *The Letters of Percy Bysshe Shelley*, ed. F. L. Jones (Oxford, 1964), I, 152.

111 *Hellas* / *The Complete Poetical Works of Shelley*, ed. Thomas Hutchinson (Oxford, 1904), pp. 491, 516, 5·8, 522f.

V. PAGEANTRY

112 William Drummond of Hawthornden / *The Poetical Works*, ed. L. E. Kastner (Manchester, 1913), II, 118; I, 149.

113 models pairing off beneath the trees / See Otto Kurz, "Gli Amori de' Carracci," *Journal of the Warburg and Courtauld Institutes*, (June-December 1951), XIV, 3–4, 221–33.

Arcades ambo / Vergil, *Eclogues*, vii, 4.

114 Thomas Nashe / *Works*, ed. R. B. McKerrow (London, 1904), II, 282–5.

Christopher Marlowe / *Hero and Leander*, I, 385–484.

John Donne / "The Second Anniversary," 70.

Joseph Hall / *Works* (Oxford, 1863), XII, 193 (*Virgidemiarum*, III, i).

T. A. / *The Massacre of Money* (London, 1602), Az.

John Donne / Satyre v, 35.

115 Thomas Howell / "Of the Golden worlde," *Howell's Devises 1581*, ed. Walter Raleigh (Oxford, 1906), p. 53.

Thomas Bastard / *Chrestoleros: Seven Bookes of Epigrames* (Manchester, 1888), p. 64.

"it were enough. . ." / Francis Bacon, "A Frame of Declaration for the Master of the Wards," *Works*, ed. Montagu, VI, 32.

"Well, shepheard, well. . ." / Michael Drayton, *The Shepheards Garland, Works*, ed. J. W. Hebel (Oxford, 1931), I, 87.

Phineas Fletcher / *The Purple Island*, I, xvi, xvii, xlix-lii.

William Browne / *Poems*, ed. Gordon Goodwin (London, 1894), I, 269, 279.

116 Fulke Greville / *The Remains*, ed. G. A. Wilkes (Oxford, 1965), pp. 35, 39.

A broadside ballad / Frank Kermode (ed.), *English Pastoral Poetry* (London, 1952), p. 57.

"haplesse Hap" / Drummond, op. cit., I, 90.

"sleep securely all the night. . ." / Isaak Walton, *The Compleat Angler*, I, iv.

117 every segment of British history / Thomas Heywood, *An Apology for Actors*, in *Early Treatises on the Stage* (London, 1853), pp. 52–3.

"the Worldes Child-hood" / Thomas Heywood, *Troia Britannica* (London, 1609), pp. 3–4.

Homer as prologue / Thomas Heywood, *The Golden Age*, I, i, 21–7.

118 ". . . not liv'd to get." / *The Poetical Works of Sir William Alexander*, ed. L. E. Kastner and H. B. Charlton (Manchester, 1921), I, 263.

George Chapman / *Bussy D'Ambois*, II, 203, 204; III, ii, 95–107.

119 *Eastward Ho* / III, iii, 14, 15.

Masque of the Middle Temple / 369.

120 Philip Massinger / *The City Madam*, V, i, 105–10.

Samuel Daniel / *The Queen's Arcadia*, III, i, 991–2, in *Complete Works*, ed. Grosart, III, 249.

121 Shakespeare's diction / *King Lear*, III, iv, 111; *Sonnets*, iii, 12; *Lucrece*, 59, 60; *Titus Andronicus*, IV, iii, 4; *3 Henry VI*, III, iii, 6; *2 Henry IV*, V, iii, 99, 100; *Twelfth Night*, II, iv, 47–9.

122 Samuel Johnson / "Prologue Spoken by Mr. Garrick at the Opening of the Theatre-Royal, Drury Lane, 1747."

"in a holiday humour. . ." / Shakespeare, *As You Like It*, IV, i, 69

C. L. Barber / *Shakespeare's Festive Comedy* (Princeton, 1959).

". . . in the golden world." / *As You Like It*, I, i, 120–5;

"To liberty. . ." Ibid., I, iii, 140.

"from Fortune's office. . ." / Ibid., I, ii, 43, 44.

123 Touchstone / Ibid., V, iv, 58.

old Adam / Ibid., II, iii, 57.

a later song / Ibid., II, vii, 175, 176.

". . . good in everything." / Ibid., II, i, 15-7.

Marshall McLuhan / *Understanding Media* (New York, 1964), pp.
58, 59.

124 Shakespearean Comedy / *Two Gentlemen of Verona*, IV, i, 39, 40;
Merchant of Venice, II, vii, 65; *Winter's Tale*, IV, iv, 89, 90. See
also Frank Kermode's introduction to the New Arden edition of
The Tempest (London, 1954).

"*melior natura*" / Ovid, *Metamorphoses*, i, 21.

125 *The Tempest* / II, ii, 33–4; II, i, 143–68.

126 letter from More to Erasmus / *Opus Epistolarum*, ed. Allen, II, 414
(29-2-499)

127 "the *locus classicus*. . ." / A. O. Lovejoy, *Essays in the History of
Ideas*, p. 238.

Montaigne / Tr. Florio, loc. cit., I, 222.

"Spring come to you. . ." / *Tempest*, IV, i, 114, 115.

128 "the qualities o' th' isle" / Ibid., I, ii, 337.

". . . the nimble marmoset." / Ibid., II, ii, 173, 174.

". . . the acorn cradled." / Ibid., I, ii, 463, 464.

"O wonder!" Ibid., V, i, 181-4.

129 Ben Jonson / *Bartholomew Fair*, Induction, 130.

130 *Volpone* / I, i, 14, 15, 33–6; III, vii, 171, 172.

131 *The Alchemist* / I, i, 135; II, i, 2; IV, i, 25; I, iv, 29; V, v, 81, 82.

the traditional changes / see C. F. Wheeler, *Classical Mythology
in the Plays, Masques, and Poems of Ben Jonson* (Princeton, 1938).

The declination / Jonson, *Epigrams*, lxiv, cxxii.

epistle to the Countess of Rutland / *The Forest*, xii, 21–6.

"Saturnes raigne" / Ibid., iii, 50.

132 *The Sad Shepherd* / Prologue, 13, 14; I, iv, 36, 18, 40–7.

the English masque / See A. H. Gilbert, *The Symbolic Persons in the Masques of Ben Jonson* (Durham, North Carolina, 1948).

133 the royal procession / *The King's Entertainment*, 523, 524.

an encomium at a tournament / *Prince Henry's Barriers*, 341, 342.

The Golden Age Restored / 163–168.

Pleasure Reconciled to Virtue / 29–36; 107; 189–91; 325–7; 226–35.

134 a recent essay / Lionel Trilling, "The Fate of Pleasure," *Beyond Culture* (New York, 1965), pp. 57–87.

135 Edgar Wind / *Pagan Mysteries in the Renaissance* (London, 1958), pp. 78–88.

De voluptate / See Franco Gaeta, *Lorenzo Valla* (Naples, 1955), pp. 17–39.

Henry Reynolds / *"Mythomystes,"* in *Critical Essays of the Seventeenth Century*, ed. J. E. Spingarn (Oxford, 1908), I, 175, 176.

136 Douglas Bush / *English Literature in the Earlier Seventeenth Century* (Oxford, 1962), p. 384.

"Mortals that would follow me. . ." / *A Mask Presented at Ludlow Castle*, 1018–23.

137 Mythography . . . iconology / See Stephen Orgel, *The Jonsonian Masque* (Cambridge, Mass., 1965), pp. 150–185.

"hidden strength" / Milton, *A Mask*, 418.

"the sage and serious doctrine" / *Ibid.*, 786, 787.

"the sage and serious Spenser" / Milton, *Areopagitica*.

"eternal Summer dwels" / Milton, *A Mask*, 988.

Paradise Lost / iv, 267; iv, 241, 314, 751–2.

138 wives are the sole exception / Tommaso Campanella, *La Città del sole*, ed. Norberto Bobbio (Turin, 1941), p. 136.

Paradise Regained / iii, 277; 377.

VI. Historiography

139 "Happy the people. . ." / Thomas Carlyle, *History of Friedrich II of Prussia called Frederick the Great*, XVI, i.

Brahman lore / See Willibald Kirfel, *Die Kosmographie der Inder nach den Quellen dargestellt* (Bonn, 1920), pp. 91f.

"Jam tomorrow..." / Lewis Carroll, *Through the Looking Glass*, v.

140 "Past, and to come..." / Shakespeare, *2 Henry IV*, I, iii, 108.

"*más versado*..." / Miguel de Cervantes Saavedra, *Don Quijote de la Mancha*, I, vi.

141 "*ordén desordeñada*" / Ibid., I, i.

"I was borne..." / Cervantes, *Don Quixote*, tr. Thomas Shelton (London, 1896), I, 170.

142 "Happy time..." / Ibid., I, 92, 93.

"*el felícismo tiempo*" / Cervantes, *Don Quijote*, II, i.

"But now sloth triumphs..." / *Don Quixote*, tr. Shelton, III, 22.

143 "more compassion than cruelty..." / Ibid., IV, 173.

an interest he has elsewhere expressed / See Américo Castro, *El Pensamiento de Cervantes* (Madrid, 1925), p. 179.

Jorge de Bustamente / See Rudolph Schevill, *Ovid and the Renascence in Spain* (Berkeley, 1913), pp. 153, 154, 175.

a voluble concern for the golden age / See *Don Quijote de la Mancha*, ed. Francisco Rodríguez Marín (Madrid, 1947), I, 314–22.

Juan del Encina / See Erika Lipsker-Zarden, *Der Mythos vom goldenen Zeitalter in den Schäferdichtungen Italiens, Spaniens und Frankreichs zur Zeit der Renaissance* (Berlin, 1933), pp. 43–6.

Mosén Diego de Valera / *Crónica de los reyes católicos*, ed. J. de M. Carriazo (Madrid, 1927), p. cxi.

Charles V / Ariosto, *Orlando furioso*, XV, xxv.

Bernardo de Valbuena / *Siglo de oro en las selvas de Erífile* (Madrid, 1821), pp. 2, 52, 53.

144 "*O siglo de oro*..." / Lope Felix de Vega Carpio, *Obras escogidas*, ed. F. R. Sainz de Robles (Madrid, 1946), II, 356.

Francisco Martínez de la Rosa / *Obras*, ed. D. C. Seco Sorrano (Madrid, 1962), II, 230.

Erasmus / *Opus Epistolarum*, ed. Allen, II (1910), 527; II, 487; III (1918), 587.

145 the golden age of Pope Leo / George Berkeley, *Works*, ed. A. A. Luce and T. E. Jessop (London, 1950), III, 203 (*Alciphron*, v, 25).

The conception of a Renaissance / See Konrad Burdach, *Reformation, Renaissance, Humanismus* (Berlin, 1926), 3–78; Johan Huizinga, *Men and Ideas*, tr. J. S. Holmes and Hans van Marle (New York, 1959), pp. 243–87; W. K. Ferguson, *The Renaissance in Historical Thought* (Boston, 1948); B. L. Ullmann, "Renaissance: the Word and the Underlying Concept," *Studies in Philology* (April, 1952), XLIX, 2, 105–18.

"*Maintenant toutes disciplines. . .*" / François Rabelais, *Pantagruel*, viii.

146 discourse on arms and letters / Cervantes, *Don Quijote*, I, xxxviii; *Don Quixote*, tr. Shelton, II, 136.

Tam Marti, quam Mercurio / Sir Walter Ralegh, *Works*, ed. William Oldys (Oxford, 1829), I, 22.

"the concurrence of Armes and Learning" / Louis Le Roy, *Of the Interchangeable Course, or Variety of Things in the Whole World; and the concurrence of armes and learning*, tr. R. A. (London, 1594), p. 108. See also W. L. Gundersheimer, *The Life and Works of Louis Le Roy* (Geneva, 1966).

147 "Those blessed ages. . ." / Cervantes, *Don Quixote*, tr. Shelton, II, 139, 140.

Jean de Montreuil / *Opera*, ed. Ezio Ornato (Turin, 1963), I, i, 241. Cf. *The Portable Renaissance Reader*, ed. J. B. Ross and M. M. McLaughlin (New York, 1953), p. 66.

Erasmus / *Opus Epistolarum*, ed. Allen, II (1910), 527.

Gyraldus / *Lili Gregori Gyraldi Opera omnia* (Leyden, 1696), II, 608.

Henri Estienne / *Apologie pour Hérodote*, ed. Paul Ristelhuber (Paris, 1879), II, 52.

148 Sir Walter Ralegh / *The History of the World* (London, 1614), p. 183.

the four seasons / See D. C. Allen, "The Degeneration of Man and Renaissance Pessimism," *Studies in Philology* (April, 1938), XXXV, 2, 219.

the growth of historical consciousness / See Herbert Weisinger, "Ideas of History during the Renaissance," *Renaissance Essays from the "Journal of the History of Ideas,"* ed. P. O. Kristeller and P. P. Wiener (New York, 1968).

Sir Thomas Browne / *Hydriotaphia, or Urn Burial*, v.

Robert Burton / *The Anatomy of Melancholy*, III, i, 3.

149 the youth of the world / Francis Bacon, *Of the Dignity and Advancement of Learning,* i, in *Works,* ed. Spedding, Ellis, and Heath, III, 291.

John Selden / Quoted by Herschel Baker, *The Race of Time: Three Lectures on Renaissance Historiography* (Toronto, 1967), p. 21.

Godfrey Goodman / Quoted by Victor Harris, *All Coherence Gone* (Chicago, 1949), p. 41.

Hakewill's sturdy answer / George Hakewill, *An Apology of the Power and Providence of God* (Oxford, 1630), p. 24.

150 Secondo Lancelloti, / *L'Hoggidí, overo Il Mondo non peggiore ne più calamitoso del passato* (Venice, 1637), pp. 171–9, 521–50.

"Say not thou. . ." / *Ecclesiastes,* vii, 10.

the Ancients and the Moderns / See R. F. Jones, *Ancients and Moderns: A Study of the Background of the Battle of the Books* (Saint Louis, 1936), and Hans Baron, "The *Querelle* of the Ancients and the Moderns as a Problem for Renaissance Scholarship," *Journal of the History of Ideas* (January, 1959), XX, 1, 3–22.

Ben Jonson / *Timber,* 124ff.

151 The millennium / *Isaiah,* lx, 17.

Isaac Newton / "Observations upon the prophecies of Holy Writ," *Opera quae exstant omnia* (London, 1785), V, 312.

Joachim of Fiore / Cf. Cohn, *The Pursuit of the Millennium,* pp. 99–107.

a third realm / Leo Tolstoy, *War and Peace,* tr. Louise and Aylmer Maude (New York, 1942), p. 994 (XI, xii).

their third Reich / See Julius Petersen, *Die Sehnsucht nach dem Dritten Reich in Deutschen Sage und Dichtung* (Stuttgart, 1934).

Giambattista Vico / *The New Science,* tr. T. G. Bergin and M. H. Fisch (Ithaca, N.Y., 1948), pp. 37, 159, 244.

152 Johannes Annius / See *Berosus Babilonicus de his quae praecesserunt inundatione terrarum* (Germany?, 1511), pp. xvᵛ, xvi.

Thomas Burnet / *The Sacred Theory of the Earth* (London, 1684), pp. 176, 197.

David Hume / *An Inquiry Concerning Human Understanding,* xi ("Of a Particular Providence and of a Future State").

Thomas Fuller / *Gnomologia* (London, 1816), p. 48.

The enlightened citizens / Campanella, *La Città del sole*, ed. Bobbio, p. 158.

Seneca / *Epistulae morales*, cxv, 14.

153 "With Ovid ended the golden age. . ." / John Dryden, *Fables, Ancient and Modern*, Preface.

Gabriel Harvey / *Works*, ed. A. B. Grosart (London, 1884), I, 146.

Jean Bodin / *Methodus ad facilem historiarum cognitionem* (Paris, 1566), p. 361.

154 the visitations of Knowledge / Francis Bacon, *Advancement of Learning*, viii, in *Works*, ed. Spedding, Ellis, and Heath, III (1859), 476.

Petrarch's Dark Ages / See T. E. Mommsen, "Petrarch's Conception of the 'Dark Ages,'" *Medieval and Renaissance Studies*, ed. E. F. Rice, Jr. (Ithaca, N.Y., 1959), pp. 106–129.

Voltaire / *Le Siècle de Louis XIV*, I, i.

". . . a monstrous dream." / François de la Mothe Fénelon, *Télémaque*, ed. Albert Cahen (Paris, 1920), I, 323; II, 454; I, 331.

155 "la renaissance des lettres" / Jean Le Rond d'Alembert, *Discours préliminaire de l'Encyclopédie*.

Voltaire / *Le Mondain*, 1, 2, 19–22, 128.

156 Voltaire / *Candide*, xvi, xiv, xvii.

Philosophical Dictionary / *Dictionnaire philosophique*, *Genèse*.

His reaction to the manifesto / *Voltaire's Correspondence*, ed. Theodore Besterman (Geneva, 1957), XXVII, 230 (5792), 30 August 1755.

157 To Malesherbes / J. J. Rousseau, *Correspondance générale*, ed. Théophile Dufour (Paris, 1927), VII, 72 (26 January 1762).

"For the poet. . ." / J. J. Rousseau, *De l'inégalité parmi les hommes*, ed. J. J. Lecercle (Paris, 1954), p. 118.

158 "The first man who. . ." / Ibid., p. 108.

What should then be done? / Ibid., p. 163–4.

Prudentius / See Hakewill, op. cit., p. 293.

159 Fichte / "*Einige Vorlesungen über die Bestimmung des Gelehrten*," in J. H. Fichte, *Werke*, ed. Reinhard Lauth and Hans Jacob (Stuttgart, 1966), I, III, 65.

from Arcadia to Elysium / Friedrich Schiller, "*Über naive und sentimentalische Dichtung*."

One of the projectors of socialism / C. H. de Rouvroy, Comte de Saint-Simon, and Augustin Thierry, *De la réorganisation de la société européene*, ed. Alfred Pereire (Paris, 1925), p. 97. Cf. J. B. Bury, *The Idea of Progress*, pp. 282–9.

reverberations which echo / R. W. Emerson, "Resources," *Letters and Social Aims;* Thomas Carlyle, *Sartor Resartus*, III, v.

Edward Bellamy / *Looking Backward 2000-1887*, ed. J. L. Thomas (Cambridge, Mass., 1967), p. 314.

160 An article in the *Scientific American* / Cited by Leo Marx, *The Machine in the Garden* (New York, 1964), p. 226; cf. pp. 105–7.

". . . forward, not behind. . ." / J. G. Whittier, "Among the Hills."

"O for old Saturn's reign. . ." / George Gordon, Lord Byron, *Beppo*, LXXX.

Robert Frost / "The Last Follower"; cf. "It Is Almost the Year Two Thousand."

John Berryman / *His Toy, His Dream, His Rest* (New York, 1968), p. 59.

161 *A Vision of the Last Judgment* / William Blake, *Poetry and Prose*, ed. Geoffrey Keynes (London, 1927), pp. 829, 830.

Zola / See Harry Levin, *The Gates of Horn: A Study of Five French Realists* (New York, 1963), p. 332.

The laureate of modern nostalgia / Gustave Flaubert, *La Tentation de Saint Antoine* (Paris, 1924), pp. 458, 625.

"regrets for the golden age. . ." / Edgar Allan Poe, *Oeuvres en prose*, tr. Charles Baudelaire (Paris, 1951), p. 1064.

Cesare Pavese / *Il Mestiere di vivere* (Turin, 1952), pp. 249, 344.

162 " 'A marvellous dream. . .' " / F. M. Dostoevsky, *Podrostok*, vii.

163 "A dream? What is a dream?" / F. M. Dostoevsky, *Son smeshnogo cheloveka*, v. Cf. Elizabeth W. Trahan, "The Golden Age—Dream of a Ridiculous Man," *Slavic and East European Journal* (Winter, 1959), XVII, 4, 348–71.

164 Schiller / "*Hoffnung*."

Oscar Wilde / "The Soul of Man under Socialism."

René Dubos / *Mirage of Health* (New York, 1959), p. 220.

Charles Péguy / *Oeuvres complètes* (Paris, 1927), III, 230.

Sigmund Freud / *Civilization and Its Discontents*, tr. Joan Rivière (London, 1951), p. 48.

165 "... desponding view of the present." / T. B. Macaulay, *A History of England*, I, i.

"To complain of the age. . ." / Edmund Burke, *Select Works*, ed. E. J. Payne (Oxford, 1874), I, 3.

Friedrich Schlegel / "Gespräch über die Poesie," *Kritische Ausgabe*, ed. Hans Eichner (Paderborn, 1967), II, 289–90, 295.

166 Thomas Warton / *The History of English Poetry* (London, 1781), p. 490.

"... the times of ELIZABETH. . ." / Richard Hurd, *Works* (London, 1811), III, 213.

167 Nick Greene / Virginia Woolf, *Orlando* (New York, 1928), pp. 91, 90.

John Florio / *His First Fruits* (London, 1578), p. 61ᵛ.

the entire human condition / Montaigne, *"Du repentir."*

Index

Index

DATE DUE
